SHAKESPEARE SURVEY

SHAKESPEARE SURVEY

AN ANNUAL SURVEY OF
SHAKESPEARIAN STUDY & PRODUCTION

22

EDITED BY
KENNETH MUIR

CAMBRIDGE
AT THE UNIVERSITY PRESS
1969

Published by the Syndics of the Cambridge University Press
Bentley House, 200 Euston Road, London, N.W.1.
American Branch: 32 East 57th Street, New York, N.Y. 10022

© Cambridge University Press 1969
Library of Congress Catalogue Card Number: 49-1639
Standard Book Number: 521 07612 9

Shakespeare Survey was first published in 1948. For the
first eighteen volumes it was edited by Allardyce Nicoll
under the sponsorship of the University of Birmingham,
the University of Manchester, the Royal Shakespeare
Theatre and the Shakespeare Birthplace Trust.

Printed in Great Britain
by Alden & Mowbray Ltd at the Alden Press, Oxford

EDITOR'S NOTE

The first eight articles in this volume were delivered as lectures at the Thirteenth International Shakespeare Conference at Stratford-upon-Avon in September 1968.

Shakespeare Survey 23 will contain a number of articles on Shakespeare's language. No. 24 will be a miscellaneous volume but will include some of the papers from the 1970 Conference. Contributions, which should not normally exceed 5000 words, should reach the Editor (Department of English Literature, The University, P.O. Box 147, Liverpool, L69 3BX) by 1 September 1970.

K. M.

CONTRIBUTORS

C. L. BARBER, *Professor of English, State University of New York at Buffalo*

RALPH BERRY, *Professor of English, University of Massachusetts*

NORTHROP FRYE, *Professor of English, Massey College, University of Toronto*

MICHEL GRIVELET, *Professor of English, University of Dijon*

G. R. HIBBARD, *Reader in English, University of Nottingham*

ERIC IRVIN, *Australia*

V. Y. KANTAK, *Professor of English, The Maharaja Sayajirao University of Baroda*

HARRY LEVIN, *Professor of English, Harvard University*

GARETH LLOYD EVANS, *Senior Lecturer and Staff Tutor in Literature, Extra-Mural Department, University of Birmingham*

WILLIAM H. MATCHETT, *Professor of English, University of Washington*

ROBERT ORNSTEIN, *Professor of English, Western Reserve University, Cleveland*

RICHARD PROUDFOOT, *Lecturer in English, King's College, University of London*

LEAH SCRAGG, *Lecturer in English, University of Manchester*

GUNNAR SJÖGREN, *Sweden*

JOHN W. VELZ, *Professor of English, University of Texas*

ROGER WARREN, *Leverhulme Fellow in Drama, The University of Southampton*

HERBERT S. WEIL, JR., *Professor of English, University of Connecticut*

ROBERT WEIMANN, *Professor of English, Humboldt University, Berlin*

CONTENTS

[Notes are placed at the end of each contribution, except in the Reviews section]

LIST OF PLATES

BETWEEN PP. 118 AND 119

I. *A.* Plan of Elsinore

B. Page from Danish Court Records
(Rigsarkivet, Copenhagen)

C. Playbill for a production of *Henry IV* at the Theatre, Sydney, 8 April 1800
(The Mitchell Library, Sydney)

II. *A. Julius Caesar*, Royal Shakespeare Theatre, 1968. Directed by John Barton, settings by John Gunter. Charles Thomas as Mark Antony

B. Ian Richardson as Cassius and Derek Smith as Casca

III. *The Merry Wives of Windsor*, Royal Shakespeare Theatre, 1968. Directed by Terry Hands, settings by Timothy O'Brien. Brewster Mason as Falstaff

IV. *As You Like It*, Royal Shakespeare Theatre, 1968. Directed by David Jones, settings by Timothy O'Brien. Janet Suzman as Rosalind

V. *A. As You Like It.* Janet Suzman (Rosalind) and Michael Williams as Orlando

B. King Lear, Royal Shakespeare Theatre, 1968. Directed by Trevor Nunn, settings by Christopher Morley. Patrick Stewart as Cornwall, Susan Fleetwood as Regan, Sheila Allen as Goneril, Eric Porter as Lear, Diane Fletcher as Cordelia and Terrence Hardiman as Albany

VI. *Troilus and Cressida*, Royal Shakespeare Theatre, 1968. Directed by John Barton, settings by Timothy O'Brien. Helen Mirren as Cressida and David Waller as Pandarus

VII. *A. Troilus and Cressida.* Helen Mirren (Cressida), David Waller (Pandarus) and Michael Williams as Troilus

B. Troilus and Cressida. Alan Howard as Achilles, with the Myrmidons

VIII. *A. Doctor Faustus*, Royal Shakespeare Theatre, 1968. Directed by Clifford Williams, settings by Abd'elkader Farrah. Terrence Hardiman as Mephistophilis and Eric Porter as Faustus

B. Doctor Faustus. Hugh Keays Byrne as Sloth, Sara Kestelman as Lechery and Eric Porter (Faustus)

Plates IIA to VIIIB are reproduced by permission of the Governors of the Royal Shakespeare Theatre (Photos: Gordon Goode).

OLD AND NEW COMEDY

BY

NORTHROP FRYE

The Old and New Comedy forms in Greek literature are highly stylized and conventionalized forms, each the product of very specific cultural and historical conditions that can never recur. Each may be of course imitated in later ages: the *Comedy of Errors* adapts Plautus, and there is some imitation of Aristophanes in *The Knight of the Burning Pestle*. But more important than the possibility of imitation is the fact that the two Greek forms are species of larger dramatic genera. The *kind* of comedy they represent may and inevitably will recur, when a larger pattern of cultural and historical factors makes it possible.

I begin with New Comedy, as the more familiar, and as having something more like a continuous line of tradition. The distinguishing feature of New Comedy is the teleological plot: perhaps this feature had something to do with Aristotle's approval of it. As a rule the main theme of this plot is that of the alienated lover moving towards sexual fulfilment. New Comedy reaches a *telos* in its final scene, which is superficially marriage, and, more profoundly, a rebirth. A new society is created on the stage in the last moments of a typical New Comedy, when objections, oppositions, misunderstandings and the schemes of rivals are all cleared out of the way. This newborn society is frequently balanced by a recognition scene and a theme of the restoring of a birthright, the recognition (*cognitio*) being connected with the secret of somebody's birth in the very common device of the foundling plot. Much simpler and more popular is the comedy in which a hero, after many setbacks, succeeds in doing something that wins him the heroine and a new sense of identity.

In such a structure the characters are essentially functions of the plot. However fully realized they may be, they are always organically related to the roles on which the plot turns, whether senex, parasite, bragging rival or whatever it is. The *commedia dell'arte* indicates with particular clarity how a group of stock characters related to a stock plot is the basis of the comic structures of Shakespeare and Molière, both of whom show many affinities with the *commedia dell'arte*. In Ben Jonson's 'humour' theory the New Comedy conception of character as a plot-function is rationalized in a most ingenious way. The character as plot-function has something predictable at his basis: the 'humour' is a character who is completely dominated by a predictable reaction. But predictability of response is also one of the main sources of the comic mood, as has been emphasized in most theories of comedy and laughter down to Bergson. Thus the 'humour' is the appropriate type of character for a New Comedy plot because in the humour comic structure and comic mood are unified.

The imagery and characterization of New Comedy belong to an extensive area of literary symbolism which I shall call Eros symbolism. Eros symbolism includes all the medieval poetry in which an alienated lover is stimulated by his love to make some gigantic achievement, whether his goal is explicitly sexual, as it is in *The Romaunt of the Rose*, or spiritual and sublimated, as it is in the *Purgatorio*. The two climaxes of the Eros quest we may call, following Milton, the *allegro* and the *penseroso* forms. The Biblical archetypes of Dante's quest are the journey of man towards the garden of Eden, the journey through the wilderness to the Promised Land, and the vision of the *hortus conclusus* of the Song of Songs which in its Christian form is the epiphany of the virgin mother and divine child. Here the transcendence of a sexual goal goes along with the vision of a divine childhood which is partly the poet's childhood as well, for Dante in Eden regains his generic childhood as a son of an unfallen Adam. In all these quests we notice the figure of the lonely old man who can see but not enter the sacred garden. This figure is represented by Moses in the Old Testament, by Joseph in the New, and by Virgil in Dante. He corresponds in New Comedy to the defeated or reconciled senex. In Shakespeare we notice how in *As You Like It* the quadruple marriage is contrasted with the melancholy Jaques, who goes off to consult a hermit, and how in *The Tempest* the festivities of Ferdinand and Miranda are an emotional contrast to the world-weariness of Prospero.

New Comedy develops two main forms, the romantic form of Shakespeare and the more realistic and displaced form of the Neo-Classical tradition, of which the greatest name is Molière. The more realistic such comedy becomes, the more it is in danger of becoming a sentimental domestic comedy, like the *comédie larmoyante* of the eighteenth century. A combination of realistic treatment and comic structure has a tendency to sentimentality inherent in it, as its theme approximates very closely the favourite rubric of the agony column: 'Come home; all is forgiven'. Molière avoids this by focusing nearly all the dramatic interest on a central senex or blocking figure, whose particular folly, whether avarice or snobbery or hypochondria, keeps the tone well away from the sentimental. But in Sheridan and Goldsmith the effort to keep the texture dry and witty is more of a strain. The domestic virtues do not appear to have attracted the loyalty of a major dramatic genius, unless we wish to call Beethoven a major dramatic genius. *Fidelio* is a bachelor's tribute to the domestic virtues, but the extraordinary unevenness of the music indicates some doubts even in his mind. Naturally, too, anything in the nature of a 'well-made play', like the plays of Scribe and Sardou, or in general of what Bernard Shaw called 'Sardoodledom', belongs to the New Comedy tradition.

Eventually the New Comedy structure tends to desert the stage for the domestic novel, where a sentimental tone is easier to accommodate. The foundling plot reappears in *Tom Jones*, and reaches perhaps its culmination in Dickens. For in Dickens, while the story normally ends in marriage, a great deal is made of the mystery of birth. The production of the parents of the hero or heroine, even when they are bare names unrelated to the story, like the father of Oliver Twist or the parents of Little Nell, seems to be a feature of great importance. And, of course, the whole conception of characterization in Dickens is very close to that of the Jonsonian humour, except that the looser fictional form can find room for a greater number of peripheral characters who are not directly concerned in the central plot.

When drama revives in Great Britain towards the end of the nineteenth century, the formulas of New Comedy are used increasingly for purposes of parody, parody being the usual sign in literature that some conventions are getting worn out. We begin with parodies of foundling and mysterious-heir plots in Gilbert and Sullivan, notably in *Pinafore* and *The Gondoliers*; then we have Wilde's urbane treatment of the foundling plot in *The Importance of Being Ernest*, where the hero has to overcome a refusal to 'marry into a waiting room, and contract an alliance with a parcel'. Wilde is followed by Bernard Shaw, who was well aware of the extent to which some standard New Comedy devices, such as the hero's being attracted by a girl whom he does not know to be his sister, had already been parodied by Ibsen. Among Shaw's parodies of recognition scenes we may note the ingenious device that enables Undershaft to adopt his son-in-law as his successor in *Major Barbara*, and the discovery in *Arms and the Man* that Captain Bluntschli is of the highest social rank possible in his country, being an ordinary Swiss citizen, besides being made rich enough, by inheriting a hotel business, to upstage his rival Sergius. In the next generation, the writer who most closely followed the New Comedy structure as laid down by Plautus and Terence was P. G. Wodehouse. In other words, the teleological New Comedy structure seems to have dropped out of the centre of serious literature in the twentieth century.

In this situation writers of comedy clearly have to do something else, and what they are doing may be easier to understand if we think of Old Comedy, not simply as the form of Aristophanes, but as a genus of comedy—I should be inclined to suggest that it is *the* alternative genus—which is open to writers bored or inhibited by the other conventions. The structure of Old Comedy is dialectical rather than teleological, and its distinguishing feature is the *agon* or contest. This feature makes for a processional or sequential form, in which characters may appear without introduction and disappear without explanation. In this form characters are not functions of a plot, but vehicles or embodiments of the contest. For a dramatic contest is as a rule not simply between personalities as such, but between personalities as representatives of larger social forces. These forces may be those of a class struggle, as they are in Brecht, or they may be more concrete situations like a war or an election, or they may be psychological forces or attitudes of mind. Such a form is the appropriate one for introducing historical figures. We recall how Socrates and Euripides appear in Aristophanes: in Bernard Shaw, who shows the transition to Old Comedy conventions very clearly, we have the caricatures of Asquith and Lloyd George in *Back to Methuselah*; and this prepares the way for more recent plays about Churchill, the Pope, and various analogues of Hitler. Or such characters may come from literature: I think, as a random example, of Tennessee Williams's *Camino Real*, which begins with Don Quixote and Sancho Panza entering from the audience, in a way curiously reminiscent of *The Frogs*.

We notice in Aristophanes that while the *agon* may conclude with the victory of something the dramatist approves of, it may equally well be a victory of something patently absurd, as in *The Birds*. A comic structure based on a contest in which absurdity is the victor of the contest is clearly anti-teleological, the greatest possible contrast to the more idealistic New Comedy form. Although Aristophanes himself is a high-spirited writer, full of jokes and slapstick, the form he uses, in its larger context, is the appropriate form for black or absurd comedy. The darker tone latent in Old Comedy was recognized in Elizabethan times: Puttenham says, for example: 'this bitter poem called the old *Comedy* being disused and taken away, the new *Comedy* came in place, more civil and pleasant a great deal'. It was perhaps the more deeply sardonic tone of *Every Man Out of His Humour* that made Jonson speak of it as closer to Old Comedy, though it is still within the conventions of New Comedy in its structure. In our day the black comedy is normal, but half a century ago, when Chekhov showed characters slowly freezing in the grip of a dying class, many audiences found it difficult to believe that *The Cherry Orchard* or *The Three Sisters* were comedies at all.

New Comedy may go either in a romantic or in a realistic direction: the natural development of Old Comedy is towards fantasy, which now seems to us a peculiarly modern technique. Where characters are embodiments of social or psychological conflicts, the conception of the individual as defined by sanity, wakefulness, and ordinary experience is only one of many possible points of view. In New Comedy we are continually aware of the predominance of the chain of being: we notice this, for example, in the rigid social hierarchy of Shakespearian comedy, which the action of the comedy never essentially disturbs. Old Comedy, by contrast, may be called the drama of unchained being. In Aristophanes characters may be gods, as in *The Birds*, or the dead, as in *The Frogs*, or pure allegories, as in *Peace*. A similar tendency to introduce characters who are not coterminous with the bodies of individuals is marked in the theatre of the absurd, especially in Ionesco. One form of this is the archetypal characterization that we find, for instance, in *Waiting for Godot*, where the two main characters identify themselves with a number of representative figures, such as the two thieves crucified with Christ.

Waiting for Godot is also, in one of its aspects, a parody of the vaudeville dialogue, which bears much the same relation to Old Comedy that the *commedia dell'arte* does to New Comedy. In more sophisticated versions of such dialogue, as we have it in Nicholls and May, it becomes more clearly a verbal *agon*. When the contest is one of incident rather than words, we may have the loose sequential structure of some of the early Chaplin films, where there is a series of collisions between the hero and a number of unsympathetic antagonists, very similar in form to, for example, the last part of Aristophanes' *The Acharnians*. In New Comedy the essential meaning of the play, or what Aristotle calls its *dianoia*, is bound up with the revelation of the plot, but such a meaning may be crystallized in a number of sententious axioms that express reflexions arising from the various stages of the plot. Menander was famous for his sententious or proverbial utterances, one of which was quoted by St Paul: Terence was highly prized for the same quality in the Renaissance, and the same characteristic recurs in Shakespeare, as in the well-known line from *A Midsummer Night's Dream*: 'The course of true love never did run smooth'. Old Comedy is less sententious but more argumentative and conceptual than New Comedy, hence it can find a place for the long harangue or monologue, which tends to disrupt the action of a New Comedy, and so appears in it only as a technical *tour de force*, like the speech of Jaques on the seven ages of man. In Aristophanes we have the parabasis or direct address to the audience; in Shaw the parabasis is transferred to a preface which the audience is expected to read along with the play; and many recent comedies not only include but are based on monologue, as we see in several plays of Beckett and in Albee's *Zoo Story*.

Two other characteristics of Old Comedy may be more briefly mentioned. As we see in Aristophanes' use of a chorus, Old Comedy, because of its looser processional form, can be more spectacular and less purely verbal than New Comedy. In New Comedy, once we go beyond the incidental songs that we find in Shakespeare, music and spectacle tend to caricature the complications of the plot, as in *The Marriage of Figaro*. But Old Comedy is in its nature closer to musical comedy, and we notice again how the plays of Shaw, despite their intensely verbal texture, make surprisingly good musical comedies. Again, the fact that Old Comedy is less preoccupied with the game of love and the rituals of courtship make it a better medium for a franker and more explicit treatment of the workings of the sexual instinct. Even the scurrility which is so conspicuous in Aristophanes recurs in *Mac Bird* and similar forms of undercover drama.

Of modern dramatists, perhaps T. S. Eliot shows most clearly the conflict between the two types of comedy. Eliot begins his dramatic efforts with the exuberant and superbly original *Sweeney Agonistes*, subtitled 'Fragment of an Agon', where, besides the obvious and avowed influence of Aristophanes, many of the features noted above appear, such as the assimilation to musical comedy and vaudeville forms. When he settles down to write seriously for the stage, however, we get such confections as *The Confidential Clerk*, where the main influence is Euripides' *Ion*, usually taken as the starting point of New Comedy. But this play seems, in comparison with *Sweeney Agonistes*, a somewhat pedantic joke, an attempt to do over again what Oscar Wilde (and, for that matter, Gilbert) had already done with more freshness.

Shakespeare's comedies conform for the most part to a romantic development of New Comedy. But Shakespeare was a versatile experimenter, and there is at least one play which falls within the genus of Old Comedy as we have been dealing with it here. This play is, of course, *Troilus and Cressida*. Here the characters are well-known figures from history or literature; the structure is a simple sequential one, built up on the background movement of Helen from Greece to Troy and the foreground movement of Cressida in the reverse direction; the characters are both embodiments and prisoners of the social codes they adopt, and so far as the action of the play itself is concerned, the only clear victor of the contest is absurdity. The reasons why this play seems to us a peculiarly 'modern' one should be clear by now.

New Comedy, especially in its more romantic or Shakespearian form, tends to be an ideal structure with strong analogies to religion. The sense in which Christianity is a divine comedy is a New Comedy sense: here history is a teleological drama of which the hero is Christ, and the heroine who becomes his bride is also a reborn society. Similar affinities between romantic New Comedy and religious myth may occur outside Christianity, as we see in *Sakuntala* and other Indian comedies. Old Comedy is a more existential form in which the central theme is mockery, which may include mockery of the gods, above or below. The presiding genius of New Comedy is Eros, but the presiding genius of Old Comedy is more like Prometheus, a titanic power involved by his contempt for the gods in a chaotic world of absurdity and anguish. The fictional counterpart of New Comedy is the classical novel as it develops from Fielding to Henry James; the fictional counterpart of Old Comedy is the kind of satire that we have in Lucian, Apuleius, and more particularly Rabelais, where the theme of descent into a lower and more chaotic mode of existence occupies a prominent place. A hero may escape from this chaos, as Odysseus does from the cave of Polyphemus, or all the characters may remain involved in it. Such titles as *Huit Clos* and *Endgame* suggest that the latter is the more conventional form today. Whatever its conventions, the dramatic genus of Old Comedy is the one now established on our stage, and as we enter the age of anarchism it is likely to remain there.

AN APPROACH TO SHAKESPEARIAN COMEDY

BY

V. Y. KANTAK

Anything like a serious probing into the nature of Shakespearian Comedy, an attempt to discover, as it were, its governing principle, has been rare. One may hold the view that such an effort is hardly necessary, that, as has been suggested in the case of Tragedy, each Comedy could best be studied for its peculiar kind of unity of theme, structure, and effect, rather than as illustrative of the Shakespearian comic idea.

Shakespeare, at any rate, seems to write his Comedy with little concern for conformity to the established genre. The tradition associated with the form gave but a general direction to his attitudes. 'What distinguishes Shakespeare's Comedies from most contemporary ones is the amount of blending. Each play is sharply individualized, and yet nearly every one contains in different proportion all the elements of the others.'[1] The peculiar blend of several modes has produced a kind of 'polyphonic music', to use Miss Bradbrook's phrase, asking of the reader a continual switching of interest and also a capacity to respond with a kind of multi-consciousness to the situation. This 'manifoldness' of Shakespeare's comic form discourages any attempt to define its organizing principle. So that when we ask what is that common element, that particular kind of excellence that beginning with *Love's Labour's Lost* reaches definitive form in *A Midsummer Night's Dream, Much Ado About Nothing, As You Like It, The Merchant of Venice* and *Twelfth Night*, the temptation is to define it in terms of theme and content rather than the quality of artistic structure. We could say, for instance (as has been finely said), that in these Comedies more than in any other of the European comic traditions love is realized 'as a force making for proper happiness and social reconciliation over a wide area of human experience'[2] embracing varying degrees of the sane and the eccentric, that the ideal of social balance they present is 'the power to live with one's own absurdity with ease and with confidence'.[3] And this is achieved mainly through a kind of all-inclusiveness—width rather than depth. 'And what is wrong with width?' asked Gordon.[4] Yet one of the most striking features of Shakespearian Comedy is the animated unity with which every remote detail, the minutest gesture, as in a dance, seems to vibrate. And, as in a dance, the centre always holds. In our appreciation of it what we seriously lack is an adequate idea of the form in which Shakespeare embodies his complex comic vision, a fresh stand-point from which to approach the varied achievement of the Comedies.

In the absence of such a controlling idea the plays have been approached in a partial, so to say, in a piecemeal, fashion. From the point of view of plot and structure they can only appear to be lax, and present a complete contrast to the tense structure and movement of the great Tragedies dominated by single heroes. Despite the admixture of intrigue, theirs is mainly the relaxed progression of an episodic narrative more akin to the structure of the Histories. Many have found *As You Like It*, for instance, recklessly careless in construction, whereas with a change of perspective we should have perceived how deceptive the simplicity of the structure of Shakespearian Comedy, in fact, is; how a subtle workmanship welds together diverse traditional elements—the Morality Play, Farcical Interlude, jesting, pageant and pastoral—in the service of a higher purpose.

Similarly, they can be seen simply as triumphs of Shakespeare's sympathetic power of character creation. We may utilize Keats's happily phrased insight into Shakespeare's 'negative capability' and place almost the whole secret in Shakespeare's power to identify himself imaginatively with all sorts and conditions of men and women, his habit of giving everyone a case, even to the Devil if he comes in human guise—and he always does! There is something undoubtedly in this mystique of the head and the heart by which Shakespeare identifies himself with the object of his mirth, romps whole-heartedly with his fools, redeeming all follies, leaving none in the stocks, thus combining in a single gesture of the spirit detachment and sympathy. Such an approach, however, has many inconveniences. For one thing it leans heavily on psychology for ultimate warrant and often glances off to a spurious analysis of the personal image of the writer. Hazlitt saw special evidence of Shakespeare's personal magnanimity in his treatment of grotesques for public entertainment and Pater imagined there was in Shakespeare's own genius an element of that delicate raillery he endows a Berowne with. Again, a naturalist interest in character is stressed almost always at the expense of the total design. It is as though the plays in which Berowne, Touchstone and Bottom appear were designed merely to make them possible. And then, after all, if characterization be the main concern we should look elsewhere rather than to the Romantic Comedies.

But perhaps the greatest obstacle to a fresh approach is the persistence of an old critical attitude to the nature of the comic form. The traditional view of Comedy as a social corrective continues to influence our thinking, often in devious ways. That is somehow the standard comic form, and Shakespearian Comedy the deviation, though doubtless we allow a margin of incidental variety. The long success of the essentially satiric types—from Aristophanic and Plautine Comedy through Jonson, Molière, and the Comedy of Manners down to Shaw—has something to do with this. But one sometimes wonders if the well-known Anglo-Saxon concern for the social norm like the Jonsonian assertion of solid common sense—an otherwise healthy attitude in itself—or like a more general form of it as reflected, say, in Wyndham Lewis's *Time and Western Man*, hasn't also something to do with it. Even recent attempts, like Nevill Coghill's, distinguishing two kinds of Comedy and relating Shakespeare's practice to the medieval comic spirit rather than to the classical, have not been of much help.[5] After all, 'a story beginning in sadness and ending in happiness' can hardly be an adequate description of the essential qualities of Shakespearian Comedy. Nor is it easy to assume that its spirit resides in any such simple aspect of plot.

It is conceded, of course, that in Shakespeare neither plot nor character is really articulated around a satirical view-point, that even when the characters seem to be founded on a moral failing—Falstaff, Shylock, Jaques, Malvolio, Duke Frederick or Don John—the response they evoke in the play's setting and final effect is distinct from reproof or indignation. It is also recognized that the social norm of the Shakespearian comic vision is not conservative like that of classical comedy. It doesn't assume an order that is regarded as sacrosanct, an unquestioned propriety in the established fitness of things, but rather 'speculates imaginatively on modes not of preserving a good already reached, but of enlarging and extending the possibilities'.[6] Its spirit, in other words, is essentially, even embarrassingly, exploratory. This is more to the point, but despite all such qualifications the Bergsonian view of Comedy as the natural weapon of society to bring errant individuals to heel has a way of asserting itself in a new and more generalized form. Let us say that Shakespearian Comedy upholds no particular set of social values. Well then, it upholds social value as such. 'Comedy assumes that society must be made to work, that creatures must somehow learn to live together...That is the central and typical area of Comedy. However much Shakespeare may stray from it into farce, fantasy, or melo-drama he comes to rest in the social norm'.[7] And, of course, to clinch the argument the great *normality* of Shakespeare can always be invoked.

One of the consequences of this attitude has been that all too neat a separation of the spheres of Tragedy and Comedy has become axiomatic. 'For Tragedy life is the relationship of the moment and eternity, of the individual and the absolute, of man and God. For Comedy life is the reality of actual existence, the solving of the problem as to how man may ameliorate his condition here and now among his fellows. Comedy is social rather than metaphysical'.[8] I have no quarrel with these large generalizations except to suggest that they tend to obscure rather than reveal the characteristic force of Shakespearian Comedy. For what if, one may ask, Shakespeare's Comedy turns out to be, in fact, no less *metaphysical* than his Tragedy?

There has been something like a critical impasse and one hopefully looks for a break-through. Is it possible to approach Shakespearian Comedy from a larger stand-point so as to bring into proper perspective those elements which have suffered neglect? Any fresh appraisal that may be suggested should go some way in explaining the inexhaustible appeal of these Comedies with a proper appreciation of their peculiar 'doubleness', their ambiguity, their 'montage-like' structure. It should at the same time bring out their special closeness to the Tragedies, making it possible for us to recognize that the two seem to have grown from a common root, though so different, in their full manifestations, in mood and feeling. My purpose is to suggest that some very perceptive writing to come out in our time—like Susan Langer's *Feeling and Form* and perhaps C. L. Barber's *Shakespeare's Festive Comedy*—indicate possibilities of new openings and a fresh stand-point. For one thing there is here no unwarranted narrowing-down of the scope and effect of Shakespearian Comedy. There is a recognition that its subtle strength derives in no small measure from pre-rational modes of feeling and expression. And Comedy is viewed above all as a celebration of life—a celebration in a very special sense.

The joyous release of a Shakespearian Comedy can only be described in terms of the basic rhythm of life Langer speaks of, the sense of exhilaration that comes of our ability to face the changes and chances of life as we confront it. It is in some ways the most elementary kind of self-assertion we live by, the way living things declare their superiority to non-life by being able to maintain an organic balance. On the other hand this would also reveal the curious affinity this kind of Comedy has to the fine arts—why, for instance, dance should come to mind as the only appropriate analogy to describe what happens in it. Similarly, the new interest in 'festive' comedy might help us to understand the means Shakespearian Comedy characteristic-ally employs. Of the presence of the saturnalian element and its importance as a structural principle in the Comedies there is little doubt. But our neglect to recognize its place and relevance has severely limited our appreciation of Shakespeare's comic vision—in the celebrated case of Falstaff, for instance.

Falstaff is perhaps the clearest example of Shakespeare's use of the ritual prototype—Lord of

Misrule, Vice or Revel—for a comic purpose. It is not difficult to perceive the scapegoat aspect of the saturnalian ritual in Falstaff's rejection. Hal's action clearly carries out an impersonal pattern, the sacrificial ritual the prince has to perform as part of his assumption of office as king in cutting himself free from the guilt which he inherits along with the tarnished crown of his father. Though the underlying pattern of action is unmistakable, when we come to explain the great rejection our partiality for character-realism and concern for the moral norm begin to gain on us. We tend to reduce the rejection to a plain question of human relationship in the way we judge of the truth and perfidy of people in their common dealings with one another. The whole problem is commonly treated as one of a temporary lapse from moral responsibility and its timely recovery. 'The way you feel on this old controversy depends on how far you allow your head to intervene in the promptings of the heart', Tillyard says.[9] Shakespeare triumphs so long as he wants us to be on Falstaff's side; his hand is not sure when we begin to transfer our allegiance. But when, on the death of the king, Falstaff is ready to heap honours on Pistol and Shallow and imagines that the laws of the kingdom are at his commandment, we know that Falstaff has over-reached himself and that his day is over. Our minds force us into the realm of duty and the rascal gets his reward.

Somehow, those who are constant in their allegiance to Falstaff and those who transfer their allegiance to the Prince seem equally swayed by these moral considerations of the declared surface. One recalls Middleton Murry's comment, 'it is not Falstaff who needs to be pitied but Prince Hal'.[10] The rejection seems to backfire and the Prince becomes answerable to a charge of moral depravity, a shade blacker than ever Falstaff was charged with, namely, personal perfidy and ingratitude, which ranks considerably higher in Shakespeare's protocol of guilt. And then, it is argued that it is not Hal so much as Shakespeare who rejects Falstaff as a menace to his comic art, and that he painfully recovers from that contamination by exposing the Falstaff values in Thersites and Parolles. Such, indeed, are the poisoned wells from which we derive our greatest comic delights!

It is true we have since gained some understanding of the great gesture of Falstaff's expulsion and of the extreme artistic boldness of placing him in the world of historical reality that a Chronicle play claims to image. As Auden said, to quote a recent example, Falstaff's true home is music, the *Opera Buffa* world governed not by will or desire but by innocent wish.[11] And this opposition is brought home to us by the fact that there are at least two incidents in the *Henry IV* plays where the incongruity that results is too much even for Shakespeare's art, and a patently false note is struck. These are Falstaff's action in thrusting his sword into the corpse of Hotspur, and Colville's 'comical' surrender to him. There is no way in which an actor can play the scenes convincingly.

And what is gained from this sharp opposition that is allowed to develop within the plays even at some risk to their formal homogeneity? It does result in a clarification; but that clarification is not confined to casting aspersions on the character of the Prince—a blot on his scutcheon—or to imputing moral depravity to the Plantagenet family; it is far more general, far more potent than what satire or irony would have achieved. It not only calls into question the Tudor idea of kingship and government, the enthusiasm and ruthlessness that builds empires, but extends to all action in the interest of public causes, to the conduct of the worldly man who dedicates himself to some public end or other, politics, science, industry and so on, and thinks nothing of sacrificing personal life and relations if they conflict with the public vocation. At the farthest reaches of its expanding implications there are even hints of the Hamlet-problem of action in a vicious world. And it is important to grasp the sources of this suggestive power. The comic illumination that results depends on the tension established between the two poles, the historical and the ritual. So juxtaposed, Falstaff becomes the means of an implicit judgement of great moment. But such a polarization shifts the emphasis away from simple moral terms. The characteristic action is 'saturnalian' not 'satiric'.

In the comedies, the pattern of the action is a mingling of 'festive' gesture and the social situation in which it arises, but the festive character is dominant. *Much Ado About Nothing* or *Twelfth Night* may be potentially Comedies of Manners, *The Merchant of Venice* can be read as a Tragedy of Shylock or as a plea for minority toleration, and so forth, but their 'social' comment can easily be over-emphasized. After all, what does the sociology of Shakespeare's plays amount to? Is it any more than asserting that social security is generally attained through marriage? What makes them different is that the spirit that informs them is akin to the release experienced in a work like Cervantes' *Don Quixote*. We detect in it something of the liberating quality of great Farce and even perhaps something of the impulse behind the Theatre of the Absurd.

The dramatic mould it takes has many features that give it a strange power to induce reflexion which can only be described as a kind of metaphysical power. Its structure, so deceptively casual and simple, is in fact highly complex and the general air of relaxation is only strategy used for an intense purpose. Even the titles—*A Midsummer Night's Dream*, *Much Ado About Nothing*, *As You Like It*, *Twelfth Night or What You Will*—have a deliberate casualness and ambiguity as though asking a certain freedom of manœuvre without commitment. Shakespearian Comedy mainly works by a method of contrast, by merely providing a place propitious for chance encounters, rather than by development of an action to a studied resolution. It is naturally dominated by place, not time—the Park at Navarre, Messina, Illyria, Venice-Belmont, the wood near Athens, Arden Forest—each with a distinctive ethos which determines character and event, the elements to be placed in apposition and the nature of their dialogue. And the festive release works as the opportunity to enlarge vastly the range and quality of these encounters affording a richer clarification. So that one may justly ask if some of the great moments of Shakespearian Comedy are not rather like the great moments of Shakespearian Tragedy. One thinks of Dame Quickly's report of Falstaff's death in that light. How can we explain the placing of the two lyrics at the close of *Love's Labour's Lost*? The gay masque of quaint lords and sweet ladies suddenly melts and 'Dick the shepherd blows his nail...While greasy Joan doth keel the pot'. And then we are left to ponder the final judgement thrown at the departing vision, 'The words of Mercury are harsh after the songs of Apollo'. We might call it a flash of comic insight but it might more appropriately be called 'tragic' considering the quality of reflexion it induces. So also the effect of Feste's nonsense song on which *Twelfth Night* closes. Feste's quizzical 'The rain it raineth every day' does sound 'perilously like a tune whistled through the surrounding darkness'.[12] And this is especially so because the lit-up world of the play has achieved only a very 'chancy' and tentative kind of happiness. The relevance of Feste's song dawns on us with a tragic force for which there is no parallel outside Shakespeare or Cervantes. This power to draw opposite polarities into sudden confrontation is one of the marked features of that comic form Shakespeare made his own.

I must refer, however tentatively, to another—the curious manner in which the image of life as a stage-role becomes integrated with the comic idea. This is seen at its clearest in *As You Like It*, a play which besides being the most harmonious example of the *genre*, has seemed to many to have had a special closeness to Shakespeare's mind in the sense Johnson's remark, 'His tragedy seems to be skill, his comedy to be instinct' probably implies.[13] Shakespeare employs holiday motives directly in *Love's Labour's Lost*, *A Midsummer Night's Dream* and *Twelfth Night*. In *As You Like It* the sense of 'holiday' is more subtly conveyed as a leaven of the action that affects event, word, and gesture. The 'excess' suggestive of revelry that secures momentary release from the strain of life and social responsibility is derived from many sources, partly formal—there is formal pageant like the deer-horn procession or masque of Hymen and, indeed, the distanced pastoral; but there is also the 'holiday-exile' of the Duke Senior. The plot elements are more completely blended; the pastoral modulates into the natural mode with perfect ease and a marvellous unforced simplicity of tone is achieved. The tragical matter of the first Act—Oliver's villainy, the boyish quarrel, the breaking of the ribs, the humorous Duke's tantrums and fits of malice—are all finely toned down and brought into harmony with the festive element so that the sharp reaction and turbulence caused by a Shylock's demand, a Claudio's brutality or the tragical fate of a Malvolio are wholly avoided.

At the same time it is clear that Arden is no place for empty frivolity. There is a tone of serenity about Arden. What happens on this singular stage acquires the character of a ritual somehow without ceasing to be a natural event. The transitions from one to the other are smoothly made. Things like Jaques's malice or Touchstone's rascally intentions in regard to Audrey are 'distanced', being essentially 'festive' gestures, and do not arouse the sharp sting of moral censure, but when Rosalind gives a piece of her mind to Phoebe we at once credit her with extreme earnestness. But she too joins the ritual dance. The 'festive' figures like Touchstone, Jaques, Silvius, Corin, Phoebe, Audrey, and even the Duke Senior and his entourage, can move freely in and out of the two dimensions of 'every-day' and of 'holiday' reality. Life can be lived on widely different planes. There is a constant attempt to define what those different points of view could be. There is Touchstone's 'Hast thou any philosophy in thee, shepherd?' There is Orlando's absurd poetizing, and the Duke Senior's reflexions on 'this our life exempt from public haunt', finding good in everything. Jaques too has his point of view. They are all engaged in enacting their several demonstrative roles. And, of course, there is Rosalind and she is both actor and spectator.

'Playing' and masquerade has somehow a deep connexion with the clarification festive comedy brings about through release. It is as though we fashioned a comic strategy out of Polonius's words, 'And thus do we of wisdom and of reach,/ With windlasses and with assays of bias,/ By indirections find directions out'. That old buffer, himself a comic prototype, spoke better than he knew. After all, what he was lecturing Reynaldo about was how to put on an act in order to achieve a clarification! Such a sense of 'playing' is perhaps inseparable from revelry and the release implicit in it. In the Romantic Comedies, the characters are all engaged in some kind of posturing at different levels of conscious involvement and the masquerade takes many forms. In this way, not only do the lords of Navarre indulge their peculiar humour but Beatrice and Benedick, Orsino and Olivia.

But nowhere perhaps does this 'playing' become so subtle an instrument of revelation as in

As You Like It; nowhere is it so pervasive. And this 'playing' is not confined to figures like Touchstone and Jaques; the Duke Senior himself has a touch of it. And, of course, it is firmly centred in Rosalind who is chief actor, director–producer, and audience all in one. It is as though she were to possess a double identity as ritual prototype and naturalistic character, presenting a kind of fusion of the ceremonial and the historical in an easy combination. With one part of her mind she gives way to the saturnalian release and holds it in check with the other. Her mood of revelry has an underlining of the ardent, serious nature of a clear-sighted girl intent upon her greatest adventure which must lead to a 'world-without-end' bargain—to use the words of the Princess of *Love's Labour's Lost*. Early in the play she says, 'From henceforth I'll devise sports; Let me see, what think you of falling in love?' And she keeps this attitude throughout the multiple play-acting of the mock-wooing scenes till she steps down from her role of impresario to join the country copulatives in her own person. It is a difficult balance she maintains, all the time seeing herself playing a role without losing any of the impetuous drive of youthful impulse. Part of the fun is that she can observe herself in the grip of impulse and laugh at her own ridiculousness as though she were upon a stage. 'Alas the day! What shall I do with my doublet and hose? What did he when thou saw'st him? What said he? How look'd he? Wherein went he? What makes he here? Did he ask for me? Where remains he? How parted he with thee? And when shalt thou see him again? *Answer me in one word*.'

This seeing of earnest life as a playing is a source of the comic but it is also a serious mode of apprehending reality possible only to the most poised. 'All the world's a stage, and all the men and women merely players'—but Jaques perverts its truth, as he perverts everything with his spurious reflexion, and the ludicrous image of the pantaloon of the last stage that sums up the strange eventful history has to be immediately corrected by the entry of 'reverend old age' (not 'unregarded age in corners thrown'). But it is Rosalind who fulfils the meaning of his words, making it the basis of a comic vision of life, an excellent example of how profoundly Shakespeare's art is impressed with this larger sense of life as a mode of playing. There seems to be for Shakespeare, one might almost say, no wisdom possible without such a realization.

The renaissance man, it has been said, was engaged in modifying the ceremonial conception of life to create a historical conception, and the historical view expresses life as drama. This imaging of life as a drama played out on the stage of the world has serious implications for an understanding of Shakespeare's Tragedy as well as his Comedy, and is something which I have always felt is still to be explored and fully grasped. When we do recognize its importance in our appreciation of Shakespeare's total meaning, we also begin to realize how his Comedy and Tragedy are really a unity. We cannot rightly see this relationship unless we approach his Comedy from a larger viewpoint than has been commonly attempted so far.

NOTES

1. E. M. W. Tillyard, 'The Nature of Comedy and Shakespeare', *Essays Literary and Educational* (1962), p. 19.

2. G.K.Hunter, 'The Later Comedies', in *Shakespeare: The Writer and His Work* (1964), p. 181.

3. *Ibid.* p. 182.

4. George Gordon, *Shakespearian Comedy and Other Studies* (Oxford, 1944), p. 34.

5. Nevill Coghill, 'The Basis of Shakespearian Comedy', *Essays and Studies of the English Association* (1950), pp. 1–28.

6. H. B. Charlton, *Shakespearian Comedy* (1938), p. 278.

7. Tillyard, *op. cit.* pp. 17, 25.

8. Charlton, *op. cit.* p. 226.

9. Tillyard, *op. cit.* p. 21.

10. John Middleton Murry, *Shakespeare* (1936), p. 175.

11. W. H. Auden, *The Dyer's Hand* (New York, 1962), p. 184.

12. Hunter, *op. cit.* p. 238.

13. *Johnson on Shakespeare*, ed. Walter Raleigh (Oxford, 1908), p. 19.

SHAKESPEARE, MOLIÈRE, AND THE COMEDY OF AMBIGUITY

BY

MICHEL GRIVELET

Exactly three hundred years ago, in September 1668, in the presence of the Russian ambassadors, Molière was performing his great success of that year, *Amphitryon*, a comedy based on a play of Plautus which, as it happens, Shakespeare had also used in his only imitation of the Latin poet. In the eyes of one who has been invited to speak of Molière on the occasion of a Shakespeare Conference—a rather perplexing privilege—the coincidence is too remarkable not to seem, as Duke Vincentio would say, 'an accident that Heaven provides'. I see no reason to deny myself the benefit of this happy coincidence, especially since there is much more in common between *The Comedy of Errors* and *Amphitryon* than their comparatively unimportant debt to Plautus.

It is currently said that Shakespeare, whose plot is chiefly drawn from the more down-to-earth, naturalistic, *Menaechmi*, went to the play of *Amphitruo* for the sake of additional comic effects, the double master–servant theme, and the incident of the husband locked out of his own house. This may be true, but does not invalidate deeper motives. Always a very intelligent reader, he may well have been shrewd enough to recognize that *The Menaechmi* and *Amphitruo* are substantially the same kind of story.

To begin with, *Amphitruo* is not merely about an unfortunate husband; it is also, and in fact primarily, about the birth of twins. It tells how Alcmena, the innocent yet adulterous wife of general Amphitryon, gave birth to Hercules, the demi-god, as well as to a mortal named Iphikles. The Latin play is an already late version of a very old legend which, through the Greek dramatic poets and Pindar, can be traced back to Homer and beyond. Twins, it appears, were always, for early humanity, a subject of scandal and concern. In his study of *The Double*, Otto Rank, the follower of Freud, has collected evidence showing that primitive societies regarded the birth of twins as something supernatural, both evil and holy. Hence the ritual murder of twins and the no less widespread cult rendered to them, for instance as founders of cities. As late as the Middle Ages, it was believed that twins could only be born of an adulterous mother. Viewed in this perspective, the myth of Amphitryon seems to be just a tale embodying a deeper complex of mental attitudes towards the riddle of twin birth.

On the other hand, *The Menaechmi*, like *Amphitruo*, makes much of the love rivalry between two men identical in appearance. While one of the brothers has all the bad luck, is cheated of his pleasure with Erotium, the courtesan, and must nevertheless endure the abuse of a provoked wife, the other, heartily welcomed by everyone, enjoys both a good dinner and the lady. For reasons obvious enough in a context of Christian and highly domestic ideals, Shakespeare has toned down this aspect of the plot. But even then his Adriana, dutiful wife though she is, narrowly escapes going to bed with the wrong Antipholus. And thus the case reveals itself as one not of mere dissipation but of potential incest, just as incest may seem to be committed by Alcmena whose two men are as identical as twins. It is easy enough to see moreover that in

15

the triangular relationship the real Amphitryon plays the part of a staid husband, already past his best, while all the illicit intoxication, the daring, the youth of love is on the side of Jupiter. Thus the suggestion of incest which attaches to the triangle points to its great archetype. As Charles Mauron says, the magic resemblance between two brothers modulates into the magic resemblance between father and son.[1] You have, of course, recognized the inevitable Oedipus situation.

The subject treated by Shakespeare and by Molière is then a highly serious subject, rooted in the deepest anxieties of the human mind. And yet, in spite of its seriousness—or perhaps because of it—it has long proved to be particularly fit for comic treatment. The sight of two similar faces side by side, as Pascal observes in his *Pensées*, is one of the acknowledged sources, if not the main source, of the comic: 'Deux visages semblables, dont aucun ne fait rire en particulier, font rire ensemble par leur ressemblance.'[2] Bergson, Freud and others, have turned the remark to their own account in various theories about laughter. The paradox of this exhilaration is perceptible in the very first scene of *The Comedy of Errors*, when Egeon relates the 'sad story' of his 'own mishaps'. He takes great care not to omit anything: the two pairs of twins born in the same hour 'and in the self-same inn', the two identical halves of the family 'fastened at either end the mast' when the storm rages, the 'two ships from far' distant from one another 'by twice five leagues' at the moment of the encounter with the mighty rock,

> Which being violently borne upon,
> Our helpful ship was splitted in the midst;
> So that in this unjust divorce of us
> Fortune had left to both of us alike
> What to delight in, what to sorrow for.   (I, i, 102–6)[3]

Who could imagine a more unrelenting series of symmetries! Real as the sorrow may be in that romantic tale, there is no mistaking the delight arising from such a neat cluster of contrasts in similitude. Playfulness is also the note struck at the opening of *Amphitryon*, in the Prologue— of Molière's invention—between Night, a charming young goddess, and a weary Mercury. He desires her to stop in order to have a word, or rather 'two words', with her:

> Tout-beau, charmante Nuit; daignez vous arrester.
> Il est certain secours, que de vous on désire;
>   Et j'ay deux mots à vous dire,
>   De la part de Jupiter.   (I, i, 1–4)[4]

Since nearly all the plays of the French poet are written either in prose or in sustained alexandrines, the strict medium of the Grand Siècle, it is here no small surprise to come upon the light-heartedness of free verse. The style is no other than that of La Fontaine whose *Fables*, at least the first of them, belong to that same year, 1668. Their mocking spirit seems to preside over the whole play, lifting it from the still religious atmosphere of Plautus' *Amphitruo*.

It is, I think, a sense of intellectual excitement which, in our two plays, illumines the darkness of myth with the light of comedy. Some support may be found for this view in the interpretation of the Oedipus story given by Claude Lévi-Strauss in his essay on 'The Structural Study of Myth'. Anthropology's Pope, as he has recently been called, writes as follows: 'The myth has to do with the inability, for a culture which holds the belief that mankind is autochthonous (see, for instance, Pausanias, VIII, xxix, 4; vegetals provide a *model* for human), to find a satisfactory transition between this theory and the knowledge that human beings are actually born from the union of man and woman...Although the Freudian problem has ceased to be that of autochthony *versus* bisexual reproduction, it is still the problem of understanding how *one* can be born from *two*...'[5] This statement does not only add pointedness to the connexion we have noted—for there is a striking symmetry between the problem of *one* being born from *two* and that of *two* being born from *one*—it also tells us a great deal about the spirit of both *The Comedy of Errors* and *Amphitryon* by showing how a whole complex of human experience, inherited from a long cultural past and feeding on our unconscious fears, can be reduced to the simple terms of intellectual perplexity.

This is, I submit, why we may be allowed to touch with professorial clumsiness upon two works so deftly devised for fun and delight. *The Comedy of Errors* and *Amphitryon* are remarkable instances of the ambiguity of comedy. They turn the deepest causes of man's bewilderment into a joke, but it is a perilous balance which keeps them on the side of laughter. This uncertainty has philosophical implications and, moreover, they deal so explicitly with its cause that it may not be entirely misleading to treat them as comedies of ambiguity. As Molière observes 'c'est une étrange entreprise que celle de faire rire les honnêtes gens',[6] which I might perhaps render as: What a strange undertaking to attempt to make professors laugh!—if my purpose was not, more soberly though no less strangely, to lecture about it. By ambiguity I simply mean man's doubtfulness about being one or two, identical with himself or not. And, starting from what Shakespeare's play has to say about this, I chiefly propose to examine Molière's answer and what it tells us concerning the nature of his comedy.

In *The Comedy of Errors*, the fun arises mostly from the fact that the pieces of the family puzzle, the elements of the solution, are all there, ready for use, in the same city of Ephesus. Only the most perverse of chances would bring about a fatal mistaking of identities. Our real fear is lest the two Antipholuses or the two Dromios should happen to meet and thus, by inevitable recognition, spoil the game. Our hilarity breaks out every time a fresh mistake averts this danger. It is particularly exquisite when, as in the scene of the husband locked out, we can almost see the two pairs of twins side by side though in no position to see one another. This, it should be remembered, is precisely where Shakespeare refines and improves upon Plautus. But it is not so much the doubling of the stakes, the doubling of the twins, which makes the difference as the awareness that, while this to-do is going on, the Syracusan Antipholus is inside with Adriana and that, a moment before, he was saying:

> To me she speaks, she moves me for her theme;
> What, was I married to her in my dream?
> Or sleep I now, and think I hear all this?
> What error drives our eyes and ears amiss?
> Until I know this sure uncertainty,
> I'll entertain the offer'd fallacy.
>
> (II, ii, 181-6)

This situation is one of greater intensity than the corresponding one in Plautus, and it is markedly different from that in Molière. In the French play, all is already lost—or won—

Jupiter having fully succeeded as the lover of Alcmena when Amphitryon is kept out of his own house. Shakespeare, it would seem, is above all a master of comic suspense. We are here on the brink of the irreparable. Whether we fear more that this should happen than that it should not is a debatable question and, perhaps, a matter of taste. In any case, our comic pleasure owes much to the extreme precision and the extreme precariousness, to what we may call with Antipholus the 'sure uncertainty' of the equilibrium. This, I suggest, is the distinctive Shakespearian ambiguity.

It is rash, I confess, and dangerous to generalize from one play; especially from one which critics have often set apart as uncharacteristic. But after all, Harold Brooks has shown—in his essay on 'Themes and Structure in *The Comedy of Errors*'—how pregnant this play is with Shakespearian ideas.[7] The great themes of order, of appearance and reality, are already there, and specially conspicuous among them is the idea of relationship. From the start, the Syracusan Antipholus gives us to understand that adequate relationship is somehow indispensable to his own sense of identity, even though in seeking relationship he endangers this identity:

> I to the world am like a drop of water
> That in the ocean seeks another drop,
> Who, falling there to find his fellow forth,
> (Unseen, inquisitive) confounds himself.
> So I, to find a mother and a brother,
> In quest of them, unhappy lose myself. (I, ii, 35–40)

And indeed the first mistake he is trapped into making about the identity of Dromio renders his relationship to the world more insecure and fills him with fears for his personal integrity. Yet, before long, he will be willing to be 'transformed' and even created 'new' by Luciana, if she accepts his love instead of exhorting him to love her sister.

The irony is that Antipholus seems thus to be speaking the language of incestuous passion while he is expressing his 'soul's pure truth', just as Adriana is unwittingly wanton when she urges the same Antipholus to be true to her as a husband should. Virtuous words in equivocal situation—this is an entanglement which seems to have had a kind of fascination for Shakespeare. It is repeated, with subtle variations, in several of the major comedies. The first instance perhaps which comes to mind is that of Olivia, just married to Sebastian, and pressing Caesario to acknowledge that he is her husband. There is also the tremulous equivocation of Rosalind–Ganymede with Orlando—and with Phoebe—in the forest of Arden. The enchantment comes from everyone's many-hued uncertainty about himself. The delicacy, the changeableness of the vagaries which lead us into Illyrias of sensibility is all the more poignant as it is short-lived. 'Every wise man's son doth know' that 'journeys end in lovers' meeting' and Shakespearian comedies in happy reasonable marriages.

We may say then, even if this is rather too blunt to be entirely adequate, that Shakespearian comedy thrives on ambiguity ultimately overcome. Personal identity, at first untried and unsure of itself, barely emerging like Viola from the hazards of the sea, is put to the test of misunderstanding and self-contradiction, until, by adjusting itself to society, it comes into its own.'Know thyself' is the maxim and the assumption of Shakespeare's comedies. He does not, in them, face the sceptic's problem, that of a rift in personality which, once and for all, precludes all possibility of self-knowledge. This is why the stories of twins, for which he has an obvious fondness, suit his purpose so well. For the similarity of two distinct faces, fraught as it is with comic horror, does not in the end prove irreconcilable with nature. It is finally robbed of its awful magic. Once the Antipholuses and Dromios have met, they are just ordinary brothers. Each pair of twins has lost nothing of its deceitful symmetry, yet, now that the riddles have been solved, the world of errors will comfortably disintegrate.

When we turn to Molière, we find something very different. The plot he uses has two striking characteristics. First, it stages the confrontation of two identical faces, those of Sosia and Mercury, at the very start. Secondly, the two pairs of identical persons it involves are not twins. He drops all reference to Iphikles, the twin of Hercules in the original story. Plautus has a highly complicated and impossible theory of how Alcmena, already three months pregnant by her husband when she is visited by Jupiter, eventually gives birth, on the same day, to a ten-month Iphikles and to a seven-month Hercules, the demi-god being therefore a premature infant as well as a prodigy. But Molière will have none of this. He is not to be bothered by offspring, heroic or not. His only concern is with the loveliness of Alcmena, the ardours of Jupiter, the puzzled anger of Amphitryon on the one hand, and, on the other, the wrangles of Mercury and Sosia who, with impeccable duplication, is also provided with a wife. These two symmetrical triangles invite splendid speculations on the problems of conjugal geometry. We are distinctly in another world from that of Plautus whose earthiness does not exclude a genuine sense of the religious significance of myth. The atmosphere of Molière's play owes nothing to Roman 'pietas' or plebeian taste. It is aristocratic, courtly and, in spite of the classical names, more in touch perhaps than any other of his works with the everyday life of the monarchy towards 1668. Although there is no scholarly ground for believing that this was intended, yet the main plot reads like a plain transcription of Louis XIV's liaison with the beautiful Madame de Montespan. The play is decidedly, perhaps excessively, human.

But, at the same time, the fact that the doubles of Amphitryon and Sosia are not their twins but gods in disguise forbids the kind of solution which, in Shakespeare, brings all troubles to an end through tranquil acceptance of human relationships. In Plautus we have to do with a tragi-comedy in which human bewilderment and suffering are balanced by genuine joy at the birth of a hero. In Molière there can be no happy ending. After having fully enjoyed the privilege of being Amphitryon at the most opportune moment, Jupiter pretends to untie the whole unintelligible knot by reappearing as his own divine self. He then argues that Alcmena's husband need not be dismayed since there can be no dishonour in sharing with *him*:

> Un partage avec Jupiter
> N'a rien du tout qui déshonore. (III, x, 1898-9)

But Sosia, for one, is not to be duped by such fine words. His comment, in an aside, is that

> Le Seigneur Jupiter sçait dorer la Pilule. (III, x, 1913)

To gild the Pill! The phrase, in this our age of contraceptives, can hardly pass without additional irony, especially as it is pronounced just before we are told of the forthcoming birth of Hercules. In vain does a well-meaning friend of Amphitryon attempt some dubious congratulation. The last word is left to Sosia who remarks that in affairs of this kind it is always best to say nothing:

> Sur telles Affaires, toujours,
> Le meilleur est de ne rien dire. (III, x, 1942–3)

Thus the play ends in cautious derisive silence.

Ambiguity, in fact, has asserted itself as unconquerable from the very beginning. This is what the long, but otherwise subsidiary, scene between Mercury and Sosia signifies. Sosia is confronted at the door of his master's house with a double. Not so much a double who looks like him and behaves like him (in fact, his appearance and behaviour, though similar, are markedly different) but one who claims to be what he, Sosia, thought that he was. The poor servant is denied the use of his own name, given a sound thrashing whenever he tries to raise an objection, abused by the other individual, who has the cheek to call *him* executioner if he starts crying for help:

> Comment, Bourreau, tu fais des cris? (I, ii, 366)

Stubborn as he may be and, for a while, still unconvinced that blows make any difference except that he is now 'Sosie battu', the victim must finally give in, the other having for him, to speak like La Fontaine, 'La raison du plus fort' which is, of course, 'toujours la meilleure'. Besides, Mercury, with divine omniscience, knows every detail of the servant's past and the proofs he gives of this private knowledge seal the conviction of the poor bewildered fellow that the individual he faces can be no other than himself. But a final question remains: if he who thought himself to be Sosia is not Sosia, what is he? For he has to be something:

> Je ne saurais nier, aux preuves qu'on m'expose,
> Que tu ne sois Sosie; et j'y donne ma voix.
> Mais si tu l'es, dy-moy qui tu veux que je sois;
> Car encore faut-il bien que je sois quelque chose. (I, iii, 509–12)

The question, however, is left unanswered until, a little later, Amphitryon insists on being told everything. Sosia can only account for what has happened by saying that there must be two of him, that he has two selves, two 'Moi'. And now he flatters himself with the thought of his exact likeness to a smart *alter ego*:

> Des piez, jusqu'à la teste, il est comme moi fait;
> Beau, l'air noble, bien pris, les manières charmantes:
> Enfin deux gouttes de lait
> Ne sont pas plus ressemblantes (II, i, 783–6)

now, on the contrary, wishing to exculpate himself, he argues that the other fellow has the advantage of a stronger arm and a better courage. Vainglory mingles with hatred in his declamation against the tyranny of this other self:

> Ce Moy, qui le seul Moy veut estre:
> Ce Moy de Moy-mesme jaloux:
> Ce Moy vaillant, dont le courrous,

> Au Moy Poltron s'est fait connoistre:
> Enfin ce Moy, qui suis chez nous:
> Ce Moy qui s'est montré mon Maistre;
> Ce Moy, qui m'a roüe de coups.　　　　　　　　　　　(II, i, 814–20)

The results of Molière's comic strategy are here perceptible and, for all his debt to Plautus and Jean Rotrou, his immediate predecessor, bear witness to the originality of his genius. His frontal attack on the problem of personal identity enables him to explore, almost systematically, the animosities, the dramatic tensions which are at work within a divided personality. Their significance is not, however, fully disclosed in Sosia's row with his double. Unlike Jupiter, Mercury is not interested in the wife of the man whose identity he has usurped. And thus the antagonism loses much of its sting and of its meaning. For, in Molière no less than in Shakespeare, though with a different effect, love is the ultimate test.

Alcmena is conspicuously absent from the denouement of the drama of which she is the centre. Molière spares her the revelation, made by Jupiter in the last scene, that there were actually two Amphitryons, one her lover, the other her husband. The dictinction is one which she precisely refuses to admit, confident as she is that her husband is also her lover:

> Je ne sépare point ce qu'unissent les Dieux;
> Et l'Epous, et l'Amant me sont fort précieux.　　　　　　　　　(I, iii, 620–1)

There is in this some ground for the view which Jean Giraudoux, in his *Amphitryon 38*, takes of the heroine as the embodiment of woman's profoundly natural and virtuous simplicity—a simplicity which men and gods with their theories, their dogmas and their complications, do their best to destroy, though in vain. But Giraudoux was always a dreamer. Molière's Alcmena, the victim of a stratagem, is a pathetic figure and a disturbingly seductive one. She may have something of the miraculous innocence which Giraudoux sees in the character. She may be, as Thomas Heywood says in his *Silver Age*, 'honest in her worst dishonesty and chaste in the superlative degree of inchastity'.[8] But she remains unaware of her paradox. A suspicion of moral indifference and indiscriminate dedication to love attaches to this incomplete knowledge. There is about it that sense of feminine elusiveness which—with far less reason than general Amphitryon—general Othello was unable to bear.

But Amphitryon's manner of bearing it has nothing particularly commendable. When he learns from Sosia's double that another Amphitryon

> Est auprès de la belle Alcmène,
> A jouir des douceurs d'un aimable entretien,　　　　　　　　(III, ii, 1552–3)

his immediate concern is not with his love, his personal relationship with Alcmena. It is with his own image in the eyes of others, his honour. The question for him is whether he ought to conceal the dishonour of his house from the world or avenge himself publicly. His attachment to his wife is that of the owner to his property. The mutual bond comes first in his eyes and not the freedom of mutual enjoyment. In this he shows himself a mere husband.

The real point of Molière's play, however, is that Jupiter is also, in his way, a failure. And yet it is to him that Alcmena first appears with all the tender charm of one who finds it natural

21

to be both wife and mistress. In lines of a fervour and grace not unworthy of a character in Racine, she expresses, not so much pride in the victory of one so dearly loved, as her still trembling preoccupation with his safety:

> Et, de quelque Laurier qu'on couronne un Vainqueur;
> Quelque part que l'on ait à cet honneur suprème;
> Vaut-il ce qu'il en couste aux tendresses d'un Cœur,
> Qui peut, à tout moment, trembler pour ce qu'il aime? (I, iii, 561-4)

But, listening to words meant for Amphitryon, Jupiter is perplexed with care as well as increased passion. Though prevented from being too explicit about it, he would prefer to be loved, not as the husband which he is not, but exclusively as the lover which he is:

> En moy, belle et charmante Alcmène,
> Vous voyez un Mary; vous voyez un Amant:
> Mais l'Amant seul me touche à parler franchement;
> Et je sens près de vous que le Mary le gesne. (I, iii, 589-92)

The fashionable casuistry of courtly love which he uses cannot disguise the fact that he is above all self-seeking. The favours of Alcmena would be nothing to him if not freely given to his own absolute freedom, regardless of any human title or duty. They *are* actually nothing to him, for he has had them already. This scene, the first in which we see him with her, is a scene of leave-taking after the night. 'I would wish', he says,

> Qu'à vostre seule ardeur, qu'à ma seule personne,
> Je dûsse les faveurs que je reçois de vous. (I, iii, 573-4)

To have enjoyed the beauty and tenderness of Alcmena is then not enough. He must still strive for the impossible, that is strive to be and not to be Amphitryon; to be known as his quintessential and divine self while passing for the worthy general. In the end, of course, he has to admit his defeat: what he has obtained was not won by himself and for himself but given to the husband.

The self-regarding, inconstant, lover and the inadequate husband, Jupiter and Amphitryon, are recognized human types. They seem to make of the play a kind of domestic comedy. In the same manner, the master–servant relationship which it so fully explores is the occasion for many remarks on contemporary society. The element of social criticism which is commonly regarded as characteristic of Molière is by no means absent from *Amphitryon*. But the merit of this play is to show with unusual clarity that, whatever the social or other implications of a comedy, its essence finally resides in the understanding and interpretation of human personality. A comedy is always a psychomachia and its worth depends upon the skill and penetration with which the author manipulates the forces at war in man's consciousness—and his unconscious. Thus, as in Sosia's dispute with Mercury, Jupiter and Amphitryon stand for the two 'Moi' of a divided individual. But this time the division is seen as due to love and the terror it inspires. The simplicity of love is too much for man and he is tempted either to rush into the dream of infinite desire or to recoil and fall back upon reassuring positions, the security of ownership, the guarantee of marriage. Another and no less important meaning is added to the moral of this fable by Jupiter's own part in the disaster. Molière has reduced him to a very human stature and does not ask us to believe in his mythological grandeur. Yet Alcmena's lover retains something of his prestige as king of the gods and master of the universe. We cannot entirely forget that he is the supreme representative of order, the intelligence of the world. His symbolic function in psychological drama is therefore invested with the highest mental dignity. He stands for what is, or at least ought to be, supreme in man: the power of reason. It is then of no small consequence that he should have come to grief by practising upon Alcmena's honesty: confronted with the mystery of love, reason has been found to be a fraud.

In an article published a few years ago, Lionel Gossman has argued that Molière's play was intended, under the influence of Gassendi, as an answer to Descartes and his hypothesis of the wicked genius.[9] Wishing to meet even the most extreme objection against his view that the ego provides a sure basis for knowledge, Descartes had supposed, in his *Méditations*, that there is no truthful God but a certain *Malus Genius*, a spirit of deceit, endowed with no less power than cunning. What the hypothesis, however, was made to demonstrate is that, even though the wicked genius renders it impossible for reason to determine which appearances do and which do not correspond to reality, doubt cannot reach the I itself. With Molière, on the other hand, the wicked genius prevails. The ego's intense preoccupation with itself is finally self-destructive and reason, confounding itself, confuses everything.

Even if one is reluctant to admit that such things were dreamt of in Molière's philosophy, *Amphitryon* remains a deeply significant play, significant not only in itself, but also, as I should now like to indicate very briefly, for the light it throws on the whole of Molière's theatre.

Just before he meets his double at the beginning of the comedy, Sosia is seen soliloquizing in front of his master's house. He has been sent by Amphitryon to tell Alcmena of her husband's imminent return after complete victory over the enemy, and, in order to make it impressive enough, he decides to prepare his speech. What in Plautus is a rather tedious recital of past events, becomes in Molière the full rehearsal of a scene with three different characters. Like Launce with his shoe, staff, hat and dog, Sosia with his lantern plays many parts: that of Sosia as he imagines himself making his speech, that of Alcmena interrupting and asking questions, that of Sosia as observer, commenting upon the fertility of his own invention. The point is that Sosia is twice himself: voluble and boasting on the one hand, overwhelmed with admiration on the other. Thereupon Mercury enters to act the part of a still more vocal and pugnacious Sosia, while the other must be content with being abused and beaten. The meaning is clear: Sosia has brought down upon himself the visitation of supernatural mischief by indulging his own propensity to histrionics.

Now we know that the role of Sosia was taken by Molière himself. We also know that his extraordinary virtuosity as an actor was noted by his contemporaries. Donneau de Visé, for instance, writes that 'He seemed to have several voices all speaking in him; and with a step, a smile, a lowering of an eyelid, and a tilt of the head, he could give more of an idea of things than the greatest talker could have done in an hour.'[10] We may say that the character of Sosia, though not exactly a self-portrait, provides Molière with a means of dramatizing his own destiny and reflecting upon his own work. The son of a good bourgeois family, he had, at the age of twenty, given up the security of the legal profession in order to throw himself body and soul into the mad adventure of the boards. It was a choice he would never cease to debate in his comedies. There had been both exhilaration and misgiving about it, the exhilaration of freedom, the misgiving that he might lose himself. With the development of his thought and art, a growing sense of the excitement and impending danger is felt in his plays. The mounting tension is specially perceptible in the three major ones. They succeed one another, it is worth noting, in the years immediately before *Amphitryon*: *Tartuffe*, the first two versions of which are dated 1664 and 1667, *Dom Juan* in 1665, *Le Misanthrope* in 1666. In each case the bold lively challenge to bourgeois virtue meets the resistance of a stubborn attachment to common sense and responsibility. In each case the outcome of the conflict is different.

Tartuffe, the hypocrite, acts the part of the devout holy man with such perfection that, catching the confidence of religious-minded Orgon, he all but succeeds in robbing him of his young wife, his house and his property. The menace to personal integrity is here all the more subtle as the liar plays the game of truth, the actor that of puritan hatred of the stage. And as Molière goes on fighting his great quarrel with the enemies of the theatre, the figure of Tartuffe, in the successive versions, seems to become increasingly disquieting. The threat, however, is still muffled. Hypocrisy being the tribute paid by vice to virtue, it looks less alarming and calls for a less open reaction from sincerity.

Dom Juan, the universal seducer, embodies the theatrical impulse with aristocratic panache and fearlessness. The spirit of play-acting seems to glory in his inconsequence and intrepidity. He is handsome, he is clever, he is humorous, his irreligion is full of humanity. One would easily take him for a modern hero of irreverence and rebellious thought. Three hundred years later, on a warm night of May, he would have adorned the Latin Quarter with barricades and bonfires, taken the Odéon by storm, inscribed the maxims of 'contestation' on the incredulous walls of the Sorbonne. No one would have more truthfully declared: 'The more I make love, the more I want to make the revolution.' At the same time, there is resentment at his faithlessness. He is denounced as a bad man, though of gentle birth. But the denunciation is voiced on the whole clumsily by a blockhead of a servant, a lachrymose wife, a pompous petulant father. Dom Juan is silenced in the end by the Statue of the Governor, but the charm of his vitality remains, while morality, a mere piece of stone, can win but little sympathy. It is as if the histrionic tendency was still felt to be more promising than dangerous.

In the next play, *Le Misanthrope*, the attraction of irresponsible versatility is not diminished; on the contrary, it is now seen in the shape of the adorable Célimène. But here the protest of honesty is invested with all the personal and social distinction, the mental and moral vigour of Alceste. A blunt man himself, he is passionate and even quarrelsome in his demand for truth in others. Yet he cannot help loving the young widow, a born actress, who excels at imitating her acquaintances to make fun of them, a woman of fashion who delights in all the frivolous intrigues of society. It would be, if they were to marry, the most incredible and the most blissful match. The issue is left beautifully, distressingly, undecided. *Le Misanthrope* is Molière's greatest play because it states his inward struggle with perfect and almost unbearable equanimity. The infinite variety of life, which the stage tries to mirror, could not be more alluring to the man of the theatre than under the appearance of wit and charm in the person of Célimène. But against this seduction, the plain man rises, resentful and loving, prompted to the most severe indictment of society—so severe that there seems to be an intimation of revolution about it— and above all urging his claim to remain true to himself, and to be known and loved for what he is really, personally. There was, one imagines, a brief, breathtaking, moment when Molière almost thought the reconciliation, the fulfilment, possible.

To this illusion *Amphitryon* deals the decisive blow. Tartuffe had already caused some anxiety. It was rather disturbing to think that so determined a villain could be mistaken by everyone for a saint. Vituperated as the author of a most vicious attack on religion and society, Molière had pleaded with his powerful enemies, and no doubt with himself, that the play ran on the difference between a genuinely devout man and one that is falsely so. The trouble is that it is practically impossible for the observer to make the distinction. It was only at the last minute and not very convincingly, that the Impostor, as Tartuffe is also called, had been prevented from doing his worst by the king's police. This time it is the king, I mean Jupiter, who is the impostor, as he himself proclaims in the last scene:

> Regarde, Amphitryon, quel est ton Imposteur.   (III, x, 1890)

This means that Molière has given up not only what hope he may have had in social order as safeguard of personal identity but also much of his determination to see it safeguarded. We live in a world of appearances. We *are* a world of appearances, ever-renewed in the endless metamorphosis of play-acting. There is obviously no cause in this for renouncing laughter. It is even about to become more reckless, more riotous than ever, in *Les Fourberies de Scapin*, for instance. There is no reason either why Molière should not indulge the taste of his royal master for the unreal world of 'comédies-ballet'. At the same time, there is a feeling that something—or somebody—has been hurt and rendered helpless. Most of the last plays—*L'Avare*, *Le Bourgeois Gentilhomme*, *Le Malade Imaginaire*, to name only a few—are about mad or foolish old men, who cling desperately to some treasure, some whim, some vanity, while their sons and women-folk humour, cajole, and bait them gleefully. Five years after *Amphitryon*, on 17 February 1673, while acting the part of the imaginary invalid with his usual energy, Molière fell ill and died before the end of the night. It was a most appropriate death in which, so to speak, the actor had killed the man.

We may seem to be a long way from Shakespeare. Shakespearian comedy does not incline towards the worrying of fathers by the younger generation. 'Wronging the ancientry' may be one of the many grudges which the Old Shepherd in *The Winter's Tale* has against the age 'between ten and three-and-twenty'. But the function of youth in this play is rather to restore a father to the fullness of life and authority by bringing about the resurrection of a seeming-dead mother. The theme in *Pericles, Prince of Tyre* is very much the same. And this leads me back to *The Comedy of Errors* which also owes a great deal to the story of Apollonius of Tyre. It was not quite true to say, as I have done, that every single piece of the family puzzle is given at the start. We must wait until the last scene to be introduced to the Abbess and it is only some eighty lines before the end that we learn that she is Aemilia, the mother. The late and unexpected revelation of her presence—a procedure which, as Bertrand Evans remarks,[11] is otherwise unexampled in Shakespeare—the religious atmosphere with which she is surrounded and her own religious dignity, the salutary part she plays in preventing Adriana for the last time from taking hold of the wrong husband, everything tends to enhance her figure and to give it the halo of supernatural sanctity. In her maternal hands, the healing of ambiguity is not merely nature rediscovered, it is also the disclosure of a mystery. The play ends on the idea of new birth mixing, not without strangeness, with that of marriage. In the mystic experience of love, Shakespeare seems to say, man newly made overcomes his contradictions. While, for Molière, perplexity can only be eased by letting protean life overwhelm all care for consistency.

But the real purpose of Shakespeare's as well as Molière's comedy is not to offer a way out of ambiguity. It is much rather to face it. The escapes which they propose may well have mostly to do with their own obsessions. There is indeed in these escapes something curiously reminiscent of the terror inspired by the two tragic errors linked together in the Oedipus story: killing the father and marrying the mother. Which of the two sacrilegious deeds each dramatist found most unthinkable may be reflected in his attempt to turn the other alternative into a comic issue. But Shakespeare and Molière are at their comic best in the spirit which prompts them to laugh and make us laugh at our anxious fear of the great tragic doom. The lesson which they teach is one that nobody could have learnt and taught better than the two most complete men of the theatre at a time when the theatre was the most complete 'glass of fashion'. They say that, since man cannot help being an actor, it is better for him to know that he is one; better for him not to believe that he is simply what he is. That, indeed, is the darkness of ignorance which leaves Malvolio 'more puzzled than the Egyptians in their fog'. On the other hand, there is such honesty in Shakespeare and Molière that they cannot and will not surrender the claims of sincerity. I sometimes fancy that no one more than they hated the stage to which they devoted the best of their lives. It is a perfectly ridiculous situation and the abstract of man's predicament. To laugh at it may not be wisdom itself but it is, perhaps, the beginning of wisdom.

© MICHEL GRIVELET 1969

NOTES

1. *Des Métaphores obsédantes au mythe personnel* (Paris, 1963), p. 293.

2. *Pensées*, ed. Leon Brunschvicg, II, 133 (Paris, 1935), p. 389.

3. All quotations are from *The Comedy of Errors*, ed. R. A. Foakes, The New Arden Shakespeare (1962).

4. All quotations are from *Amphitryon*, ed. Pierre Mélèse, Textes Littéraires Français (Paris, 1950).

5. *Myth*, a symposium edited by Thomas A. Sebeck (Indiana University Press, 1958), pp. 91–2.

6. *La Critique de l'École des Femmes*, scene vi.

7. Harold Brooks, 'Themes and Structure in *The Comedy of Errors*', Early Shakespeare, Stratford-upon-Avon Studies 3, ed. J. R. Brown and Bernard Harris (1961), pp. 55–71.

8. Thomas Heywood, *The Silver Age*, II. i (Heywood, *The Golden and Silver Ages*, ed. J. P. Collier, The Shakespeare Society, 1851, p. 110).

9. 'Molière's *Amphitryon*', PMLA, LXXVIII (1963), 201–13.

10. As quoted by René Bray, 'The Actor', in *Molière: A Collection of Critical Essays*, ed. Jacques Guicharnaud, Twentieth Century Views (Englewood Cliffs, New Jersey, 1964), p. 15.

11. Bertrand Evans, *Shakespeare's Comedies* (Oxford, 1960), pp. 8–9.

COMIC STRUCTURE AND TONAL MANIPULATION IN SHAKESPEARE AND SOME MODERN PLAYS

BY

HERBERT S. WEIL, Jr.

In the final moments of Edward Albee's *The American Dream*, the mother—a bit tipsy—begins to seduce The Young Man, who has just been adopted by her family to replace another young man, now lost. Mommy mumbles:

Something familiar about you. You know that? I can't quite place it.

Then Grandma interrupts and speaks directly to the audience:

Well, I guess that about wraps it up. I mean, for better or worse, this is a comedy, and I don't think we'd better go any further. No, definitely not. So, let's leave things as they are right now—while everybody's got what he wants...or everybody's got what he thinks he wants. Good night, dears.

Albee's Grandma protests too much. Certainly she knows that, for a traditional comedy, the audience does not expect the kind of situation that has been developing. Although Albee tries to answer critics of his play by insisting in his brief preface that it is a comedy, he goes on to ask a few lines later:

Is my play offensive? I certainly hope so; it was my intention to offend—as well as to amuse and entertain.

Still more cynical and aggressive is the curtain speech of Irma in Genet's *The Balcony*. After she puts out the lights of the chambers in her brothel where the customers come to play out their favourite masochistic roles, she turns wearily to the audience and projects her future beyond tonight's play:

In a little while, I'll have to start all over again...put all the lights on again...dress up...distribute roles again...assume my own.

She then stops to direct the spectators:

Prepare yours...You must go home now, where everything—you can be quite sure—will be even falser than here.

At first glance, there can seem to be little basis for comparison between *The American Dream* and *A Midsummer Night's Dream* or between *The Balcony* and *Measure for Measure*. In all of Shakespeare, I think only Pandarus, who bequeathes his diseases to the audience he insults, is so abusive. But I shall attempt to suggest that second and third thoughts will uncover major similarities in the demands upon the spectator made by the best modern plays and by most of Shakespeare's comedies. These endings by Albee and Genet display an effort typical of many

27

modern plays not only to involve the spectator but also to confuse him. Such explicit statements to the spectator insist that he be conscious of *some* relation between the world of the play and the world it imitates. They suggest that this relation is a displacement, not a copy. In Shakespeare's comedies, such reminders are frequent, but much more muted. He may hint, as in the epilogues of Puck, Prospero, and the King of France, that the relation of actor to audience should supersede the internal action of the play. Through Feste's song, he even suggests that the happy play-world does *not* mirror the everyday world of the audience. But unlike Irma or Pandarus or even the slightly bullying Rosalind, each of these speakers humbly submits himself and his play to the judgement of the spectators.

In contrast to the final speaker in any of Shakespeare's comedies, Albee's Grandma explicitly claims that things will get worse for the characters in the play after the customary happy ending. She seems to share Eric Bentley's view that comedy is more pessimistic than tragedy for it requires that we simply refuse to consider essential matters. In Shakespeare's comedies there may be suggestions, barely hinted or baldly stated, that the ending may not lead to eternal bliss (as in Gratiano's poor jest or Lucio's displeasure at the prospect of marriage). But never in such dissimilar villains and victims as Malvolio, Don John, and Shylock does Shakespeare suggest a future that cannot or should not be faced.

No one can really accept Albee's consciously artificial ending as a happy one. His Grandma may insist that, *because* the play is a comedy, the representation can simply stop. But certainly this arbitrary interruption of the action at a point short of its resolution has not precluded hints of behaviour that many consider outside the realm of comedy. Through his spokesman, Albee pretends to employ common attitudes toward the genre, but actually he is mocking such responses. In fact, Albee insults any member of his audience who might tend to believe in his ending. Taken literally, the overt viewpoint of Grandma may seem absurd, but it embodies one of the most pervasive—if often unformulated—prejudices about comedy. This is clearly and correctly rejected by the author, except as a resounding surface against which we may test our own conceptions.

By refusing to let the spectator accept its formal statement, the play shares the structural ambiguity of other modern plays. When we examine *Who's Afraid of Virginia Woolf?*, *The Balcony*, *Henry IV* or *Judith*, we discover that each employs a structure not immediately apparent—so that the spectator does not know what to expect. This is true whether the play ends in a disaster (as in *Sarjeant Musgrave's Dance*) or in a muted victory (perhaps *The Caretaker*) or in a neutral suspension (*Waiting for Godot*). Each play seeks effects or meanings, particularly in its conclusion, not immediately clear to most spectators. Our concern here is not that we need agree upon the genre of these plays, but simply that we observe—or remember—how little, upon our first exposure to them, their possible parallels to more traditional patterns influenced us. Yet this does not imply that there is no veiled supporting structure which becomes significant to an over-view or an after-view.

A dramatist can employ his structure either to mislead or to operate by delayed effects, as we can see by comparing Giraudoux's *Judith* with Pirandello's *Henry IV*. Because we feel familiar with the Biblical story underlying *Judith*, we should not be surprised when the play ends with the glorification of the heroine. Its ostensibly comic movement and conclusion seem, upon first impression, to be the reverse of those in Pirandello's work. But like Henry, Judith has at first seemed extremely limited, almost defined by the role she must play. Like Henry, she surprises us by her growth and transformation. In both plays, this achievement provides a false climax; Judith and Henry falter, or—to be more precise—become trapped in situations they seemingly had mastered. Judith kills the one heroic figure in her play—for which she is made a miserable saint. And Henry kills the only character who grasps the truth of his role-playing. After this act, neither he nor we can imagine for him any way out into a better world—or any further satisfaction in the world he had invented before regaining his senses. The actions of the two plays, apparently opposite in direction, move their central figures to startlingly similar final positions. Within each play, however, the *other* characters maintain divergent attitudes toward these main figures at the curtain; and, I suspect, most spectators find themselves with mixed feelings.

In Shakespeare's romantic comedies, structure is a much more reliable guide to our expectations of *what* will happen. But that the audience is not insulted or confused, and that there are no explicit forecasts of a horrible future, should not blind us to important similarities between Shakespeare's comedies and these disturbing modern plays. We are justified in treating Shakespeare's romantic fables as simple and reliable comic structures only if affirmation and joyous festivity are the sole legitimate perspectives they offer. In a talk of this length, I want to suggest only that like *The American Dream* and *Judith*, most of Shakespeare's comedies are *open* to different legitimate responses by different members of the same audience—or even by the same spectator who watches contrasting productions of the same play. We enjoy a freedom to ponder the meanings of these plays because we can—and usually should—remain detached from the characters, the obstacles they face, the choices they make. Moments of realism (like Andrew Aguecheek's 'I was adored once too') are out of the ordinary in the comedies; treatment of character varies in depth and consistency, often from scene to scene. In Shakespeare's comedies —from *Love's Labour's Lost* to *The Tempest*—we see that character does not always determine action. Nor can a character invariably be judged by what he does. Similarly unusual are reliable choral comments. We seldom identify our views and evaluations with those of a protagonist as we do with Rosalind's, or with one of the many characters who claims to be a reliable spokesman. Consequently, the action is unlikely to lead to a clear representation of a theme. Thematic unity in these plays can grow only from situations in which the spectator is asked to participate, to formulate his own attitudes, or at least to see that those offered are too facile. Any simple explanation, therefore, will be unlikely to satisfy us.

The openness and potential multiplicity of Shakespeare's comic form can be found, to varying degrees, in all of his plays. One simple way to investigate its limits is to test the reliability of alleged choral characters in two contrasting plays. In *Measure for Measure*, those characters with whose fates we have been intensely involved, repeatedly give way to new sketched figures. Instead of Isabella or Claudio, first Mariana, then Barnardine, and then Ragozine, perform the required functions of being figuratively raped or executed. These suddenly presented characters engage us less and less, and it becomes increasingly difficult to take them or their dangers very seriously. At the same time, the action no longer focuses on the stirring debates of Isabella first with Angelo and then with Claudio. Instead, the dialogues between the Duke and Lucio dominate the stage with their wild accusations and fantasies. Isabella's moral dilemma is glossed over by the strange—perhaps improvised—methods of the disguised Duke, as he, like a vaudeville performer, substitutes heads and virgins. Are we to think that this controlling character fully knows himself when he assures Isabella, 'To the love I have in doing good, a remedy presents itself?' Or when he describes himself to Lucio, 'Let him be but testimonied in his own bringings-forth, and he shall appear to the envious, a scholar, a statesman, and a soldier?'

Any spectators who have picked up the egoism, the repetitions, and the inconsistencies of the Duke will relish the contradiction implicit in the first line of the speech with which he concludes the play. When Lucio objects that he is being forced to marry a whore, Kate Keep-down, Duke Vincentio magisterially answers, 'Slandering a prince deserves it'. No matter how serious an offence slandering a ruler might be for a Jacobean audience, the punishment hardly fits the crime. Certainly the alert spectator could not forget that only five lines earlier the Duke had told Lucio, 'Thy slanders I forgive'. Even a less attentive spectator would probably notice such a flat reversal. If the subordination of Claudio, Angelo and Isabella suggests the disjunction of character, decision and ensuing action, the manner in which the Duke is presented as he comes to control the plot reinforces—rather than converts—this disjunction. His methods lead us to no new insights into the working out of such important thematic problems as the relation of mercy to justice.

In *A Midsummer Night's Dream*, the festive ending is barely qualified by our awareness of any disturbing realism or inconclusive thematic resolutions. In *Measure for Measure*, we might almost say that because character is developed beyond the requirements of the comic plot, some spectators and critics have made inappropriate demands upon the play. Some have treated Isabella and Angelo as if they should receive the development appropriate to the hero in a biography or a novel; some have managed to discover in the Duke himself a reflexion of Providence or of an ideal King James. In *A Midsummer Night's Dream*, on the other hand, the minimal characterization leads to surprising but testable inferences, as in the chapter by Jan Kott, who declares:

The entire action of this hot night, everything that has happened at this drunken party, is based on the complete exchangeability of love-partners...This reduction of characters to love-partners seems to me to be the most peculiar characteristic of this cruel dream; and perhaps its most modern quality. The partner is now nameless and faceless. He or she just happens to be the nearest.[1]

Probably most of us would agree that as long as the four lovers finally pair off to *their* mutual satisfaction, we feel no great concern over which boy goes with which girl. Nor, I suspect, do most spectators recall which lover speaks such memorable lines as, 'So quick bright things come to confusion'. Why then does there seem something drastically misleading in Kott's assertion? Partly because each lover, however two-dimensional, thinks, speaks, and acts in an identifiable manner. Neither girl is ever unfaithful; Lysander becomes untrue only temporarily and only when he has received the irresistible potion—given of course through a mistake by Puck. Only because Demetrius bears some likeness to Proteus, only because he has switched the object of his love before the action of the play started, are we justified in finding some analogy between the supernatural potion and love, or lust. To discount such observations is to risk bringing one's subjective impressions into the argument—and treating them as evidence *within* the play.

To draw earnest literal inferences from the action can be as dangerous. The complications of the plot do develop from one clearly presented mistake by Puck. To the fairy, faithful Lysander, because he is obeying Hermia's command to 'lie further off', *must* be the 'lack-love, kill-courtesy churl', Demetrius. But to notice this nice touch, lightly mocking a kind of puritanism in manners and morals, surely cannot justify us in considering the play as a serious attack on either modesty or chastity.

In fact, to treat Puck or any other fairy as a *consistently* reliable commentator is always a questionable step. To them, all the mortals are fools. When Titania awakens from her dream, she looks on Bottom and exclaims: 'O! how mine eyes do loathe his image now!' Here she echoes Oberon's description of Bottom as 'this hateful fool', lines she could not hear because she was sleeping blissfully—under the influence of the so-called 'cruel dream' which led her to return the changeling boy to Oberon and thereby effect their reconciliation. One of the splendid and joyous ironies of the play lies in contrasting the fairies' heartless and snobbish attitude toward Bottom—so close to that of Demetrius and Lysander toward his Pyramus—with the *experience* of the dream Bottom suggests in his own marvellous description. We must not try to draw overly precise inferences from the action of such a comedy. How is our delight diminished if we notice that Bottom, Peter Quince and company never quite manage to finish their play or receive their reward? And for which of us does not Bottom's dream far surpass both Hermia's dream and Titania's?

I certainly do not intend to suggest that a straightforward acceptance of Shakespeare's comic affirmations is *never* the best approach. However, because affirmation in comedy has received the most intelligent and stimulating criticism—as for example in the well-known works of Frye, Barber, and Gardner—I feel that possible alternative perspectives now need more of our attention. It is important that we should be able to understand how *Much Ado About Nothing* can succeed for the spectator who does *not* believe in Claudio's transformation after he insults Hero, Leonato, and Antonio both in the church and after he believes Hero to be dead.

If we talk about comedy in the traditional sense of a work with a happy ending, we *must* mean a happy ending that *convinces* the spectator. Frye has pointed out that 'except for death, life has little to suggest in the way of plausible conclusions...The requirements of literary form and plausible content always fight against each other.'[2] We might apply this to suggest that for a comedy that has depth or complexity, the ending will be completely convincing only in so far as we attend to its formal aspects—and to no others. When credible motivation is used, even intermittently, as for Duke Vincentio, Angelo, Bassanio, Claudio, and Valentine, the adequacy of the epiphany must remain in some doubt.

If the basic form of a Shakespearian comedy is open, admitting attitudes which coexist with the predominant festivity, then its essence may well lie close to the ambivalence of the history play brilliantly argued at Stratford-upon-Avon seventeen years ago by A. P. Rossiter:

I mean by 'Ambivalence' that two opposed value-judgements are subsumed and that both are valid... All simplifications are not only falsifications, they amount to a denial of some part of the mystery of things.[3]

It might be thought that by accepting multiplicity as a formal principle for Shakespearian comedy, we risk chaotic permissiveness. But when the form is open or the theme problematic, it becomes even more important for the critic to weigh evidence with care.[4] We can hardly agree with my student who doggedly argued that Troilus did not love Cressida because he never discussed marriage.

From the perspectives we have been sketching, *Troilus and Cressida* and even *Antony and Cleopatra* are not a cynical reaction to the joyous romantic comedies. Instead, they develop a strand that has been present—if less insistent—through most of Shakespeare's comedies. Alert critics and directors will probably find many effective multiple perspectives beyond those we now recognize. But the consummate achievement will probably remain the second scene in Act v of *Troilus and Cressida*. When Cressida commits herself to Diomedes while Troilus and Ulysses watch together and Thersites watches alone, we have at least five clear perspectives on the action. We have the biting cynicism of Thersites—balancing the simple disillusion of Troilus so that the urbane cynicism of Ulysses almost becomes a sane rationalism by contrast. We have black and cruel humour from Thersites, an anti-hero in Troilus whose strange sexual fears and whose weird self-analysis—'Truth is my vice'—have all been justified. In his relativistic universe, Troilus identifies all virtue with that he has misplaced in Cressida. And she is a modern heroine—a Judith of Giraudoux—with an open-eyed awareness of what she is doing and what she is losing.

This scene offers a detached over-view for the spectator, multiple perspectives, the shattering of illusions, the self-conscious drawing attention to artifice and to form. Of the traditional characteristics of comedy, it lacks only joyous humour and a happy ending. And something like these is provided by the unexpected growth in wisdom and compassion by the commentators, Ulysses and Thersites. For these two, Shakespeare provides a surprising development of character that foreshadows one significant type of modern comic resolution—that used for George in *Who's Afraid of Virginia Woolf?* and Aston in *The Caretaker*. If an ending of this type succeeds, it does so primarily because it develops from its own very special context within the play and because it is appropriate to the abilities and potentialities of its specific hero. Our initial dissatisfaction with these endings (as with the more problematic conclusions of *Measure for Measure*—and perhaps *The Merchant of Venice* or *The Jew of Malta*) seems a necessary stage toward any full appreciation. We might say that the dramatist aims at our *delayed* recognition of the rightness of his ending.

But the comic vision need not be so modest. Its triumphs range from the simple existence of Sebastian to the conversion of Oliver and the repentance of Angelo. The words of Albee's Grandma: 'For better or worse, this is a comedy, and I don't think we'd better go any further'— can apply only if comedy pretends to the *whole* truth—and therefore tries to become an escape from the world it imitates. Shakespeare's best comedies make no such claim. Instead, they present for us *part* of the truth and invite us to relate that part to whatever whole we can imagine or understand.

NOTES

1. Jan Kott, *Shakespeare our Contemporary* (New York, 1966), pp. 219–20.

2. Northrop Frye, *Fables of Identity* (New York, 1963), p. 36.

3. A. P. Rossiter, *Angel with Horns and other Shakespeare Lectures*, ed. Graham Story (New York, 1961), p. 51.

4. Ambivalence is also one of the best tools we have to consider laughter and vitality—which seem so difficult to relate convincingly with any depth or precision to the rest of the play. The idea of ambivalence helps us distinguish between immediate impact and our delayed responses, or between impact and function. For example, in *Marat/Sade* it is invaluable to help discuss the relation of the playful tone and surface of the songs to their brutal subject-matter. Celia and Rosalind employ such a contrast much more lightly when they jest about sexual looseness. And Shakespeare's Cressida vividly creates such a tension in her early banter with Pandarus, where the rhythm seems to set up a series of clichés that are contradicted by her words.

LAUGHING WITH THE AUDIENCE: 'THE TWO GENTLEMEN OF VERONA' AND THE POPULAR TRADITION OF COMEDY

BY

ROBERT WEIMANN

Laughter with the audience can be and has been approached from at least two quite different angles: on the one hand from that of the theatre and social custom and ritual, on the other from that of aesthetics and the theory of comedy. Dover Wilson was perhaps the first to remark, many years ago, that Shakespeare 'gets his audience to laugh, quite as often *with* his characters as *at* them'.[1] In more recent years, the social and dramatic background of the actor–audience relationship has been brilliantly explored by Anne Righter and C. L. Barber, and this has— in connexion with the reassessment of the Elizabethan platform stage by G. F. Reynolds, Richard Hosley, W. C. Hodges, Glynne Wickham, Bernard Beckerman and others—con- siderably modified our conceptions not only of the Elizabethan theatre but of the theatrical modes and possibilities of Shakespearian comedy and, of course, of laughter in this comedy.

Now such laughter on the comic stage has both a history and a theory, and from a compara- tive point of view it may perhaps be desirable to try and link up the historical (or theatrical), and the theoretical (or typological) aspects. Quite to integrate them must in the last resort involve both a historical view of theory and a theoretical view of history, and it would of course call for a vast amount of documentation.[2] It seems therefore more fruitful just to raise the problem (without necessarily suggesting all the answers) and to do so within the limited context of one Shakespearian play. I shall take as my text *The Two Gentlemen of Verona*, where laughing with the audience can be studied in its dramatic functioning and where it serves, perhaps for the first time in Shakespeare's work, as an essential means of organizing, controlling and evaluating experience through a larger comic vision. Here, then, it assumes something of a structural significance, in the light of which some problems as to the reading of this early and experimental, but seminal, comedy can perhaps be viewed from a fresh angle.

I

But before we come to the play itself, let us take a hasty glance towards a theoretical problem which has repeatedly come up in recent criticism of Shakespeare, particularly in the course of the 1968 Stratford Conference: the nature of comedy and the question of *types* or *kinds* of comedy. If the comedy of laughing with the audience were to be fitted into a typological scheme, or into a system of types, it would certainly not be classed among what has traditionally been called 'New Comedy'. In the largely neoclassical tradition of Menander, Jonson, Molière, Lessing, Ostrowski and Ibsen, the audience, if indeed it laughs at all, definitely laughs *at* but never *with* the comic figure. The comic figure so laughed at, usually is the comic *character* of dramatic illusion, but hardly ever the comic *actor*. The resulting laughter is inspired not by a more or less traditional feeling of social unity between audiences and *actors* but by a critical view of the contradictions between the norms of society and the unconventional standards of comic *characters*, be they the dupes or intriguers, the cheats or butts of society. The informing comic vision is essentially critical (or satirical, ironical, etc.) because the resolutions it offers are so many ways of exposing the human inadequacy of the antisocial attitudes of hypocrisy, vanity, snobbery, bureaucracy, as well as all kinds of mechanical or inorganic ways of isolation from the given norms of living.

It is, at any rate, this kind of comedy, which the classic writers on the subject (such as Meredith) are discussing, and it is this kind of comic effect with the psychology of which Bergson, in *Le Rire*, is concerned. While some of the more important recent studies on the subject, such as Jurij Borew's long book *On the Comic*, follow this tradition and consider laughter mainly as a 'weapon', as directed 'against any phenomenon which deserves to be criticised and condemned',[3] we have to go as far back as Hegel to find a more relevant, though still very general, theory of what I (for the sake of brevity) call laughing with the audience. Hegel in his *Aesthetics* draws attention to the fundamental distinction in comedy, 'whether the acting characters are for themselves comic or whether they appear so only to the audience'.[4] While the latter appear—to Hegel—as merely ridiculous, the former are more truly comic in the sense that they enjoy the 'blessed ease of a subjectivity which, as it is sure of itself, can bear the dissolution of its own ends and means' ('*die Seligkeit und Wohligkeit der Subjectivität, die, ihrer selbst gewiß, die Auflösung ihrer Zwecke und Realisationen ertragen kann*'). Hegel gives no examples, but is probably thinking of the security and ease of such comic characters in Aristophanes as Dikaiopolis in *The Acharnians* or Trygaios in *Peace*. Such a comic figure is truly comic, when 'the seriousness of his will and purpose is not to himself serious', and when his own mode of existence is free from any *Entzweiung*, any disunion or disruption of self and society.[5] Now this theoretical or comparative approach to comedy, which my summary very much oversimplifies, suffers, in our present context, from several weaknesses which result from the highly speculative nature of these theories but especially from the fact that they completely ignore the practical and historical experience of the theatre as a social and technical institution. As recent research into Shakespeare's platform stage has made clearer than ever before, his theatre is, historically speaking, a highly complex and transitional institution in which there was room for (in Lyly's words) the most astonishing 'mingle mangle', for a true 'gallimaufray' of medieval and traditional as well as Renaissance and classical conventions, from which no single formula of comedy can be abstracted. Consequently, laughter in Shakespearian comedy cannot be reduced to any one comic pattern, or structure, or mood, and to realize this is to realize the limitations of any typological system, and the limited extent to which Shakespeare's comedy can be fitted into the categories of such a system.

II

If, then, we understand the various types of Shakespearian comedy and laughter against the historical background and the various social traditions of Shakespeare's theatre, we hardly have to remind ourselves that, in *The Two Gentlemen of Verona*, laughing with the audience is part of a larger whole: it is limited and defined by its context of speech, character and plot. To study the traditional popular mode in comedy, then, is first of all to be aware of this dramatic context which, in *The Two Gentlemen*, is largely built up by several conventions of speech and disguise, and various degrees and ways of audience awareness, such as are mainly associated with the characters of Speed, Launce and Julia.

To suggest the significance of this context, I can look at only two such conventions. First of all there is the series of *comic asides* by Speed in the first scene of the second act; Valentine, addressing Silvia in the style of courtly romance, greets her as 'Madam and mistress' with 'a thousand good morrows'—which Speed, turning aside, echoes as 'a million of manners' (II, i, 88 ff.).[6] While Silvia and Valentine are exchanging their high-flown compliments and Silvia is wooing her Valentine, in Speed's words, 'by a figure' (the figure of his self-written love-letter), the clown continues to comment aside. These comments are definitely not over-heard by Silvia and Valentine: they form no part of their dialogue, nor are they in the nature of any monologue or self-expression. Rather, they address the audience as from the angle of some kind of comic chorus; and it is through the comic chorus quality of Speed's comments that a dramatic interplay between the wit of the audience and the wittiness of the clown is achieved. The resulting laughter, both in the yard and on the scaffolds, shares the same per-spective towards its object. The object (Silvia's and Valentine's high-flown addresses) is part of the play world, but the perspective of his comic asides links the clown with the real world of everyday experience. This involves some contact not simply between the audience and the character Speed, but between the audience and the actor of Speed's part who, as comic chorus with his asides, enjoys a perspective of awareness which is not strictly limited by the play world. The resulting unity of mirth, between the audience and the actor–character, cannot be dismissed as a clowning concession to the groundlings or as to so much genial atmosphere; for it turns out to be highly functional and quite relevant to any reading of the play as a whole. Its func-tional achievement can be measured by the degree to which it succeeds in the building up of a wider comic vision through which the main theme of friendship and courtly love (so under-lined, in this scene, by words such as 'mistress' and 'servant')[7] is dramatically controlled and comically evaluated.

Another and different kind of context in which the audience laughs with, rather than at, a comic person, is marked by Launce's famous leave-taking speech (II, iii). Again, this is in the tradition of direct address, and, as it is spoken on Launce's first entrance, still harkens back to the extended self-introduction of the older comic figure in Tudor drama. But the way in which this speech achieves a comic concurrence of actor and audience is quite different from Speed's asides which, while they provoke laughter on the stage, direct this laughter at others. Launce, however, enters by himself, and while he and his family experience are the objects of his own mirth, he is also its free and willing subject—subject in the sense of *Subjekt* or ego, or self. His, indeed, is (in Hegel's words) the 'blessed ease of a subjectivity which, as it is sure of itself, can bear the dissolution of its own ends'. For the comic tension between the ridiculousness of the object and the hilarity of the subject (the *Subjekt*) of this speech is altogether remarkable, and it points to the dramatic quality of its comic achievement. This achievement, I suggest, can be measured by the degree to which the given tension between the fictitious object and the actual medium of this speech is solved in terms of the unity (and the contradiction) between the illusory character Launce and the real actor behind this character. For Launce to become the clowning object and the laughing subject of his own mirth and that of the audience, reveals an astonishing stability in his relations to the social whole. These relations connect the character and the actor, illusion and reality, so that the imaginative flexibility of his relation to the play world has much to do with the social security of his relation to the real world. And it is one of Shakespeare's supreme achievements in *The Two Gentlemen* to make these two relations not simply co-exist, but so interact that the resulting phenomenon attains a dramatic coherence and artistic integrity which, I think, is hardly surpassed in any of the mature comedies.

To suggest the comic effects of such laughing with the audience, one can say that Launce, much like Falstaff, is not merely witty in himself but the reason that others have and enjoy their own wit. The audience, or at least a certain section of it, is made to share the implicitly burlesque approach to the experience of leave-taking, but the actor, in performing this, shares the audience's hilarious experience over the scene so enacted. The clowning actor has, as it were, a public capacity for distancing the dramatic illusion and for undermining the social prestige of the main theme of courtly love and friendship; he is, at any rate, still very close to the social attitudes of a popular audience, but the audience in their turn, are no passive spectators, but share in the post-ritual community of theatrical mirth. The comic actor, in fact, does not merely play *to* the audience: to a certain degree he still plays *with* the audience, though already much less directly so than Richard Tarlton did, when he took up his cue from a so-called 'theamer' among the onlookers, or when he reacted upon a thrown apple with a piercing couplet.[8]

But a traditional element of audience awareness survived the decline of the extemporal mode of clowning, and Shakespeare, who condemned the latter, revived the former on a newly literary basis, at a time when, in the nineties, the popular platform dramaturgy of the clowning convention was attacked with increased vigour, as in the words of Joseph Hall who took up Sidney's assault upon the 'hotch-potch' tradition by his scornful but immensely suggestive comments on the clowning convention, especially the mode of entering of the clown, who, apparently, would emerge laughing, and grinning, and gasping, in the midst of the 'applauding crowd' that greeted him with 'gladsome noise'. Says Hall:

> midst the silent rout,
> Comes leaping in a self-misformed lout,
> And laughs, and grins, and frames his mimic face,
> And justles straight into the prince's place:
> Then doth the theatre echo all aloud,
> With gladsome noise of that applauding crowd.
> A goodly hotch-potch! when vile russetings
> Are match'd with monarchs, and with mighty kings.
> A goodly grace to sober Tragic Muse,
> When each base clown his clumsy fist doth bruise,
> And show his teeth in double rotten row,
> For laughter at his self-resembled show.[9]

These lines seem to me to be the most telling contemporary account we have of laughing with the audience, and they provide us with a highly significant hint at its popular background and origins. Hall, I think, attacks not the Shakespearian clown, but the clowning figure in the popular drama of the eighties and early nineties, the immediate predecessor of Launce. The early Elizabethan clown, Hall says, shows 'his teeth in double rotten row / For laughter at his self-resembled show'. The clown, to be sure, is no mere object of laughter; he himself laughs and grins at his own performance, and the 'self-misformed' nature of this performance is such that it does not so much create the illusion of a dramatic role, as incorporate the actor's own clowning pure and simple; it is, in short, 'his self-resembled show'.

The tradition of the 'self-misformed lout' (about which Hall is so scornful) reaches, of course, much further back than Tarlton, and the actual background of this tradition is suggested by Shakespeare himself when, upon Launce's quibbling speech, he makes Speed reply: 'Well, your old vice still: mistake the word...' (III, i, 279). The allusion, which is itself in the form of a pun, is unmistakable.

Among Shakespeare's three explicit references to the Vice, the one in *The Two Gentlemen* is the earliest, and it is here that, after the Plautine servants in *The Comedy of Errors* and the dictionary humour of Costard, in *Love's Labour's Lost*, Shakespeare first harkens back, quite deliberately, to the most popular figure in the morality tradition. Launce has been called by Isaacs 'the beginning of the true Shakespearean clown'; as such he is of course no vice, and— with Tarlton before him—not even his direct descendant, but the dramatic function of his laughter and audience awareness are very much indebted to the farcical–allegorical anti-hero of the morality plays. If the contemporaries viewed Will Kempe as 'Jestmonger and Vice-regent general to the Ghost of Dick Tarlton',[10] then this witty phrase itself was a quibbling reminder of the continued relevance of the Vice tradition which, as early as *Mankind*, can be shown to produce the comic concurrence of audience and actor.

When, for example, in this undoubtedly popular play the allegorical Virtue Mercy wards off the impertinent assault of vicious Myscheff ('Ye ben culpable / To interrupte thus my talkynge delectable'), the vicious reply reads: 'I say, ser, I cumme hedyr to make you game'. And when Mercy continues to persist—in heavily latinized terms—on his 'clerycall manere' and his 'doctryne', we have an even more telling reply from Now-a-days, another figure of Vice, who says to Mercy:

> Men haue lytyll deynte of yowur pley,
> Be-cause ye make no sporte.   (260 ff.)[11]

Mercy, a most serious virtue, is here addressed not as an illusory figure of dramatic allegory but as an *actor* who provides no sport. The comic figure of Vice identifies himself with the point of view of the audience whose traditional right to indulge in 'sporte' (line 78), in 'game' (69), in 'reuel' (82), in 'mery chere' (81) he maintains. His frame of reference is not provided by a moral convention or an allegorical illusion but by an awareness of the actual conditions of, and the expectations roused by, a fifteenth-century travelling troupe's performance. The comic figure's reproach to Mercy, in fact, says not that 'Men do not enjoy your *role*'; he says, rather, 'Men haue lytyll deynte of yowur *pley*'. The traditional criterion of the comic figure is not the impersonation of the *role* but the 'self-resembled show' of the actor.

The comic concurrence of audience and actor is well-nigh complete; and, indeed, there is more than laughing with the audience; there is *singing* with the audience when, somewhat later, the figures of Vice strike up a bawdy 'crystemes songe' (325 ff.), in which all the onlookers are expected to join (*cantant omnes* is the original stage direction). The figures of Vice—in their reckless fashion—sing and play and laugh with the audience, and in their quibbling, riddling impertinency they can again and again 'mistake the word' and thereby establish a traditional community of laughing, gasping and guessing. I call this community traditional, because the popular origins of this kind of wordplay are considerably older than *Mankind*, and can quite definitely be traced in the speech of the Wakefield Garcio (*Mactacio Abel*), the 'Lechys man' Hawkyn (*Mary Magdalene*) and the cheeky boy Colle in the Croxton *Play of the Sacrament*. Parallel with these there is, of course, the topsy-turvy patter of Jack Finney in the mumming plays and, behind all these, finally, the more ancient topsy-turvydom of the late rituals of release and inversion, such as have survived in the Middle Ages through the good luck of their semi-toleration.

III

Shakespeare, who used, and experimented with, the Vice and the Tarlton traditions, also absorbed the clown's 'laughter at his self-resembled show', but he did so critically, on a newly limited and functional basis. For the comic acting of William Kempe, even though Kempe was acclaimed as Tarlton's 'Vice-regent generall', was increasingly integrated into a socially much more heterogeneous division of theatrical labour. Accordingly, the clown Launce—if indeed acted by Kempe—no longer carries the comedy before him, but, more modestly and more effectively, assumes a functional role in a larger whole, thereby fulfilling—much as Speed does—the structural task of helping to organize and control the play's larger comic perspective. He becomes, as Speed does, an important element in the 'implicit judgment' of the play.[12]

As has recently been shown by Harold F. Brooks,[13] this involves a series of comic parallels between the clowning and the romantic scenes—a burlesque kind of parallelism which is quite essential to any understanding of the peculiar poise of the play's meaning; including, I suggest, the vexed problem of the play's denouement through Valentine's outrageous generosity (which of course can be and has been variously understood in terms of textual corruption, or source study, or the history of ideas on friendship, etc.).[14] Whatever the explanation, the resulting comic vision on courtly love yields a highly complex image in which the joint actor–audience perspective of laughter helps to define and to control, though not necessarily to belittle, the main theme of love and friendship.

The point, then, is not that Shakespeare absorbed the clown's 'self-resembled show', but the really interesting question is as to how and by which means this tradition was integrated into the much more self-contained structure and the larger meaning of Shakespearian comedy. To attempt an answer to this question, one might first of all suggest that, in *The Two Gentlemen*, the real performance of the comic actor's true clowning is achieved through the role of the fictitious character of Proteus's comic servant. The real performance of the actor and the imaginative role of the servant interact, and they achieve a new and very subtle kind of unity. Within this unity, the character's relations to the playworld begin to dominate, but the comic ease and flexibility of these relations are still enriched by some traditional connexion between the clowning actor and the laughing spectator—a connexion which has its ultimate origins in the rituals of a less divided society. The continuity and the flexibility of this position (which, in the last resort, involves some kind of freedom from shame and isolation) are remarkable.

To be sure, such freedom is a social and historical phenomenon, which has a lot to do with, say, Elizabethan economic history, the contemporary division of labour, the extent of the enclosure of the commons, etc., but this freedom becomes so meaningful to the art of Shakespeare's comedy precisely because it finds an imaginative equivalent in the structure and the dramaturgy of the play itself. To illustrate the dramatic nature of this equivalent one can observe that the joint audience–actor perspective of the play world involves a mutual extension of awareness, if I may here use Bertrand Evans's fruitful term in a somewhat wider and perhaps slightly different sense. Such awareness, one would suggest, reflects and interconnects both the social security of the *actor's* relation to the real world and the imaginative and spatial flexibility of the *character's* relation to the play world, his implicit insight into and criticism of, the action of the play.

This extension of mutual awareness, or what I have called the comic concurrence of actors and audiences, is of course not restricted to Speed's asides or Launce's direct address. A more exhaustive treatment of the subject would have to consider Julia and the problem of disguise— a vast problem, almost too huge to be mentioned here, although like the clowns, the disguised person (such as Julia) is the character who is usually laughed with, but rarely laughed at, by the audience. Julia's disguise, just like Speed's asides and Launce's direct address, form perhaps the most sustained context in which the comic character is comic for himself, that is to say, in which that character himself enjoys the comic situation that he is either watching (as Speed does) or creating by himself (as in the case of Launce).

In *The Two Gentlemen,* as in the mature comedies, this awareness is as characteristic of the disguised person as it is of the clown or fool. In our examples it is shared by Speed who alone can interpret the figure of the self-written love letter by which his master is wooed; but it is also, if more indirectly, shared by Launce whose privileged perspective is implicit in the burlesque quality of his parallel action so that, in a later scene, again in direct address, he can say, quite explicitly:

I am but a fool, look you, and yet I have the wit to think my master is a kind of knave: but that's all one, if he be but one knave...   (III, i, 262 ff.)

Here, Launce is utterly secure in the actor's awareness of his own comic function ('I am but a fool', he says, and in saying this he harkens back to the 'self-misformed lout' who never was afraid of his self-resembled show). But at the same time he is and remains a character, and as a character he is equally secure in his awareness of other characters: he is aware—as Valentine is not—of the true significance of Proteus's doing.

To express this awareness, he (much as the old Vice does) uses two very revealing figures, a proverb together with a pun. The proverb, as the New Cambridge editor notes, says 'Two false knaves need no broker', but Proteus, being but one knave, does need his broker, that is his go-between. In using the proverb in this quibbling or perhaps riddling fashion, Launce renews and emphasizes his comic concurrence with the audience and he again appeals, from within the romantic comedy, to the Elizabethan world of everyday experience. But, by using the proverb incomplete, almost in the way of a riddle, he does more than simply express his

41

privileged awareness: he uses this awareness so as to make the audience, as it were, participate in the playing of the game or the solution of the riddle. Basically, this invites the same kind of participation that the gravediggers in *Hamlet* provoke by their quibbling riddling question as to who was the first gentleman, or that the porter in *Macbeth* so ostensibly challenges ('and drink, sir, is a great provoker of three things', II, iii, 24 ff.). Through these riddling jests, of which of course Tarlton was the supreme master, the audience in their turn, being still very keen on sports and mirth, are imaginatively invited to join in the building-up of the comic perspective of the play. It is on the basis of the popular tradition that the clown achieves his comic concurrence with the audience. It is a concurrence which, in Shakespeare's comedy, does not merely relate the play world to the real world but which makes the representatives of the real world, through the associations of proverb, pun and riddle, and disguise, form an implicit element in the dramaturgy, the judgement, and hence the larger comic vision of the play.

© ROBERT WEIMANN 1969

NOTES

1. John Dover Wilson, *Shakespeare's Happy Comedies* (1962), pp. 23 ff.

2. For a more comprehensive documentation see the present writer's *Shakespeare und die Tradition des Volkstheaters: Soziologie, Dramaturgie, Gestaltung* (Berlin, 1967).

3. Jurij Borew, *Über das Komische* (Berlin, 1960), pp. 19, 22, 166.

4. J. W. F. Hegel, *Ästhetik*, ed. Friedrich Bassenge (Berlin, 1955), p. 1091.

5. *Ibid.*; cf. p. 1075.

6. Quotations from William Shakespeare, *The Complete Works*, ed. Peter Alexander (London/Glasgow, 1951).

7. Cf. II, i, 87; 90; 97; 123. This seems unique in Shakespeare. The play's debt to the romance tradition is fully brought out by John Vyvyan, *Shakespeare and the Rose of Love* (1960). See also H. B. Charlton, *Shakespearian Comedy* (1952), pp. 27 ff.

8. Cf. *Tarlton's Jests and News out of Purgatory*, ed. J. O. Halliwell (1844), pp. 14, 22 f., 27, 44.

9. *Virgidemiarum Libri Sex*, Book I, Satire III; in *The Works of Joseph Hall* (Oxford, 1839), XII, 162.

10. *An Almond for a Parrat*, in *The Works of Thomas Nashe*, ed. R. B. McKerrow (1905), III, 341.

11. Quotations from *The Macro Plays*, ed. F. J. Furnivall and A. W. Pollard, E.E.T.S., E.S. XCI (1904).

12. See J. R. Brown, *Shakespeare and his Comedies* (1957), pp. 11 ff.

13. H. F. Brooks, 'Two Clowns in a Comedy (to say nothing of the Dog): Speed, Launce (and Crab) in *The Two Gentlemen of Verona*', *Essays and Studies 1963* (1963), pp. 91–100.

14. See, for example, R. M. Sargent, 'Sir Thomas Elyot and the Integrity of *The Two Gentlemen of Verona*', *PMLA*, LXV (1950), 1166–82; also the introduction to the New Cambridge Shakespeare, pp. xiii ff.; Vyvyan, *op. cit.* pp. 130 ff.; E. Th. Sehrt, *Wandlungen der Shakespeareschen Kömodie* (Göttingen, 1961), p. 14; etc.

SHAKESPEARIAN AND JONSONIAN COMEDY

BY

ROBERT ORNSTEIN

We can view Shakespeare and Jonson either as the twin pillars of Elizabethan comedy or as its opposite poles: one romantic, positive and attractive; the other satiric, negative and (now and then) repelling. If we take the latter view, it is partly because Jonson indicated his contempt for the absurdities of Shakespeare's romantic fables. Instead of improbable fictions like *Pericles*, he offered to his audiences the comic truth in 'deeds and language such as men do use'. In his plays the audiences were to find 'an image of the times', a living record of their affectations and follies. Jonson's determination to strike out on a new path of satiric realistic comedy was, no doubt, inevitable and right. But in deliberately rejecting the earlier romantic mode of comedy, Jonson, I suspect, denied something of his own genius, for there is in his earliest masterpiece, *Every Man in His Humour*, a sweetness and amiableness of temper not to be found again in his art. The point of view, if not the subject matter, of *Every Man in His Humour* is almost Shakespearian. Here, near the start of his career, was a tolerant amused acceptance of humours that blunts the edge of corrective satire. Contemptuous as he was of romantic fabling, Jonson had, moreover, an instinct for romantic variety and multiplicity which, though severely disciplined in *Volpone* and *The Alchemist*, burst forth in the noisy carnivals of *Epicene* and *Bartholomew Fair*. The maker of elegant courtly masques fashioned his comedies out of the coarse and common stuff of Elizabethan life, that Shakespeare preferred to ignore or varnish. Even the lowest have the virtues of their vulgarity in Shakespeare's comedies: pimps are irrepressibly cheerful, madams generous and soft-hearted; tavern cheats are ineffable liars and extempore comedians.

Although it ran against Jonson's grain to gloss reality so, he was not enamoured of the merely surly and sordid. His great characters have art, spirit, and versatility. Others are imaginative if not imaginary toads in real Bear Gardens, creatures of grandiose illusions and pipe dreams. Indeed, Shakespeare's comic characters seem by contrast a sober crew. Like Bottom they are somewhat astonished to find themselves living out the fables that poets have feigned, but they make the best of their poetic lot, their hairy ears, their father's will, or their pastoral exile. To discover true romantic obsession, we must turn, not to the Duke Orsino, who plays at being melancholy, but to Volpone, or Sir Epicure Mammon, or to that model of bourgeois propriety, Dame Purecraft. Even the more prosaic of Jonson's characters are rapt in visions of magical bounty or expectations of the millennium. Believers in the miraculous, they would be elevated, sublimed, rarefied; they would sleep with de Medicis, converse with Fairy Queens, marry Counts or madmen. Shakespeare's heroes and heroines sometimes wonder whether they wake or sleep. Jonson's characters dream with their eyes wide open, panting for and fantasizing the new-found luxuries of an acquisitive society, in which nearly everything is possible to those who know where to look for it.

How much we really learn about Elizabethan society from Jonson is difficult to say, even though the affectations that society breeds and the hypocrisies that it sanctions are increasingly his comic subject. Often we know nothing of Jonson's characters but their social role; they are

43

proctors or druggists, costermongers, cutpurses, merchants, or bakers. But these occupational tags are merely conveniences, because we see these characters only when they leave their shops to pursue their fantasies. Indeed, although Jonson's scene is panoramic, his dramatic action is narrowly focused at the point where bourgeois greed meets underworld guile.

Jonson's comedies remind us how little Shakespeare's comedies tell us of the rise of capitalistic enterprise and of the mercenary hungers of his age. Perhaps Shakespeare was too comfortable and too successful an entrepreneur to satirize the commercial hungers of his contemporaries. Or perhaps he saw the craving for position, title, land, and inheritance as a tragic rather than comic theme. His Volpone is Edmund; his Mosca, Iago. In any event, the love of money rarely tinctures the purer affections of his heroes and heroines. Only when Bassanio and Petruchio seek their fortunes in marriage, and Claudio and Angelo alter their wedding plans because of dowries, do money and marriage intermingle. In other instances the plighting of troth is a marriage of true minds—and of adequate fortunes.

The marriage quest in Jonson's comedies, however, is almost always something of a capitalistic enterprise in which women are treated as commodities. Some prizes like Bridget Kitely are worth conveying to a friend; others like Dol Common and Dame Pliant are suitable for renting out; even when the bride turns out to be a boy, as in *Epicene*, he is literally worth a fortune. In *The Alchemist* and *Bartholomew Fair*, angling for rich widows and heiresses becomes a variation of the confidence game, which respectable gentlemen like Lovewit, Quarlous, and Winwife play better than do common cheats. The enforced engagement of Grace Wellborn to the simpleton Cokes is a prosaic instance of the commodity of marriage. The voluptuousness of Volpone and Sir Epicure Mammon are fantastic examples of the convergence of greed and desire; theirs is a speculative fever for rare, extravagant concupiscence.

For Jonson the curious schemes and casuistries of lust are more comic than lust itself. Similarly we laugh, not so much at avarice, in his plays, as at the cunning and folly that avarice enlists, at the wittiness with which men pursue their own confusions. There are, to be sure, simple gulls in Jonson's plays—easy marks, credulous dupes aching to be fleeced. But none are so simple as those who have a taste of wit or would be politic.

Of course wit and folly go hand in hand in Shakespearian as well as Jonsonian comedy, for we might weary of Beatrice and Benedick's sallies of wit were it not for the interruptions of Dogberry and Verges. If we are to have springes, moreover, we must have woodcocks. If there are to be clever pretences, someone must be fooled; if there are to be ingenious schemers, there must be innocents to be duped. In Shakespeare as well as Jonson, the obverse of the comedy of wit is the joke of credulity, but somehow when Jonson tosses the comic coin it nearly always manages to come up tails. Though he offers a rogues' gallery of subtle knaves, Jonson speaks to us primarily of folly, of the universal longing to be well deceived, to believe in impossibilities, to take punks for princesses, boys for girls, lunatics for husbands. In Shakespeare's comedies, there is more pretending than deceiving, more willingness to play roles than to be taken in by them. Even in *Much Ado About Nothing*, there is more wit than credulity, and the end of deceit is the unmasking of true affections. Only in *Twelfth Night* does gulling become a central theme, and then the beguiling of Malvolio comes a bit too close for comfort to Jonson's comedy of affliction.

'Be anything but a fool', seems to be the first Jonsonian commandment, but cleverness is not its own excuse for being in his comedies. Only once, in *Every Man in His Humour*, is wit benign, genial, and attractive. Only in the merry Justice Clement is intelligence playful and compassionate. Later comedies offer Moscas and Subtles but no Falstaffs, and certainly no Prosperos. Almost from the beginning, in young Knowell and Wellbred, Jonson's clever sophisticates are somewhat chill and incapable of sympathy with the gulls they manipulate. The descendants of Knowell and Wellbred, moreover, are Clerimont, Truewit, and Dauphine, who fill their idle time with Otters and Daws, La Fooles, and Collegiate Ladies. The last generation of Jonsonian wits in the great comedies is the least attractive: the cynical fortune-hunters Quarlous and Winwife, who have the scruples of cutpurses and a thin veneer of urbanity, that is quickly rubbed off by the hurly-burly of the Fair.

It never occurred to Jonson that the fumbling of a Dogberry might confound the schemings of a Borachio. Nor did he have Shakespeare's confidence that intelligence can be wisely and generously used. Wit was for him masculine and calculating; for Shakespeare, in the comedies, it was feminine and intuitive—the special province of Portia, Viola, Beatrice, and Rosalind. Look not for mind in Jonson's women; they have little to offer, unless one will settle for Dol's common sense or Grace's disillusioned sobriety. We might say that Jonson exposes the perversities of wit that deviates from the standard of right reason. But reason is scarcely evident and hardly ever right in his comedies. After *Every Man in His Humour* intelligence turns acid if not sour. In the 'comical satyres', it grows envious as well as critical. What is first intimated in *Volpone* becomes more obvious in later comedies: namely, that wit and folly have common roots in human vanity. In *Epicene* Truewit and La Foole make up one society. In *Bartholomew Fair* the clever and the foolish meet as audience to Littlewit's motion.

When the earnest are blind and hypocritical, and the clever knavish, who shall judge? The law, right reason codified, becomes a comedy of errors. The successor to the honest Justice Clement is that eminent advocate Voltore, whose forked tongue deserves to be dipped in gold. And the travesty of the trial scenes in *Volpone* is modest compared to the last judgement of *Epicene*, where a pair of fraudulent authorities learnedly dispute the grounds in canon law for the annulment of a marriage. That way madness lies, and will appear in the wretched Troubleall, who has lost his wits serving Justice Overdo.

Despite the rigours of exile there are banquets in the Forest of Arden, even as despite Malvolio's edicts there are cakes and ale in Olivia's household. After *Every Man in His Humour*, however, the festive occasions of Jonson's comedies have neither innocence nor grace. A dwarf, eunuch, and hermaphrodite provide the entertainments in Volpone's house. The marriage feast of *Epicene* is an affliction contrived to extinguish Hymen's torch. The joke of impotence, briefly touched on in *Volpone*, is broadly relished in the mumbo-jumbo of the divorce proceeding in *Epicene*. Indeed, before the masculinity of Mistress Otter, the Collegiate Ladies, and the epicene bride, sexuality quails. Generation almost sickens as Clerimont describes to Morose the pangs of marital intercourse, and as men who are not men boast of having seduced women who are not women. The shrill clamour about contraception and frigidity is reinforced by an element of disgust for the flesh itself—for ageing bodies, anointed with unguents and reeking of sweat, tricked out with artificial eyes, teeth and hair.

One should not be squeamish about Jonson's comic realism. Perhaps the descriptions of grotesque toilettes and bizarre couplings, the insistent vulgarities and obscenities, and the endless allusions to bodily functions can be interpreted as Rabelaisian reminders that man does not live by Seneca alone. But is there any danger in Jonson that we might take too intellectual a view of the human condition? The bawdy jests and recurrent allusions to time, wind, and weather in *As You Like It* speak of realities excluded from the pastoral idyll. The great festive indulgence of appetite in *Bartholomew Fair*, however, does not call us back to nature, because all is adulterated and sophisticated: the food, the drink, the trashy goods, the dramatic entertainment. The only natural thing at the Fair is that enormous simpleton Bartholomew Cokes. The only other innocents are the puppets, who lack all sexuality.

Or perhaps it is the other way around. Perhaps at the Fair all is natural: the hustling, the cheating, the gluttony and lechery, the mindless vapours, waspish animosities, the scurrilous art, the pig and punk. Why not let copulation thrive? There must be more Littlewits to populate the earth, more marriage settlements to provide for spendthrift rakes, more whores to accommodate the illicit appetites of respectable citizens. Ultimately the licence of the Fair and the warrants of respectable society are indistinguishable. At their stalls everything is for sale: wine, wards, and wives, propriety, and salvation. Nay, as the Induction suggests, even judgement is for sale. Each man may play the critic according to his purse. The trade in the flesh is brisk and expanding. Only the art of the stage is barren: Damon and Pythias appear as Punch and Judy. The legendary passion of Hero and Leander stoops to the stews, and to a grossness which might make Pompey blush. All the world's an obscene puppet motion, fashioned by Littlewit, and enjoyed by simpletons.

Superficially the ending of *Bartholomew Fair* is the classic denouement of comedy. As disguises are shed, true identities are restored. Quarrels end in reconciliations, and in a spirit of good fellowship and cheer, all go off to celebrate the marriages to be. But what marriages are these! And what identities! The rod of correction is set aside, not because compassion triumphs, but because one cannot scratch a whore without discovering a wife. What is revealed is not our common bond of humanity but the commonness, the baseness, and enormity of our humanity. I suggested earlier that Edmund in *King Lear* might be considered Shakespeare's Volpone. I would also suggest that *Bartholomew Fair* might be considered Jonson's *King Lear*: his study of what is natural and sophisticated, rational and animal in man. What a piece of work is a man that he should judge his fellows—hog in appetite, fox in stealth, dog in madness, wasp in anger, blind hypocritical fool: Adam, flesh and blood.

In Jonson's comedies life is irredeemable, not because it is shockingly depraved, but because it exists outside of time and change. His comic actions merely disclose the impossibility of transformation in lives that are wholly momentary, compelled by appetite, obsessed by fantasies, but untouched by memories or chastened by regret. Shakespearian comedy prevails over the wind and rain of Feste's song, even as it prevails over the tempests of the late romances, paradoxically, because it admits the possibility of tragic experience. Youth's a stuff will not endure, and happiness is even more fragile, but where there is sorrow there can be wisdom; when there is remorse, there can be a change of heart. When there is memory, the present is not all, nor is the past lost for ever.

History, I suppose, testifies to the truth of Jonson's comedies. For centuries life has been, in the main, crass, vulgar and mindless. But the value of life does not exist 'in the main'. It exists in the rare particulars, in the special Shakespearian instances.

TWO MAGIAN COMEDIES: 'THE TEMPEST' AND 'THE ALCHEMIST'

BY

HARRY LEVIN

Non hic Centauros, non Gorgonas, Harpyiasque
Invenies: Hominem pagina nostra sapit.

If another confrontation between Shakespeare and Jonson is still allowable, then the challenger should be allowed to arm himself with one of his Latin epigraphs. So, on the title-page of *Sejanus*, the author warns the reader not to look for centaurs or gorgons or harpies; these particular pages will savour of man. The distich is quoted from Martial, an acknowledged kindred spirit of Jonson's, and it seems a curious point of departure for a tragedy, since Martial's epigram (x, iv) had excluded from his life-like pages such monstrous figures as Oedipus and Thyestes. Jonson cut the quotation conveniently short, yet it hints at the limitations that might emerge from a critical comparison of *Sejanus* or *Catiline* with *Coriolanus* or *Antony and Cleopatra*. For the younger playwright, always more interested in human machinations than in the workings of destiny, tragedy could be reduced to conspiracy. Hence it differed from comedy only to the extent that, in the words of the Prologue to *Every Man in His Humour*, crimes may differ from follies. That prologue, introducing a revision which shifted the setting from Italy to England, heralds a more realistic drama by condemning the extravagances and ineptitudes of the popular theatre. After casting an invidious glance at such rivals, and appealing for the more judicious laughter of the audience, it concludes by hoping: 'You, that haue so grac'd monsters, may like men'.

That Jonson should have made so sharp an issue of this distinction might not have been expected from his own work. Most of his critics have stressed his preoccupation with the anomalous. Some of the visitors to Bartholomew Fair strike us as odder than its exhibited oddities, while Volpone and Mosca and their circle of sycophants seem to be even more twisted than their deformed retinue, the dwarf, the eunuch and the hermaphrodite. But Jonson, as a classicist, was an upholder of norms who specialized in pointing out and pouncing upon abnormalities. He felt especially close in his kinship with Horace, whom he portrays and with whom he identifies in *Poetaster*. As a translator of and a commentator on the *Ars Poetica*, he gave due weight—perhaps too much—to its opening statement: its composite image of the monstrosity that the poet or painter should avoid, a woman's face joined by a horse's neck to a body covered with parti-coloured feathers and terminating in a fish's tail. Though his anti-masques are rife with queer creatures, these are rather types than sports, and their prototypes can be traced to folklore if not to classical mythology. Consequently Jonson was shocked by the boldness of Shakespeare's invention. How could he have got away with it, Jonson was constantly wondering. In the Induction to *Bartholomew Fair*, where he did his best to come to terms with the public, he expressed his reservations:

If there bee neuer a *Servant-monster* i' the Fayre; who can helpe it? he sayes; nor a nest of *Antiques*? Hee is loth to make Nature afraid in his *Playes*, like those that beget *Tales, Tempests*, and such like *Drolleries*, to mixe his head with other mens heeles, let the concupiscence of *Iigges* and *Dances*, raigne as strong as it will amongst you...

Here the attack on *The Winter's Tale* and *The Tempest* is fairly overt, and the grounds appear to be twofold. Jonson, the official purveyor of masques to the court, remained a purist with regard to the stage; he did not like to see the dramatist confound his functions with those of the choreographer. He had aired the same complaint a few years before, in prefacing the quarto of *The Alchemist*, where he appropriately cautioned the reader against being '*cos'ned...in* Poetry, *especially in Playes*'. He complained that '*now, the Concupiscence of Daunces, and Antickes so raigneth, as to runne away from Nature, and be afraid of her, is the onely point of art that tickles the Spectators*'. He also seemed to be glancing at Shakespeare *vis-à-vis* himself, in the contrast between an unfettered copiousness and a restrained succinctness, when he concluded by emphasizing the '*great difference between those, that (to gain the opinion of Copie) vtter all they can, how euer unfitly; and those that vse election, and a meane*'. The more serious charge, because it was less subject to the caprices of self-esteem, is that of affrighting nature—or, as the preface to *The Alchemist* more fittingly puts it, of being frightened by nature. This has its all too concrete embodiment in the outlandish person of Shakespeare's servant–monster, and Caliban has his rejoinder when he tells the newcomers to his island:

> Be not affeard, the Isle is full of noyses,
> Sounds, and sweet aires, that giue delight and hurt not.   (III, ii, 144–5)

Shakespeare's 'frekelld whelpe, hag-borne' (I, ii, 283) requires no defence at this stage. Not only has he been accepted by criticism as the *ne plus ultra* of original characterization, but he has fascinated later writers, who have appended their own variations to the Shakespearian theme. He has become a mouthpiece for cosmic speculation in Browning's *Caliban upon Setebos; or, Natural Theology in the Island*, for revolutionary ideology in Renan's *Caliban: Drame Philosophique*, and for a Jamesian commentary on the play itself in *The Sea and the Mirror* by W. H. Auden. He has been interpreted as a test-case for Montaigne's reflexions 'On the Cannibals', and as a prefiguration of the missing link in Darwin's great chain of being. Jonson was not the first to comment on Stephano's nickname for Caliban. 'Seruant Monster?', Trinculo queries at once and, being a professional fool, he proceeds to generalize 'the folly of this Iland' (III, ii, 5). If Trinculo belongs among Shakespeare's jesters, the butler Stephano is more of a Jonsonian type, with his petty airs and ill-supported pretensions; it is because the drunken Caliban cannot see through them that Trinculo scorns him as a 'debosh'd Fish' (III, ii, 29). From their first encounter during the thunderstorm Trinculo has been struck, as everyone seems to be, by the amphibious disposition of Caliban. We are suddenly brought home from the island to London, with a rueful allusion to the new world and a moralistic twist of social satire, when Trinculo speculates:

a strange fish: were I in *England* now (as once I was) and had but this fish painted; not a holiday-foole there but would giue a peece of siluer: there, would this Monster, make a man: any strange beast there, makes a man: when they will not giue a doit to relieue a lame Begger, they will lay out ten to see a dead *Indian*.

(II, ii, 26–31)

Similarly it occurs to Stephano, arriving shortly afterward, that he could make a fortune by bringing the mooncalf back to Naples. But Trinculo's pun, 'there, would this Monster, make a man', has a deeper reverberation. As between such freaks on display at Bartholomew Fair and the uncharitable sightseer who pays his money to gape at them, which is the monster, which the man? To press the question much farther would be to trespass on Jonson's territory. Shakespeare merely sums it up when Gonzalo, the spokesman for his humorous idealism, says of the islanders:

> though they are of monstrous shape, yet note
> Their manners are more gentle, kind, then of
> Our humaine generation, you shall finde
> Many, nay almost any.

(III, iii, 31–4)

Again it is a *double-entendre* of Trinculo's which puts Caliban into perspective: 'that a Monster should be such a Naturall' (III, ii, 36). Trinculo has the disdain of the artificial fool for a mere simpleton, yet 'this demy-divell' is really not so simple (V, i, 272). He has paid for his instruction from Prospero by instructing him in 'the qualities o' th' Isle' (I, ii, 337); his use of the language Miranda taught him ranges far beyond his imprecations; and he rises to poetic heights in recounting his dreams. Though we might not think of him as a highbrow, he makes it clear that there are worse shapes than his, when he fears that he and his fellow conspirators will 'all be turn'd to Barnacles, or to Apes / With foreheads villanous low' (IV, i, 249–50). Whether nurture will ever stick to his puppy-headed nature remains in doubt, as he is liberated by the denouement; but at least we leave him disabused of his folly and determined to seek for grace.

If the man–monster is 'not in Nature', as Dryden argues in his preface to *Troilus and Cressida*, then 'of himself' he represents a new species originated by Shakespeare. For, if the Greeks could imagine the centaur by combining the images of a man and a horse, why should not this hybrid—'begotten by an incubus on a witch'—bear witness to the copiousness of Shakespeare's imagination? The argument is subsumed by the dialogue on grafting between Perdita and Polixenes in *The Winter's Tale*. Shakespeare's attitudes toward human nature were animated by sympathetic curiosity, even as Jonson's were by acute suspicion. In the creation of Caliban, Shakespeare seemed to be pushing nature to the verge of her confine; but, though the outcome was a *lusus naturae*, it was by no means unnatural. The paradox is that Jonson, for once, was criticizing Shakespeare from the standpoint of nature rather than art. Later generations might look upon the issue as a debate between a classical sense of decorum and a romantic feeling for grotesquerie, and that difference has probably been widened by the retrospective classification of *The Tempest* as a romance. In so far as Shakespeare's comedies deal with love, derive their plots from romances, and usually take place in an aura of Romance culture, the term applies to most of them. The later ones are more precisely differentiated by their elaborate staging, their narrative qualities, and their emphasis on tragicomic vicissitude.

But the category is confusing if it obscures the inherent classicism of Shakespeare's technique, which Bernard Knox has evinced in an article relating *The Tempest* to the Plautine tradition (*English Institute Essays*, 1954). Whatever liberties he may have indulged in, Shakespeare commenced and ended his career by observing 'the law of Writ'. *The Tempest*, like *The Comedy of Errors*, defers to the unities of time and place. We may view the first scene as a prologue, which conveys to us the island through the storm. The Jacobean stage, with traps for hatches and the upper level for a bridge, was easily transformed into a ship. All that follows moves within the environs of the lime-grove surrounding Prospero's cell—where the characters finally come together 'spell-stopt'—and might readily adapt itself to a single set on a modern revolving stage (v, i, 61). After the 'Poem vnlimited' of *The Winter's Tale*, when sixteen years are leapt across in an *entr'acte*, *The Tempest* utilizes the 'Scene indiuisible'—to borrow from the terminology of Polonius. The time-span, something less than the interval between two and six in the afternoon, is announced near the outset, and we hear reminders of its passage. To achieve such unity and compression, only the last three hours of the twelve-year story could be dramatized. This means that a long retrospect must be taken, and places a heavy burden upon the exposition. After the violent action of the shipwreck comes the calm of the second scene and its leisurely narration.

If *Oedipus the King* had been an Elizabethan chronicle-play, it might have begun with the exposure of the infant hero, continued with the slaying of Laius, the outwitting of the Sphinx, and the marriage with Jocasta, and crowded into the last act all the reversals and recognitions that make up the tragedy of Sophocles. Comparably, the younger Shakespeare might have started from the court of Milan, directly presenting the intrigue, the dethronement, and the whole train of events that Prospero narrates. Here instead we relive them vicariously, through his troubled remembrance and through their first-hand impact on Miranda, who has not been aware of them before. The drama begins in its penultimate phase, with Prospero reaching his zenith. His years of adversity, like his initial prosperity, are now behind him. Another hour or two will bring the psychological moment for which he has longed and conjured: 'At this houre / Lies at my mercy all mine enemies' (II, i, 263–4). At long last they are compelled to recognize his arcane power and to grasp the personal significance of the tempest. 'O, it is monstrous: monstrous', exclaims the bemused Alonso.

> Me thought the billowes spoke, and told me of it,
> The windes did sing it to me: and the Thunder
> (That deepe and dreadfull Organ-Pipe) pronounc'd
> The name of *Prosper*: it did base my Trespasse,
> Therefore my Sonne i'th Ooze is bedded; and
> I'le seeke him deeper then ere plummet sounded,
> And with him there lye mudded. (III, iii, 95–101)

The downward thrust of this confession parallels the mock-dirge, in which Ariel has conveyed to Ferdinand an impression of his father's death by water. It contrasts with the upward movement of the tricksy sprite himself, and with the increasing ascendancy of his master. When Prospero is not an actor, he becomes a spectator, standing *'on the top (invisible)'*—the puppeteer whose 'demy-Puppets' enact a 'liuing *Drolerie*' (III, iii, 15; V, i, 36; III, iii, 21). He is the stage-manager, the book-holder, and everything is worked out under his omnipresent control.

The source of his late-won authority has been carefully analysed by students of demonology and pneumatology. This could not—in a comedy performed before the learned and superstitious King James—have been the black art of witchcraft, goety, which had led to the damnation of Doctor Faustus. Rather it was theurgy, sacerdotal science or white magic, a command over nature attained through an understanding of its phenomena and an influence over the spirits that link them to their correspondences in the spectral world. Though Prospero's book is a repository of that occult lore, books alone are not controlling forces, as he learned by neglecting his dukedom for his library. Caliban naively equates the possession of such books with the exercise of magical powers; but the only spell that works for the clowns is that which is cast by the contents of Stephano's bottle; and their parody is underscored by his toast, 'kisse the Booke' (II, ii, 145). Among Shakespeare's characters, many of whom are confronted by apparitions and portents, Prospero stands unique as a human being who controls the supernatural, through the agency of his ethereal ministers, notably Ariel. Owen Glendower vainly boasts of calling spirits, while Macbeth's witches are actually Fates. As Prospero's epilogue would make clear, if the consistent capitalization of the noun in the Folio did not, his 'so potent Art' symbolizes the art of dramaturgy (v, i, 50).

We need not identify the poet with the protagonist to regard the latter as a portrait of the artist or to look retrospectively at his ultimate conjuration as a kind of farewell to the stage. Shakespeare's fondness for dwelling upon theatrical matters happily combined with the metaphors of enchantment. Traditionally the enchanter was a demonic—not to say a diabolic—personage, such as Ariosto's Sacripante or Spenser's Archimago. The University Wits could treat him ambivalently, as a scholar straying after forbidden knowledge, like Marlowe's Faustus or Robert Greene's Friar Bacon, who could 'Make storming *Boreas* thunder from his caue'. The fact that 'our moderne writers' liked to centre their fictions on 'the persons of Enchaunters and Commaunders of spirits', as Thomas Campion would suggest in describing his masque for the Somerset wedding, helped to motivate the transformations and scenic effects. Yet Jonson, who all but held a monopoly over the genre, needed no such motivation; it is disenchantment which sets the mood for the masque of *Mercury Vindicated from the Alchemists*. His paradoxical talents might be characterized in a phrase which Auden attributes to Prospero: 'the power to enchant / That comes from disillusion'. *The Tempest* is concerned with illusion, as fabricated by magicians and playwrights and 'all which it inherit', the illusory stuff that dreams and dramas and life itself are made of (IV, i, 154). Jonsonian comedy is concerned with the theory and practice of delusion.

The conjunction of Jonson and Shakespeare was never closer or more productive than in the successive seasons of 1610 and 1611, when His Majesty's Servants introduced *The Alchemist* and *The Tempest* respectively. It is conceivable that the same actor created the parts of Jonson's criminal mastermind and Shakespeare's wonder-working sorcerer, and it is suggestive that the actors' list for *The Alchemist* was headed by Richard Burbage. To be sure, *The Tempest*—which may have been revised for the royal wedding at Whitehall in 1613—bears marks suggesting a production at the company's private theatre in Blackfriars. One of the ironies is that Jonson himself was a resident of that Puritan centre of small trade; some of his respectable neighbours appear as a chorus in Act v. Shakespeare, who had caught the local colour of Eastcheap years before, was increasingly attracted to remote and exotic locations. His lifelong interest in the sea reached its culmination with *The Tempest* where, although the uninhabited island is located in the Mediterranean, the ambiance has been affected by reports of American voyages and the winds are stirred by 'dewe / From the still-vext Bermoothes' (I, ii, 228, 229). Jonson glanced at the transatlantic horizon when he collaborated with Marston and Chapman on *Eastward Ho*; but their title reverses the direction, and their voyage founders on the Isle of Dogs in the Thames. The Prologue to *The Alchemist* proudly announces that the cockney humanist has chosen familiar ground:

> Our *Scene* is *London*, 'cause we would make knowne,
> No countries mirth is better than our owne.
> No clime breeds better matter, for your whore,
> Bawd, squire, impostor, many persons more,
> Whose manners, now call'd humors, feed the stage. (5–9)

This may sound like a somewhat ambiguous declaration of civic pride, but it brings into focus the traditionally urban perspectives of New Comedy. The roles that are named could be the typical masks prescribed by ancient convention, but they will be localized with an almost journalistic particularity. Actual dates will be cited, which topically refer to the time of the play's first presentation. That may have been the occasion when the Globe Playhouse and the other public theatres reopened after a visitation of the Black Death, the plague that still hangs so heavily over the play. The unified locale is a house in Blackfriars, presumably around the corner from Jonson's. The doorways and stairways and levels of the stage are exploited with a furtive agility which seems at times to foreshadow the bedroom farces of Georges Feydeau. The framing circumstance—the servant left by the master in charge of his house, which becomes a hotbed of trouble and frolic during his absence—was inherited from the *Mostellaria* of Plautus, and would also furnish the underplot for Thomas Heywood's *English Traveller*. The abandoned domicile of Lovewit, under the relaxed surveillance of the housekeeper Jeremie while the epidemic runs its course, provides the ideal 'caue of cos'nage' for the interaction of Jonson's coney-catchers and gulls (V, v, 115). The basic pattern was laid down in *Volpone*: a household of knaves through which troops a procession of fools.

But Volpone has been a Magnifico, his house is a Venetian *palazzo*, and the gold he worships is genuine; it crams his coffers to dazzle those would-be heirs whom he elegantly defrauds. Whereas Subtle is never more than a charlatan, a seedy and shady practitioner of the various confidence-games unmasked in the cautionary pamphlets of Greene and Dekker, and his frauds are based on no more substantial a lure than fool's gold. It is the extreme disparity between the claims and aspirations of alchemy and the alchemist's mendicant way of life, the glaring gap between the opulent promise and the sordid fulfilment, between a professed disinterestedness and the most avid self-interest, which made the subject so fruitful a premise for satirists—epitomized by Jonson in a brief epigram and expatiated upon at length by Chaucer's Canon's Yeoman. On the one hand, we are tantalized by all we hear about the great work, the mastery, the elixir, the philosophers' stone, 'the secret / Of nature naturiz'd . . .' (II, i, 63–4). On the other, we are put off by the anticlimax personified in Surly's description of Subtle:

> he is the FAUSTUS
> That casteth figures, and can coniure, cures
> Plague, piles, and poxe, by the *Ephemerides*,

> And holds intelligence with all the bawdes,
> And midwiues of three shires? (IV, vi, 46–50)

The Faustian aspect is quickly discredited by the seamy side. Yet the pioneers of science lived under such imputations of quackery and, what is worse, under the statutes against sorcery, which was punishable by death. Hence there is something of the mad scientist or the rejected prophet in Subtle—or, at any rate, in the role he acts with eloquence and conviction, the role of the trickster as mage. Like Prospero, he can confidently speak of 'mine owne great art', not admitting its fraudulence to Face even in the privacy of their collusion (I, i, 77). Their expository repartee, as contrasted with Prospero's long-drawn-out monologue, constitutes the most vivid of introductions. The quarrel between the cheaters plunges us *in medias res* and alerts us to the worst about both immediately, with a barrage of mutual invective, and a crackle of name-calling scurrility. The magian marvels of Shakespeare's isle seem very far away.

Dryden chose *The Silent Woman* to demonstrate 'the pattern of a perfect play', doubtless because it anticipated the taste of the Restoration. What he termed the *coup de maître* of Jonson is more evident in *The Alchemist*: the character-sketch that accompanies the entrance of each personage, such as the little genre-picture of Drugger in his tobacconist's shop. This presupposes a static conception of character, and it nearly immobilizes those later plays which Dryden termed 'dotages'. Shakespeare preferred to let his characters speak for themselves and to let us form our own impressions. But Jonson's approach works perfectly throughout *The Alchemist*, where it is Face's task to introduce the gulls to the cunning man. They arrive singly at first and then in couples, like the animals entering the ark, and the complications ensue when their arrivals are mistimed. Knocks at the door keep heralding new personalities until the fifth act, when the sudden appearance of Lovewit—in whose suspenseful shadow the first four acts have proceeded—precipitates the catastrophe. A diagram of the plot would show a line ascending to that point and then dropping vertically. Whereas the plan of *The Tempest* would conform to the pyramidal structure that Shakespeare favoured, rising to its apex in the third act, where the lovers plight their troth while the spirits confound both the royal party and the clownish plotters. The rest of the play has the falling cadence of resolution, recognition, reconciliation and celebration.

Shakespeare's habit of parallelism and symmetry, in relating the two secondary plots to the main one, is consummated here. All three are plots in the conspiratorial sense: the complot of Antonio against Prospero has its higher and lower counterparts in the intrigue against Alonso and the mutiny of Caliban. Each of these stratagems plays into the hands of the omniscient Prospero. Order has never been more completely imposed, nor disorder more decisively routed. But poetic justice has depended, we must note, on the sort of metaphysical aid that Jonson would have disdained. Human contrivance is bound to be outdone sooner or later by chance, and his contrivers are alert in adapting themselves to the main chance. Among them Lovewit's butler is the cleverest of servants, and Subtle has been teaching him other parts—not merely the dim-witted laboratory assistant, Lungs or Ulenspiegel, but Don Face, the insolent captain, the setter or verser who picks up customers for both Subtle and Dol Common. As for the heroine, though she has been Subtle's '*punque*', she is currently shared with Face, and shares in their '*indenture tripartite*' (*Argument*, 4; v, iv, 131). The legal phrase has a Shakespearian resonance, when we remember the compact of the rebels in the first part of *Henry IV*. Meanwhile Subtle and Face are falling out over the prospect of hooking a match with the well-endowed Widow Pliant, and in the internal conflict *sotto voce* the disciple proves himself less squeamish and more brash than his mentor.

The advent of Lovewit is therefore the cue for Face to change sides, to purchase his master's forgiveness at the price of the widow's hand. In accepting this marital bargain, the easy-going Lovewit lives up to his charactonym; he enjoys a good joke, and condones mischief when it is clever and profitable to himself. But Jonson seems slightly uneasy, when he has Face excuse himself in the epilogue: 'My part a little fell in this last *Scene*, / Yet 'twas *decorum*' (v, v, 158–9). The demotion of Face to his menial job again is some consolation to Subtle, making his ignominious get-away with Dol, though Lovewit would be well advised in future to keep a sharp eye on his buttery accounts. Whether the stricter interests of decorum have been served is an open question. Jonson could be insistently stern in the imposition of justice; typically his concluding scene takes the form of an arraignment, through which every man is put out of his humour, as it were. In *Volpone* there are two trial scenes; the logical *reductio ad absurdum* in the fourth act leaves roguery so shamelessly triumphant that Jonson had to reverse it with a heavy-handed—and much criticized—manœuvre in the fifth act. *Volpone* is the only one of his four great comedies to be clouded by this legalistic severity, and it is much grimmer than the others. *The Silent Woman* is genially resolved by a pseudo-disputation between two sham lawyers, while the reforming Justice Overdo is pilloried in *Bartholomew Fair*.

What happens to Surly, the one honest man in *The Alchemist*, exemplifies this triumph of acquiescence over asperity. Significantly enough, he is a gambler by profession; and, though he 'would not willingly be gull'd' he is willing to concede 'That *Alchemie* is a pretty kind of game, / Somewhat like tricks o'the cards, to cheat a man, / With charming '(II, i, 78; II, iii, 180–1). His cognomen allies him to Asper, the satirical moralist in *Every Man Out of His Humour*, and to those other *raisonneurs* who stand for the sterner Jonson. Since he gets nowhere as a downright sceptic among the deceivers and the deceived, Surly ventures to play a game of his own: his masquerade in the guise of a Spanish grandee. Thereby he exposes himself to the rogues he is trying to expose, and loses the widow in spite of—or rather because of—his gallantry. 'Must I needs cheat my selfe', he ends by asking, 'With that same foolish vice of honestie!' (v, v, 83–4). His impersonation of the Spaniard is carried through by Lovewit, after unsuccessful attempts by Drugger and Face. The costume for the part, 'HIERONYMO's old cloake, ruffe, and hat', is a reminder that Jonson himself, in his acting days, played Hieronimo on provincial tours of *The Spanish Tragedy* (IV, vii, 71). As a sardonic moralist, an unheeded reformer, and a sometime Roman Catholic, Jonson amiably lampooned himself in Surly's interventions. Yet they cannot seem other than surly, when they are juxtaposed to the irrepressible good nature of Gonzalo, Shakespeare's *raisonneur*.

Surly's scepticism presents an ineffectual foil to the expansive gullibility of his companion, Sir Epicure Mammon. He is Subtle's principal customer, and the diurnal timing of the play is set by the imminent maturation of his ill-starred project. 'This is the day', he apprises Surly, 'wherein, to all my friends, / I will pronounce the happy word, *be rich*' (II, i, 6–7). The explosion of the alchemist's furnace could be viewed as a Jonsonian analogue to the Shakespearian tempest. The 'voluptuous mind' that motivates this convenient disaster finds expression through a lyrical voice, the only one in the cast, projecting sybaritic fantasies by means of Marlovian rhetoric as Sir Epicure counts his chickens before they are hatched (IV, v, 74). His infirmity—should we call it elephantiasis of the imagination?—gives us an insight into the psychology of the swindler's victim, his ardent desire to be swindled. This massive suspension of disbelief achieves its climax in Sir Epicure's courtship—'all in gold'—of 'lord WHATS'HVM's sister', impersonated by Dol (IV, i, 25; II, iv, 6). The excruciating irony is to witness all these courtly compliments and arts of persuasion lavished upon a woman who, professionally speaking, is more likely to solicit than to be solicited. Jonson is careful to underline the wilful immorality of Sir Epicure's speeches, oozing with lust and glittering with luxury, by drawing upon the imagery of imperial Rome, whose decadent excesses will be surpassed:

> we but shewing our loue,
> NERO'S POPPAEA may be lost in storie. (IV, i, 144–5)

Dol's mad scene rushes to the other extreme, inasmuch as her ravings are memorized from the Reverend Hugh Broughton's deranged explanations of Biblical prophecies. These compose a poetry of sorts, as Hart Crane recognized when he made them the starting-point for one of his own poems ('For the Marriage of Faustus and Helen'), and they bring a final touch of opacity to the competing jargons of the play. The dramatic conflicts have their echo in the verbal prestidigitations. 'What a braue language here is? next to canting?' (II, iii, 42). It is considerably better than cant, the secret slang of thieves, at impressing and befuddling its hearers. The experiment in alchemy may be a failure, but the bravura of pseudo-scientific language is an overwhelming success, when Subtle lectures to Surly or catechizes Face for the benefit of Deacon Ananias. The Puritans have their own tropes and intonations, to which Jonson's ears were particularly sensitive. Ananias is an adept at casuistry, as his pastor Tribulation attests, and can put a sanctimonious construction on the sharpest chicanery. It is not surprising that Subtle treats him as a professional rival. The auditory humours mount to the highest pitch of calculated misunderstanding during the mock-Spanish interlude. The most remarkable feature of the blank verse is that it pours forth colloquial speech with as little constraint as the prose of *Bartholomew Fair*. Thus the angry boy Kastril, wanting to live by his nonexistent wits, is advised by Face to study with Subtle:

> You cannot thinke that subtiltie, but he reads it.
> He made me a Captaine. I was a starke pimpe,
> Iust o' your standing, 'fore I met with him:
> It i' not two months since. I'll tell you his method. (III, iv, 43–6)

Jonson's dramatic method is to tell us the respective methods of his dramatis personae. He is nothing if not analytic, where for Shakespeare we must use such Coleridgean adjectives as *organic* and *esemplastic*. Where Shakespeare fuses things together, Jonson sorts them out; he breaks them down, where Shakespeare builds them up. Each of Jonson's plays reveals, so to speak, the tricks of another trade. Subtle, the arch-trickster, can hoax the multitude; but Jonson is forever reminding us that, like Surly, he himself can never be gulled. When Shakespeare takes a magician for his hero, he himself submits to the mysteries of natural magic, and Prospero becomes their priestly celebrant, a king of the wood, the veritable *magus*. Though the potency of his magical book is reinforced by his staff and robes, he does not engage in abracadabras. His only incantation is a last summons and a promise of release to his agents, who remain invisible. Though it mentions some enchantments borrowed from Ovid's Medea, there is little itemizing and no cataloguing. Since the drama is illusive or dream-like, rather than delusive or misleading, it does not call for Jonsonian exposures. Jonson, who well knew how insubstantial a pageant could be, would hardly have accepted Prospero's masque as a paradigm of reality. Rather, it was what he had meant by antics that *'runne away from Nature'*—modes of escape no less evanescent, to him, than the wish-dreams of Sir Epicure.

Nor will Shakespeare's worldly cynics, Antonio and Sebastian, believe in travellers' tales of unicorns or the phoenix, until they are perforce initiated into the 'subtleties o'th' Isle' (v, i, 124). Prospero's theatrical–magical art conjures up the masque as a betrothal rite for Ferdinand and Miranda. These two favoured spectators will be actors in their turn, when Prospero *'discouers'* them to the others, *'playing at Chesse'*—a game of kings within a game of kings (v, i, 171). Ariel, the protean star of Prospero's spirit-troop, has successively figured as a nereid, as a harpy in what might be considered the antimasque, and as Circe to join in the marriage blessing. His characteristic idiom is the rhyming trochaic tetrameter, which Shakespeare reserved for his sprites and fairies, and which Milton echoes in *L'Allegro*:

> Each one tripping on his Toe,
> Will be here with mop, and mowe. (IV, i, 46–7)

The play is as full of sound effects as the isle is full of noises. Many of them are evoked by Ariel, from the barking and crowing refrains of his very first song to the pipe and tabor with which he invisibly misleads the clowns. Even the language of Caliban transposes discords into the harmony of 'a thousand twangling Instruments' (III, ii, 146). The general effect is a semi-tropical atmosphere of twittering birds, chirring insects, rustling foliage—above all, vocal winds and beating waves, set aroar and then allayed at Prospero's behest. His magic is thereby associated with music, as Ferdinand implies: 'This is a most maiesticke vision, and / Harmonious charmingly' (IV, i, 118, 119). But the charm is broken, and the dancing nymphs and reapers vanish into thin air, after the interruption of *'a strange hollow and confused noyse'* (IV, i, 138). Prospero expounds the object–lesson to the lovers. So it is with life, that elusive dream–vision. *La vida es sueño.*

Subtle's charms work on another plane. The closest he comes to staging a ceremony is the hoax he puts on for Dapper, the earliest and slightest of the gulls, a lawyer's clerk who seeks a familiar spirit in order to improve his chances at gambling. That gift is to be conferred by the versatile Dol in her most dazzling role, the Faery Queen. But before the epiphany of Gloriana, her pathetic postulant is blindfolded and pinched and squeaked at, mulcted of all his cash by Subtle and Face, and stripped of everything on his person that has the least value. 'I ha' nothing but a halfe-crowne / Of gold, about my wrist, that my loue gaue me', he swears and pleads, 'And a leaden heart I wore, sin' shee forsooke me'. Face is not wholly obdurate to this modest heart-cry:

> I thought, 'twas something. And, would you incurre
> Your aunts displeasure for these trifles? Come,

> I had rather you had throwne away twentie halfe-crownes.
> You may weare your leaden heart still.   (III,v, 43–6)

The ritual is interrupted by the knocking of Sir Epicure, and Dapper is led away to bide the interim in the privy. His touching resourcelessness is overmatched by the utter heartlessness of his cozeners; after all, the concession has cost them nothing. What is more, it measures the distance from Shakespeare, from the Shakespearian empathy with which Miranda watches the shipwreck: 'Oh! I haue suffered / With those that I saw suffer' (I, i, 5–6). Since she is her father's 'non-pareill', she is not to be compared with anybody—certainly not with Dol Common, whose surname is the trademark of her total promiscuity (III, ii, 108). When Miranda walks the island as its virgin goddess, radiating unaffected innocence, she persuades us to agree with Samuel Pepys, who described *The Tempest* as 'the most innocent play that ever I saw'. However, the description of Pepys turns into a reflexion on the Restoration theatre, when we recall that the version he saw six times was the prurient *rifacimento* of Dryden and Davenant.

Wonder is Shakespeare's epithet and synonym for Miranda, and it offers a better clue to the play as a whole than Jonson's catchword, *monster*. Monstrosity is inhumanity, a tragic theme for Shakespeare, welling to the surface when Lear's daughters are likened to tigers and serpents and kites. 'Be-monster not thy feature', Albany warns Goneril; if the heavens do not punish such offences as hers,

> Humanity must perforce pray on it self
> Like monsters of the deepe.   (IV, ii, 49–50)

True, as the concordance informs us, *monster*—along with *spirit, art, remember,* and *strange*—is one of those thematic words which Shakespeare employs in *The Tempest* more often than anywhere else. Taken together, they virtually outline the story. The strangeness of Prospero's recital, or the later sight of strangers, has its response in Miranda's wonderment, which is not unlike Desdemona's admiration for Othello's adventures. The revelation goes 'From strange, to stranger', as Alonso reacts to it (v, i, 228); the situation is 'as strange a Maze, as ere men trod' (v, i, 242). He himself does not drown, as Ariel's lyric has misleadingly predicted, or 'suffer a Sea-change / Into something rich, & strange' (I, ii, 400–1). But everyone is changed for the better by his island experience. Prospero, through his exile to a state of nature, has been better fitted for a return to society. 'In one voyage', Gonzalo rejoices,

> Did *Claribell* her husbande finde at *Tunis*,
> And *Ferdinand* her brother, found a wife,
> Where he himselfe was lost: *Prospero*, his Dukedome
> In a poore Isle: and all of vs, our selues,
> When no man was his owne.   (v, i, 208–12)

Such developments, the change and growth and diversification fostered by Shakespeare's comedy, are at odds with the attempted transmutations of Jonson's alchemy, which leaves its subjects basically unchanged. The striking consequence is that the two plays devoted to such closely related themes, and produced under identical auspices, should stand in such polar opposition as indoors to outdoors or the underworld to the upper air. That *The Tempest* came after *The Alchemist* means, of course, that Shakespeare had the opportunity to reflect and reply, as he is said to have done in the so-called War of the Theatres. He responded to Jonson's brilliant example not through imitation or refutation but, we might opine, through sublimation—remembering that this notion was held by the alchemists long before it was adopted by the psychoanalysts.

'THOU THAT BEGET'ST HIM THAT DID THEE BEGET': TRANSFORMATION IN 'PERICLES' AND 'THE WINTER'S TALE'

BY

C. L. BARBER

I

In the climactic moments of the late romances, in *Pericles* and especially in *The Winter's Tale*, a great part of the poetry is occupied in describing the principal people, praising them, doing them reverence, enhancing their meaning, while they present themselves, confront one another at gaze, or form a centre for the eyes of all beholders. This mode of presentation goes with the special sort of dramatic action which I want to outline in this paper, the transformation of persons into virtually sacred figures who yet remain persons. Before he knows that she is his daughter, Leontes says to Perdita and Florizel:

> Oh, alas!
> I lost a couple that 'twixt heaven and earth
> Might thus have stood begetting wonder as
> You, gracious couple, do.

This might be a description of a moment of a court masque where some noble couple are presented in the roles of mythological deities; at court, the real identity of Proserpina and her consort would be known; the heaven and earth would be the work of Inigo Jones. One can think of more serious parallels in baroque religious painting, where the principals are high-lighted in large space defined by streams of light connecting heaven and earth, while secondary figures gaze on them with wonder and awe. In *The Winter's Tale* secondary figures come from the presence chamber to report to us the recognition of Perdita; some of their description might fit a painting by El Greco:

I make a broken delivery of the business, but the changes I perceived in the King and Camillo were the very notes of admiration. They seemed almost, with staring at one another, to tear the cases of their eyes. There was speech in their dumbness, language in their gesture; they looked as they had heard of a world ransomed, or one destroyed...There was casting up of eyes, holding up of hands...

The fullest development of this kind of action is of course the final scene where the statue of Hermione comes alive. She is in a chapel, and the scene on one side is like a medieval miracle where a saint's statue moves, a statue, say, of the Holy Mother. Hermione finally speaks after Perdita has kneeled to her in prayer. Suggestions of a sacred or taboo figure surround the

59

seeming statue, along with an ecstasy of wonder which 'transports' Leontes. Then the fulfilment of the scene is her coming down into humanity to embrace him:

> Oh, she's warm!
> If this be magic, let it be an art
> Lawful as eating.

Along with the transformation in the direction of the sacred, the recovery of the particular human identity of the long-lost loved one is crucial—

> O Helicanus,
> Down on thy knees; thank the holy gods as loud
> As thunder threatens us: this is Marina!

As always in Shakespeare, a development of style has a profound inner logic. These final recognition scenes which become epiphanies of something sacred are arrived at by a dramatic movement which I want to contrast with the movement which is characteristic of the earlier, festive comedies. One can make the contrast by referring to the sheep-shearing feast in *The Winter's Tale*, where the holiday moment is included within the larger pattern and renews our sense of the benign power of great creating nature. Florizel, in a characteristic opening tableau, describes Perdita's transformation as queen of the feast:

> These your unusual weeds to each part of you
> Do give a life; no shepherdess, but Flora,
> Peering in April's front.

Those lines often make me think of newly created Eve peering out over God's arm on Michelangelo's ceiling of the Sistine Chapel. But this moment is framed by another kind of beginning, traditional seasonal celebration. Perdita excuses the 'transformations' of her royal lover to a shepherd and herself to a queen as the folly of holiday:

> But that our feasts
> In every mess have folly, and the feeders
> Digest it with a custom, I should blush...

The moment leads to the passionate avowal which concludes her flower speech, when she regrets that she lacks spring flowers for

>   my sweet friend,
> To strew him o'er and o'er.
> *Florizel.*   What, like a corse?
> *Perdita.*
> No, like a bank for Love to lie and play on;
> Not like a corse; or if, not to be buried,
> But quick, and in mine arms. Come, take you flow'rs;
> Methinks I play as I have seen them do
> In Whitsun pastorals; sure this robe of mine
> Does change my disposition.

In the festive comedies proper, holiday liberty frees passion from inhibition and the control of the older generation. In the usual comic movement the old are dismissed, or got round, on a tide of young feeling, whether or not they are finally reconciled and included in the new society created by the initially disruptive sexual energies of the new generation. But here in *The Winter's Tale* the festive moment is included within a larger movement where the centre of feeling is in the older generation. The festive comedies move out to the creation of new families; *Pericles* and *The Winter's Tale* move through experiences of loss back to the recovery of family relations in and through the next generation. In the comedies of youth, the perverse and repressive are laughed out of court while release leads to the embrace of passion, sanctioned by clarification as to its place as part of the natural cycle.[1] In the romances, however, fulfilment for the principal figure requires a transformation of love, not simply liberation of it. One can put this in summary by saying that where regular comedy deals with freeing sexuality from the ties of family, these late romances deal with freeing family ties from the threat of sexual degradation.

The most drastic manifestation of such degradation is the incest of Antiochus and his daughter which Pericles encounters at the outset of that play. Such a threat appears also in the source of *The Winter's Tale*, where Pandosto–Leontes, instead of welcoming the love of the young prince for his unrecognized daughter, throws the prince into prison and tries to win her sexually for himself. Shakespeare's change in the ending, keeping Hermione alive in hiding so that the play ends in Leontes' attonement with her rather than with his suicide, depends on the transformation of Leontes' relation to his daughter. For in both plays it is the recovery of the daughter that leads on to the recovery of the wife. Those recovered become ikons for a pious love which finds in them the mysterious powers which create and renew life. The ultimate justification of the wild improbabilities of the reunions is that the reality of those restored was somehow already in Pericles or Leontes:

> What is this face, less clear and clearer
> ...more distant than stars and nearer than the eye?

II

I picked out the strange line which I have quoted in my title, 'Thou that beget'st him that did thee beget', because, addressed by Pericles to his daughter, it summarizes both the effect of the beloved figures on the protagonists, in bringing them back to life, and the thing that is most emphasized in the feminine figures—their power to create and cherish life, their potential or achieved maternity. The line also recalls, in one direction, the unholy incest of Antiochus which devastated Pericles when he first sought a wife, an incest where both the riddle and Pericles' response stress that the daughter took the place of wife and mother: 'with foul incest to abuse your soul; / Where now you're both a father and a son'. In the other direction, the line points forward to the mother and wife who is found through Marina when the ecstasy of recognizing her leads Pericles to hear the music of the spheres and fall into a trance-like sleep. Pericles at the beginning of recognition literally sees the mother in the daughter, his lines beginning with an image of childbearing:

> I am great with woe, and shall deliver weeping.
> My dearest wife was like this maid, and such
> My daughter might have been: my queen's square brows;
> Her stature to an inch; as wand-like straight...

The environment of the line as Pericles speaks it is the sea:

> O Helicanus, strike me, honored sir!
> Give me a gash, put me to present pain;
> Lest this great sea of joys rushing upon me
> O'erbear the shores of my mortality,
> And drown me with their sweetness. O, come hither,
> Thou that beget'st him that did thee beget;
> Thou that wast born at sea, buried at Tarsus,
> And found at sea again!

I must pull back from following, here, the marvellous meaningfulness of this sea imagery, which in any case has been beautifully brought out by Wilson Knight and others, including Eliot in 'Marina'. Let me simply recall how the sea which here is made the locus of Pericles' rebirth was a dreadful and yet absorbing presence at Marina's birth. During the storm which is so like that in *The Tempest*, Pericles invoked Lucina, goddess of childbirth:

> O
> Divinest patroness and midwife gentle
> To those that cry by night, convey thy deity
> Aboard our dancing boat; make swift the pangs
> Of my queen's travails.

Without attempting to cope with the complex issues about Shakespeare's relationship to the text as we have it—issues on which several people at this conference have written tellingly, Muir, Edwards, Danby, Maxwell, Schanzer—one can note that the place where Shakespeare begins to use his full powers is this moment when, with the sea storm, we experience a husband's concern and reverence for his wife in labour, and his poignant helplessness:

> A terrible childbed hast thou had, my dear;
> No light, no fire. Th'unfriendly elements
> Forgot thee utterly; nor have I time
> To give thee hallowed to thy grave, but straight
> Must cast thee, scarcely coffined, in the ooze...

III

It was probably not more than two years before *Pericles* that Shakespeare had written about a tragic king who, in his Fool's words, 'madest thy daughters thy mother'. Here there is no queen, and the tragedy begins with Lear asking for everything from his daughters in return for giving himself away. Regan and Goneril, who we discover have inwardly rejected his demand for tenderness and become cruel and avidly sensual, pretend to give him what he wants—in terms that are almost incestuous:

> I profess
> Myself an enemy to all other joys
> Which the most precious square of sense possesses,
> And find I am alone felicitate
> In your dear highness' love.

Cordelia, in whom filial tenderness is intact, tries to defend herself by maintaining a balance: 'I love your majesty / According to my bond...' 'Sure I shall never marry like my sisters, / To love my father all'. The core of Lear's later anguish is in his having cut himself off from Cordelia: 'I lov'd her most, and thought to set my rest / On her kind nursery'. Lear's reunion with Cordelia, for me the most moving scene in all Shakespeare, anticipates, often point by point, the reunion of Pericles and Marina. But even as the tragedy realizes the full value of the love of parent and child, it follows out remorselessly the destructive logic of Lear's possessiveness. 'Come, let's away to prison; We two alone...' The old king has learned to ask forgiveness, learned he is not everything—and ceased to care for that. But he still wants his daughter 'to love [her] father all'. He leads her off with him to death, telling her as he does so that upon such sacrifices as hers 'the gods themselves throw incense'.

In *Pericles* the motive which leads to tragedy in *King Lear* finds resolution. Why is not the romance merely a superbly realized wish-fulfilment? Of course the given facts are simply different: Pericles is in middle age: there is a wife; the moment of *her* loss is central. And where Lear is a superb impatient egotist, Pericles is a figure of patience who lives chiefly through his awareness of others. On deeper levels, the final happy ending is earned by moving through a sequence of attitudes which have a spiritual and psychological logic and make the seemingly random adventures a visionary exploration. Components of the motive in Lear are objectified, distanced and so brought under control, with a generalized experience of suffering and misfortune which reflects the psychic cost of the process. Thus at the outset the potentiality of overt incest is recognized and felt as a destructive horror. Later, when Marina is coming to maturity, the possibility of a mother's destructive jealousy of a daughter—another tendency running counter to the final atonement—is enacted in Dionyza's attempt to murder Marina.

The total concentration of Lear on his daughters creates the tragic split between brutal sexual greed in Regan and Goneril and sacrificial tenderness in Cordelia. It fits with Lear's horror of female sexuality, which bursts out in 'Down from the waist they are centaurs...' In *Pericles*, the strange, comical scenes in the brothel bring the daughter into relation to brutal sexual desire so as literally to disassociate her from it. Boult and the Bawd and even Lysimachus assault her with brutal imagery and intention, only to be rebuked. At Stratford in the 1959 production, I gather that the astonishment of the brothel people in encountering such a creature as Marina was wonderfully funny. This comic exorcism of gross sexuality works. But it does go with a less inclusive action of reconciliation with life's range of powers than we get in *The Winter's Tale*.

In *Pericles*, the acceptance of the daughter's independent feminity is achieved not by dramatizing her own self-realization as a woman, as is done with Perdita in *The Winter's Tale*, but by
seeing her as a new embodiment of the generative powers of her mother. It is the renewed
relation with these powers which brings Pericles out of his death-like trance. That the whole
scene is elevated to a visionary level at its close fits with the fact that it is the recovery of relation
to this power in life which is crucial. In the opening scene, Pericles in describing the perversion
of the daughter of Antiochus, described the power of woman to relate man to the ultimate
forces of the universe:

> You are a fair viol, and your sense the strings;
> Who, fingered to make man his lawful music,
> Would draw heaven down, and all the gods to hearken;
> But being played upon before your time,
> Hell only danceth at so harsh a chime.

The recognition of Marina leads to mysterious music which does indeed mediate between
human and divine:

> I embrace you
> Give me my robes. I am wild in my beholding.
> O heavens, bless my girl! [*Music*] But hark, what music?
> Tell Helicanus, my Marina, tell him
> O'er, point by point, for yet he seems to doubt,
> How sure you are my daughter. But, what music?
> *Helicanus.* My lord, I hear none.
> *Pericles.* None?
> The music of the spheres! List, my Marina.
> *Lysimachus.* It is not good to cross him; give him way.
> *Pericles.* Rarest sounds! Do you not hear?
> *Lysimachus.*   Music, my lord?
> *Pericles.* I hear most heavenly music.
> It nips me into list'ning, and thick slumber
> Hangs upon my eyes. Let me rest.

He sleeps—and sees the vision of Diana, goddess of chastity and childbirth, who directs him
to her temple at Ephesus. The final scene of recognition with Thaisa is anticlimactic not only
because it is foreknown, but also because the symbolic action of recovering the relationship
has already been completed.

IV

I shall be able to consider *The Winter's Tale* only in the baldest outline, focusing only on one
of the relationships which is recovered, that between Leontes and Polixenes. The analogy of
Pericles can help, I think, to clarify the much more complex development of the later play. For
as in *Pericles* we begin with overt incest and arrive at a sublime transformation of the motive, in

The Winter's Tale we begin with the destruction of Leontes' affection for Polixenes by his pathological jealousy, and the action of atonement involves bringing the two kings back into amity *before* the recovery of the lost wife.

It is notable that the play begins with the relationship of the two men, not that of Leontes and Hermione. 'Sicilia cannot show himself overkind to Bohemia. They were trained together in their childhoods; and there rooted betwixt them then such an affection, which cannot choose but branch now.' The affection does branch, for Leontes, in the 'rough pash, and the shoots that I have...'

> Affection! thy intention stabs the centre.
> Thou dost make possible things not so held,
> Communicat'st with dreams...
> >   to the infection of my brains,
> And hardening of my brows.

There is clearly a sense in which Leontes' jealousy continues his relationship with Polixenes in a terrible negative form. Some years ago, J. I. M. Stewart, in his brilliant little book *Character and Motive in Shakespeare*, replied to the common critical view that the jealousy is purely conventional and theatrical by referring to Freud's account of projective or paranoid jealousy as a defence against homosexual attraction.[2] The defence, in Freud's account, works according to the formula, '*I* do not love him, *she* loves him'. I have found Stewart's application of Freud convincing, and I think one can make the case even stronger by close analysis of the opening scene. Beneath this level of psychological extrapolation is another, still less directly demonstrable, that relates Leontes' jealousy to very early levels of infancy, when the child, though he communicates richly with the maternal side of the mother, fears and hates the father's power to possess her sexually. The projective jealousy can put the rival in the position of the archaic father. An accepted and accepting relation to the father is a condition of positive relationships to other men, so the onset of jealousy means as important a loss of relation to the crucial man as to the crucial woman, crucial in the sense that they are those in whom is invested the core of love which has its roots in childhood and is the ground of piety toward the larger powers of life which we encounter first through the parents.

There is not time today to pursue these speculations in the text of the opening scenes, in the memories of idyllic boyhood ('to be boy eternal...What we changed / Was innocence for innocence...'), in the remarkable insistence on identification of the two kings with their sons, in the whole wonderful evocation of womanly, maternal strength in Hermione. My interest here, in any case, is structural, and my argument concerns the way the whole play moves. It seems to me that the primary motive which is transformed in *The Winter's Tale*, as father-daughter motive is transformed in *Pericles*, is the affection of Leontes for Polixenes, whatever name one gives it. The resolution becomes possible because the affection is consummated, as it could not otherwise be, through Perdita and Florizel. 'How thou lov'st us, show in our brother's welcome', Polixenes said to Hermione, and there followed the horrible sexual imagery of his wife 'sluiced in's absence...by his next neighbour'. At the onset of 'affection', he recoiled with the exclamation (appropriate equally to his own relation to Polixenes or to that which he ascribes to his wife) 'Too hot, too hot! / To mingle friendship far is mingling bloods'. Through

Perdita and Florizel, the motive towards union can welcome the daughter's loving the son as Polixenes loves the father; 'mingling bloods' becomes possible. The continuous presence of the unresolved Leontes–Polixenes relation, beyond its negative development while Leontes is in the grip of his delusion, is one of the manifest features of the play which supports this interpretation. Camillo describes Leontes' need for Polixenes as he makes plans for the flight of Florizel to Sicily, a flight which symmetrically reverses the earlier flight away from Sicily:

> Methinks I see
> Leontes opening his free arms and weeping
> His welcome forth; asks thee, the son, forgiveness,
> As 'twere i' th' father's person...

When the encounter takes place, the first thing Leontes says identifies son with father:

> Were I but twenty-one,
> Your father's image is so hit in you,
> His very air, that I should call you brother,
> As I did him, and speak of something wildly
> By us performed before.

The meaning of the recovered relation of Leontes to Perdita differs from that of Pericles to Marina because what Leontes first recovers through her is not his lost wife but his lost friend. Of course he also recovers much more, about which I can say nothing here—relation to the new life which has been evoked in the great fourth act: 'Welcome hither, / As is the spring to th' earth!' But it seems to me that he can find Hermione again because the energies of the tie to Polixenes, which originally poisoned his love, have now been transformed and fulfilled.

In the whole span of the action, we can see Leontes' jealousy and his recovery from it as the release of a motive which threatens a family tie with gross sexuality. The release leads to clarification in the third act, but the clarification is devastating, not resolving, until in Act v the motive is transformed. Indeed, from one perspective one can see that the motive cannot be fully embraced until it is transformed.

The enhancement of Hermione as she is recovered, the sanctification, analogous to baroque religious painting, expressed in her appearing first as a sacred statue and then coming alive as the warm, actual wife, has been earned by freeing Leontes' perception of the maternal in her from the perverse dependence expressed in his jealousy. One can place the spiritual process involved in such sanctification of a particular individual by imagining, for contrast, a medieval Leontes who, after similar aberration, might recover his relation to his wife thanks to the intercession of the Holy Mother. The Shakespearian situation requires the discovery of the Holy Mother in the wife.

Let me add, finally, one more suggestion which is highly speculative and must remain so. Eliot's 'Marina' provides a possible analogy: it uses the quest of Pericles to convey the recovery of relation to spiritual realities fixed in memories of Eliot's own childhood summers on Cape Anne:

> Between one June and another September...
> Made this unknowing,...my own

The spiritual action which concerned Eliot at this period was the re-understanding or relocating of motives and their objects, as Dante re-understood his relationship to Beatrice. The fruit of such re-understanding is the higher dream, visionary experience in which individual experience is not lost but transformed into something more important.

It is tempting to adapt the line I have quoted from *Pericles* to describe what happens in Paulina's chapel when Hermione's statue comes alive. 'She that beget'st him that did her beget' might read, referring now to the dramatist himself: 'He that beget'st her that did him beget'. Of course such reference is pure speculation, in one sense, or something utterly obvious in another sense. One can notice one particular feature of the scene which points, not to Shakespeare's particular life, but at least to his particular art. The statue's coming to life is dramatized by moving from the wonder of Julio Romano's sculptor's art to, literally, Shakespeare's own art.

What fine chisel / Could ever yet cut breath?

NOTES

Quotations are from *Pericles, Prince of Tyre*, ed. Ernest Schanzer (1965), and *The Winter's Tale*, ed. Frank Kermode (The Signet Classic Shakespeare, New York and Toronto, 1963).

1. See C. L. Barber, *Shakespeare's Festive Comedy* (Princeton, 1959; Meridian paperback, 1962), Chapter 1, 'The Saturnalian Pattern'.

2. London, 1949, pp. 30–9. In a brief note, 'Rooted Affection: The Genesis of Jealousy in *The Winter's Tale*', *College English*, xxv (1964), pp. 545–7, John Ellis makes the same argument as Stewart, adding the suggestion that Leontes comes to himself with the news of the death of Mamilius (after being deaf even to the oracle of Apollo) by a mechanism of projection: 'But it would seem not merely the shock which brings him to his senses, for now he has also sacrificed his victim. His sin has been carried away...'

A very interesting treatment of the father–daughter motive in *Lear* and the late romances, including *The Tempest*, is 'Still Harping on My Daughter' by Barbara Melchiori, in *English Miscellany*, ed. Mario Praz (Rome, 1960), pp. 56–74.

THE WORDS OF MERCURY

BY

RALPH BERRY

Love's Labour's Lost is probably better appreciated today than at any time since its earliest performances. It is now found to play well, it has had some extremely understanding criticism over the last two decades. Nowadays critics have slackened their efforts to expound the play as a sophisticated in-joke, a spoof on Lyly and on the School of Night. No doubt it is all that, but the concentration on the topical interest of *Love's Labour's Lost* tended to obscure its permanent value. The play retains its elusiveness, but is today generally regarded as a delicate and controlled movement towards an acceptance of reality. 'Reality' is a term that (however unsatisfactory philosophically) critics agree upon as a convenient designation for the target of the play's probing.[1] The word is not susceptible to exact definition, but it designates all those phenomena of life that are symbolized by the entry of Mercade. That entry is the key fact of the play: it is hardly possible to sustain the argument that it is 'sudden, unprovided for, external to the inner necessity of the plot, and for that reason aesthetically unsatisfactory, though theatrically effective'.[2] For the play has opened with an assault upon Time/Death (lines 1–14),[3] as it closes with the acknowledgement of Time's victory. The death-message is organically present in Scene i, as certain cells die shortly after the body's birth. And the final Act makes sense only as a reversal of the first Act: the themes of light–darkness, folly–wisdom, fantasy–reality are initiated and resolved in the exposition and conclusion.

The 'movement towards reality' is a perfectly valid way of describing the form of the play; it is, I believe, the best way of describing what *happens* in *Love's Labour's Lost*. And we can as readily see it as a set of reversals, refutations of the untenable positions taken up in Act i—just as, perhaps, the logic of the final Winter-song refutes Summer. But in this paper I want to examine the form of *Love's Labour's Lost*, not as a temporal process, but as an evolving analysis of humanity's primary symbol for reality: words. Commentators have fastened on to the word-play in *Love's Labour's Lost*, and have, I believe, missed that the play is about *words*. Words compose the central symbol of *Love's Labour's Lost*;[4] it is towards this symbol that the characters are oriented; it is through it that they define themselves. I do not mean by this that 'The contrast of different characters in terms of their different idiom, played off or chiming together, constitutes the "form" of the comedy', as M. C. Bradbrook puts it.[5] Obviously, the play contains a number of contrasting idioms, and a very considerable part of its delight lies in the virtuosity with which these idioms are exploited and counterpointed. But the play's central principle of organization creates groupings which are broader than the individual idioms in them. In essence, then, I see the personae in *Love's Labour's Lost* as falling into four main groups, characterized by different attitudes towards words; and the interaction of these groups sets up an intellectual drama that underlies the emotional and personal conflicts.

I *Navarre and his followers*

Navarre, Berowne, Dumain, and Longaville are equivocators. They are concerned with two sorts of words; words as jests, words as oaths. But they do not distinguish absolutely between the two categories; it is a very great error, for an oath cannot exist in the context of a jest, nor a jest in an oath. Essentially, they undermine words, for they see words as projections of their personal whims. The occasion that serves to expose their abuse of words is a fantastic 'study'–project manifestly opposed to 'common sense' (I, i, 57)—a term with a meaning very similar to ours. It is a denial of reality shared by all four. We need not pursue minor distinctions down to the Dumain–Longaville level (though this is possible), but the King and Berowne offer different aspects of the matter.

Navarre has the imperial tendency to want words to match his wishes. Words are his servants. There is a slight, but unmistakable, touch of oafishness about him; a favourite word of his is 'chat'; thus, to Rosaline:

> If you deny to dance, let's hold more chat... (v, ii, 228)

and, more plainly:

> Are we not all in love?...
> Then leave this chat; and, good Berowne, now prove
> Our loving lawful, and our faith not torn. (IV, iii, 279, 281–2)

It is the eternal voice of the superior officer, dismissing with a disdainful monosyllable some business that he does not comprehend, and leaving it to a clever second-in-command to arrange. 'Chat' is the utterance of a man who does not understand words, and does not respect them. Navarre is responsible for the play's most embarrassing moment, when—following the news of the death—he tries, with unbelievable lack of sensibility, to keep the old game going: 'The extreme parts of time extremely forms', and so on through a threadbare string of conceits (v, ii, 730–41). It asks for, and gets, the ultimate blank wall of language: 'I understand you not' (v, ii, 742). His penance will instruct him that words—as oaths—have a meaning and status that lie outside his authority.

Berowne is, however, the focus of the word-attitudes current in his group. He is not deceived by words: he has an ironic appreciation of all modes of language, and can switch easily from plain to tuppence-coloured. He is vitiated by a fundamental lack of faith in words as counters; the jest devalues all currency. When we first encounter him he is trying to back out of an oath, his agreement to study for three years on the King's terms, which seems likely to prove uncomfort-able: 'By yea and nay, sir, then I swore in jest' (I, i, 54). Already he erodes the status of words as oaths. But he is distinguished from the first scene onwards by a highly equivocal attitude to words. 'Necessity will make us all forsworn', he warns prophetically (I, i, 148): an attitude which the course of the play refutes. The trouble with Berowne is very clearly stated in the exchange between Margaret and Boyet:

> *Margaret:* Not a word with him but a jest.
> *Boyet:*   And every jest but a word. (II, i, 216)

Boyet's comment is a covert reproach, and a most important one. For Berowne's attack upon the integrity of words leads him to a dilemma, which he himself sees clearly:

> Let us once lose our oaths to find ourselves,
> Or else we lose ourselves to keep our oaths. (IV, iii, 358–9)

So the reality–principle asserts itself, forcing Berowne to re-examine the bases of his course of conduct. But even though Berowne talks sense, in his praise of love (IV, iii, 286–362), his ready volte-face betrays the true weakness; he accords too little fixed value to words. He has betrayed an oath, and the frivolity of that original oath is itself the fault. The reality–principle is revealed in the language, a sudden shift to Longaville's

> Now to plain dealing; lay these glozes by (IV, iii, 367)

And Berowne's

> *Allons! Allons!* Sow'd cockle reap'd no corn;
> And justice always whirls in equal measure: (IV, iii, 380–1)

is an ominous hint of retribution, recalling the earlier remark of Longaville: 'He weeds the corn, and still lets grow the weeding' (I, i, 96). Here, too, the pattern of ironic reversal holds good. Berowne's fate is to have the true meaning of 'jest' painfully instilled into him. We can pass over the oft-quoted rejection of 'Taffeta phrases' in favour of 'russet yeas and honest kersey noes' (V, ii, 402–13): it is a jesting confession, an adroit attempt to wriggle out of an insupportable situation and, in context, cannot be taken at its face-value. The end, for Berowne, comes when he has to swear *in earnest* to jest—a nice reversal of the opening scene, and a fitting punishment for his besetting vice.

In sum, the King and Berowne typify in their different ways two modes of abusing words. The King wants words to mean what he wants them to mean; Berowne has the opposite tendency, the star debater's readiness to deploy words in any cause, for or against. Wilfulness in one case, frivolity in the other, is the fault. Their common penance is to learn the meaning of oaths, hence of words in general, and to see re-asserted their status as symbols of reality.

II *The Princess and her retinue*

The Princess and her court have, for all their gaiety, the utmost respect for words as symbols of reality. 'Through them, in some sense, the voice of Reality speaks', as Miss Roesen remarks.[6] The values of the court are concentrated in its mistress, and we can readily arrive at them by examining the Princess's words. She announces them with her opening lines:

> Good Lord Boyet, my beauty, though but mean,
> Needs not the painted flourish of your praise:
> Beauty is bought by judgment of the eye,
> Not utter'd by base sale of chapmen's tongues. (II, i, 13–16)

The Princess, gracious and shrewd, stands for sound values arrived at by the senses; and she is utterly opposed to meaningless words. Shortly after, she engages in a prolonged colloquy with

Navarre. It centres first on oath-breaking (II, i, 97–106) as a largely theoretic matter, then moves to a discussion of words as pacts, that is to say of oaths in the political sphere. This episode, which puzzled Tillyard,[7] seems at first sight something of an irrelevance. We can, however, justify the legal business (II, i, 129–68) as a variant on the theme of oath-keeping. It figures the main affair of *Love's Labour's Lost*, the status of words; and the Princess is quick to accord the full value to words, if possible: 'We arrest your word' (II, i, 160)—that is, 'seize your word as security'. It is surely a reminder of the crucial position of words in the world of affairs; that the world as we know it functions on agreements that must if possible be maintained.

The Princess figures in another episode of prime importance. In IV, i, she rewards the Forester for wittily telling the truth:

> Here, good my glass, take this for telling true: (IV, i, 18)

—a testimony to the importance she attaches to true words. And her speech on the deer (IV, i, 21–35) is not only a sudden shift of mood, a glimpse into a deeper play; it is also the thematic counter to the King's opening speech in praise of 'fame'. For the Princess (moving from the deer-example, Hamlet-like, to the real point) says:

> And out of question so it is sometimes,
> Glory grows guilty of detested crimes,
> When, for fame's sake, for praise, an outward part,
> We bend to that the working of the heart;
> As I for praise alone now seek to spill
> The poor deer's blood, that my heart means no ill.   (IV, i, 30–5)

Fame, for the Princess, is merely an incitement to unnatural and painbringing activity. So it turns out for Navarre and his court, too; but the Princess has said it. She is beyond question the internal arbiter of the values of *Love's Labour's Lost*.

The Princess is seen at her most commanding in the final Act. Her attitude to words is expressed decisively in her comment on the badinage of Katherine and Rosaline:

> Well bandied both; a set of wit well play'd.   (V, ii, 29)

The metaphor is central, and exact. The Princess and her retinue see words as *games*.[8] This is not at all the same thing as jests. They may indeed make jests, but they never devalue words. The 'game' metaphor implies rules, scrupulously observed by all participants in the contest. The women in *Love's Labour's Lost* use words, but are never used by them.

When, therefore, the women come into contact, and therefore conflict, with the men, they are only superficially sharing the same idiom. In reality, two different modes of language are in collision. The feminine objective is to unmask the *meaning* of the words, that is, to relate words to the motives and purposes of the originators. The poems they regard as 'a huge translation of hypocrisy' (V, ii, 51). As for the Russian masquerade, the Princess counters this with an unmasking device:

The effect of my intent is to cross theirs:
They do it but in mockery merriment;
And mock for mock is only my intent. (v, ii, 138–40)

The women will play according to their own rules and on ground of their own choosing:

Rosaline: If they do speak our language, 'tis our will
That some plain man recount their purposes... (v, ii, 176–7)

And, in the interrogation that follows, the conceit ('...we have measur'd many miles / To tread a measure with her on this grass', v, ii, 184–5) yields to the ruthless application of the reality-principle. This passage—conceit exposed by reality—figures the whole play.

The Princess's court—and one can legitimately include the epicene Boyet in the group—upholds the value of truth, or reality. The women reason like philosophers. They use words to establish the meaning of words, and hence to relate words to the intentions of the men. This not only accords with their sexual function—the word-game is more serious for women—it expresses an intellectual role, women as realists, that we can see elsewhere in Shakespeare (Viola, Portia). At all events, they play the word-game with an essentially serious skill that deservedly puts the men to shame.

III The Clowns

The Clowns, Costard and Dull (with whom one can associate Moth) are the lower-class equivalent of the women. They, too, are realists of the first order. Within the limits of their education and intelligence, they are not to be deceived. The prime assumption of Costard and Dull is that words symbolize things. (This, be it noted, is a more rudimentary phase of the inquiry initiated by the women, into words as symbols of motives.) Costard, the 'rational hind', is certainly a reality-man. Note his reply to the charge brought against him by Armado: 'Sir, I confess the wench' (I, i, 269). The words of Armado are not for him, and his own words express a *fact*. Costard, like Moth (and Feste) knows that money is a form of reality. His brief cadenza on 'remuneration' (III, i, 134–9) shows that he is not deceived; words have to symbolize things, and he is aware of their relationship. He is quite clear that one remuneration equals three farthings, and one guerdon equals a shilling (III, i, 166–9), and he has a sardonic awareness—confirmed by Berowne—that a remuneration, in spite of its opulent aura, buys only three-farthings worth of silk (III, i, 142–7). To Costard, fittingly, are given the words that shortly precede the entry of Mercade: 'she's quick; the child brags in her belly already: 'tis yours' (v, ii, 666–7). The language, staccato and decisive, prefigures the reality that is shortly to blow the pageant away.

Dull shares Costard's position on words. He is in accord with the view that words must symbolize things. For him, a pricket is a pricket, and not a *haud credo* (IV, ii, 12–21). The triangular discourse with Holofernes and Sir Nathanial reveals Dull at his best, stubbornly holding his own; he is like a bridge player, refusing to be psyched out of his hand. And we have the exquisite pleasure of seeing in that scene one of the play's realists patronized by the pedants. 'Sir, he hath never fed of the dainties that are bred in a book', as Sir Nathaniel observes (IV, ii,

24). But Dull, not to be put down, has the audacity to try on an ancient riddle. And while his adversaries are dealing with this sudden counter-attack, he clinches the engagement with a return to his original point: 'and I say beside that, 'twas a pricket that the princess killed' (IV, ii, 47–8). It is worth noting that for all the word-play the three are actually discussing a *fact*, i.e. what sort of deer the Princess shot—buck or pricket. These three are by no means such fools as they look, and emerge well from a comparison with their (male) social superiors.

The Clowns, then, form a natural alliance with the ladies. They are intellectual, if not social, complements. (A pairing later to be refined to Viola and Feste.) In the great work of determining the status of words, the Clowns undertake the primary task: that of establishing the relationship between words and things. Without it no progress at all is possible. And we can, I think, comprehend the importance Shakespeare assigns to the Clowns' role by noting the parallelism he supplies between the Princess and Dull. Both of them use words honestly, and both are ready to admit when words have failed to communicate:

> *Dull:* Nor understand none neither, sir. (V, i, 145)
> *Princess:* I understand you not. (V, ii, 742)

IV *Armado, Holofernes, Sir Nathaniel*

Armado, Holofernes, and Nathaniel complete the spectrum of attitudes. They are concerned with words as things in themselves, rather than as symbols for other realities. Such an attitude can be dangerous, if indulged too far; and for Armado it is part of his incessant role-playing. His role as prototype of the dandy requires him to flourish words like ruffles. Since words are the mode, he uses them modishly: 'A man of fire-new words, fashion's own knight' (I, i, 177), as Berowne remarks. In his way, his circumlocutions form another denial of reality. This situation is confirmed by his incapacity at numbers: 'I am ill at reckoning; it fitteth the spirit of a tapster' (I, ii, 39). (In *Love's Labour's Lost*, money and mathematics are infallible symbols of reality. The Clowns—see, for example, Costard, V, ii, 491–5—never err in primary arithmetic.) It is impossible to determine whether his impulse to Jacquenetta is a genuine yielding to reality, or a decision to incorporate her into his role-playing. He, too, goes the way of Navarre and company: 'I shall be forsworn, which is a great argument of falsehood, if I love' (I, ii, 159–60)—and therefore constitutes a variant of their error. But while the others, at the end, see their roles shattered by reality, Armado contrives to incorporate reality into his role. The three-year penance at the plough, clearly, suits him psychologically very well. He is a disturbing testimony to the importance of words as adjuncts to one man's reality.

We can dispose of Moth in relation to Armado, though he properly belongs with the Clowns. Moth, in his scene with Armado (I, ii) is only apparently playing the same word-game. Actually, he is a better-educated version of Costard; he knows precisely what words relate to. He tells his master scornfully that the three-year study project is a mere infatuation with words (I, ii, 43–51). He has no opinion of the quality of Armado's love: 'Most maculate thoughts, master, are masked under such colours' (I, ii, 87–8). And again, he refers his sense of reality to the monetary standard I suggested earlier:

> *Armado:* How hast thou purchased this experience?
> *Moth:*   By my penny of observation.   (III, i, 25–6)

With Moth, as with the others, a man is known by the metaphors he keeps.

And there is Holofernes. He has had a bad press—Dover Wilson, for example, sees him as 'the eternal type of pedant, the "living-dead man" who will always be with us, because so long as there is a human race to be educated there will always be many to mistake the letter for the spirit'.[9] But there is a case to be made for him. Holofernes is animated by a pure, intense love of words for their own sake. It is a disinterested passion, and he admits it readily:

> This is a gift that I have, simple, simple; a foolish extravagant spirit, full of forms, figures, shapes, objects, ideas, apprehensions, motions, revolutions: these are begot in the ventricle of memory, nourished in the womb of *pia mater*, and delivered upon the mellowing of occasion. But the gift is good in those in whom it is acute, and I am thankful for it.   (IV, ii, 66–72)

Predictably, he does not care for Armado, one of his own tribe (no more does Armado care for him, v, ii, 524–5), and provides an epitome for the two of them (plus the attendant Sir Nathaniel): 'He is too picked, too spruce, too affected, too odd, as it were, too peregrinate, as I may call it' (v, i, 13–15). This is a great joy for all of us. But Holofernes is not a fool. He is addicted to verbal arabesques, but this is harmless enough. They do not interfere with his sense of reality—he functions perfectly well in the limited society which is his normal milieu. He is, in his scene with Dull and Sir Nathaniel, discussing a fact—one of specialist interest only, to be sure, but a fact nonetheless. And he does not come to grief at the end. His merciless ragging by Berowne and company expresses them, but leaves him, though 'out of countenance', with his essential dignity unshaken. He has a superb final line, in equal command of English and the situation:

> This is not generous, not gentle, not humble.   (v, ii, 621)

He has to retire, but the inner man is undefeated. Holofernes' love of words for their own sake is a faculty that Shakespeare—as well he might—treats gently enough here.

Through this grouping of the personae in *Love's Labour's Lost* we can study the intellectual centre of the play: words. *Love's Labour's Lost* is a sustained inquiry into the nature and status of words; and the characters in it embody, define, and implicitly criticize certain concepts of words. Shifting patterns of speakers endlessly debate the propositions, establishing or seeing refuted their word-concepts. The main concepts are these: first, words as jests. Ultimately, this can be a way of rejecting reality—an attempted statement that it is not so. So, though words can be used gaily, they must themselves be treated seriously. The play presents right and wrong models. Those who wish to jest must, like the Princess, use words as in games—that is, adhering strictly to the rules of usage. One must never jest by oath-breaking. An oath is sacred, for it is a wholly laudable attempt to invest words with meaning by submitting policies and actions to the agreed mediation of words. Navarre and his courtiers, then, see their confusion between 'oaths' and 'jests' refuted by events—and by the ladies. Words as symbols for things is a concept stoutly upheld by the Clowns–realists, who emerge unscathed from the play; their mission is humble, but absolutely necessary. And finally, words as things in themselves is a concept delicately criticized in Armado; they become a part of his role, to the extent that they exclude an awareness of reality. But the concept is allowed to pass with Holofernes, who—whatever his other faults—has his passion for words under control. The pressures of reality test, but do not refute, Holofernes.

And reality is the test to which all the personae must submit. It is there, throughout the play, waiting for them; it begins to throb like a pulse in the last scene, well before Mercade enters. Reality is hinted at by the three-by-three dialogue between Berowne and Costard (v, ii, 487–95): more strongly by the baiting (Malvolio-like) of Holofernes ('A light for Monsieur Judas! it grows dark, he may stumble', 622) and the Princess's Olivia-like consolation, 'Alas! poor Maccabaeus, how hath he been baited' (623): Dumain seems to sense its implications as he cries, 'Though my mocks come home by me, I will now be merry' (625–6): then Armado's 'The sweet war-man is dead and rotten' (651): Costard's rasping 'she's quick; the child brags in her belly already: 'tis yours' (666–7): the beat grows louder and more insistent, as the combatants square up, then Mercade enters.

He, Mercade–Mercury, is the messenger of the gods, bringing the tidings of mortality. His words dissolve the world of illusion, and announce the presence of a reality that must be mediated by words. Armado is the first to see it, and his language is itself a rite of confession: 'For mine own part, I breathe free breath. I have seen the day of wrong through the little hole of discretion, and I will right myself like a soldier' (v, ii, 713–15). Then the King is rebuked into using 'honest plain words'; and Berowne, the core of the King's party, has to endure the play's central penance. *Words* are the means whereby Berowne is to pass his purgatory, his initiation into the world of reality. His penance sets jokes to work; it restores the meaning of oaths, hence of words, and reasserts their status as symbols of reality.[10] That is the main point established by the close of *Love's Labour's Lost*. And the final songs, perhaps, take up the hint dropped by Armado in Act III:

> it is an epilogue or discourse to make plain
> Some obscure precedence that hath tofore been sain. (III, i, 80–1)

The burden of that epilogue is plain enough. Summer and Winter are both aspects of reality; but Winter is second, and final. The season of death ends the play, as the news of death had stilled the Worthies. It is the final message from the forces that govern the pageant. 'The words of Mercury are harsh after the songs of Apollo.'

NOTES

1. Thus Bobbyann Roesen generally in '*Love's Labour's Lost*', *Shakespeare Quarterly* IV (1953), 411–26. A. C. Hamilton writes that 'a reality does lie beneath the surface', *The Early Shakespeare* (San Marino, California, 1967), p. 139. Marco Mincoff sees the death of the King as 'a breath of stark reality against which to measure the artificiality of the courtly game of love', 'Shakespeare and Lyly', *Shakespeare Survey 14* (Cambridge, 1961), p. 20. And Philip Parsons views the later stages of the play as 'this intangible movement towards reality', 'Shakespeare and the Mask', *Shakespeare Survey 16* (Cambridge, 1963), p. 123.

2. Peter G. Phialas, *Shakespeare's Romantic Comedies* (University of North Carolina Press, 1966), p. 99.

3. Quotations are from *Love's Labour's Lost*, ed. R. W. David, The New Arden Shakespeare (1956).

4. Hamilton, *op. cit.* pp. 129–31, has noted the many occasions when 'word' is alluded to.

5. M. C. Bradbrook, *Shakespeare and Elizabethan Poetry* (1951), p. 215.

6. Roesen, *op. cit.* p. 415.

7. E. M. W. Tillyard, *Shakespeare's Early Comedies* (New York, 1965), p. 153.

8. C. L. Barber, in *Shakespeare's Festive Comedy* (Princeton, 1959), p. 95, notes that word-play is imaged with various sports—tilting, duelling, tennis, dice.

9. John Dover Wilson, *Shakespeare's Happy Comedies* (1962), pp. 73–4.

10. Hence I think M. M. Mahood's view of the conclusion overstated: 'The great feast of language vanishes to the sound of harpies' wings. There is no substance to speech', *Shakespeare's Wordplay* (1957), p. 176.

WHY DOES IT END WELL? HELENA, BERTRAM, AND THE SONNETS

BY

ROGER WARREN

An extreme version of the general modern reaction to *All's Well* occurs in a review of Tyrone Guthrie's 1959 production: 'the tone of the play and its confusion of values...raises a dozen issues, only to drop them all with a cynical, indifferent 'all's well that ends well'. No wonder Shaw liked it so much'.[1] Now I am convinced that whatever else the ending of this play may be called—puzzling, unsatisfactory, even bungled—Shakespeare was by no means 'indifferent' and certainly not 'cynical'. I think that his own personal poetry, in the Sonnets, sheds an interesting light on exactly *why* he thought the play ended well, and accounts, especially, for his uncompromising treatment of Helena and Bertram. G. K. Hunter rightly calls it a 'peculiar' play, but he emphasizes 'the peculiar force' of both the idealism and the satire.[2] Forceful writing does not reflect 'indifference'; and E. M. W. Tillyard, in finding the play 'full of suffering',[3] isolates the most important characteristic of Helena's love and Bertram's reactions, upon which the Sonnets provide an illuminating commentary.

I

First, though, certain general problems require clarification, not least the choice of the story in the first place. What meaning did Shakespeare wish to convey through dramatizing Boccaccio's story of Giletta of Narbonne? M. C. Bradbrook tries to explain it. That the ending is 'neither hypocritical nor cynical, can be granted only if the play is seen as a study of the question of "Wherein lies true honour and nobility?"'[4] But she has to account for the fact that Shakespeare 'found himself saying more, or saying other, than his purely structural purpose could justify' and so in her terms 'all did not end well'.[5] But what if the debate on virtue and nobility is purely subordinate, achieving forcible expression to place the Helena–Bertram story in perspective? For the incontestable fact is surely that the play cannot adequately be called a morality or a debate, because the extraordinarily vivid characterization of both Helena and Bertram force us to share in their fortunes. It is basically a play about them, not about a moral theme: and the ending stands or falls as it relates to them.

The gnomic passages and stiff, odd outbursts of rhyming couplets led G. Wilson Knight into an extravagant mystical interpretation: Helena functions 'almost as Christ...as a medium only'.[6] But surely nothing else in the play suggests that Helena has so symbolic a role. On the contrary, what is so striking about her is the human intensity of her love, and her capacity for all-too-human suffering. Still, I think the formality of the verse in the healing scene *is* meant to suggest some sort of faith healing, in the limited sense that the King must be persuaded that she can cure him. It has the further effect of establishing how Helena's love strengthens her courage and determination. The King explicitly makes the point: she has

> Youth, beauty, wisdom, courage—all
> That happiness and prime can happy call.
> Thou this to hazard needs must intimate
> Skill infinite, or monstrous desperate. (II, i, 180–3)

In fact, she has both: she can heal the King by her father's prescriptions and has the courage to risk all for her overpowering, and in that sense 'desperate', love. Elsewhere, the formal and gnomic elements, though admittedly odd in what is otherwise so 'realistic' a play, may be explained by Shakespeare's anxiety to underline matters which seemed to him to be important:

> Who ever strove
> To show her merit that did miss her love? (I, i, 222–3)

and, even more,

> All's well that ends well; still the fine's the crown.
> Whate'er the course, the end is the renown (IV, iv, 35–6)

seem to be placed at strategic moments to emphasize the story of Helena and her love. The awkward or (to us) worrying aspects of the plot are scarcely glossed over, and in the finale especially they are dwelt upon. This manner of writing, together with the apparently perplexing blackening of Bertram's character, which, as Hunter says, 'a historical understanding of Bertram in an Elizabethan context cannot remove',[7] bring us back to the question, 'What was it in the story that so interested Shakespeare?'

The clear-eyed, merciless presentation of Bertram supports Tillyard's suspicion that Shakespeare's 'personal feelings, unobjectified and untransmuted'[8] have slipped into the writing. Bradbrook, too, notices that not only is 'the figure of Bertram, so radically changed from that of Boccaccio's Beltramo, . . . drawn with a . . . kind of uncynical disillusion',[9] but that Helena 'is a voice of despair breaking into the play'; and although she rightly warns against too 'crude and direct [a] personal equation . . . ; Shakespeare would certainly not wish to unlock his heart on the public stage', she brings us to the heart of the matter:

In *All's Well* the juxtaposition of the social problem of high birth versus native merit and the human problem of unrequited love recalls the story of the Sonnets; the speeches of Helena contain echoes from the Sonnets...The way in which Bertram is condemned recalls also the plain speaking which is so unusual a feature of the Sonnets.[10]

By the standards of ordinary romantic heroes, Bertram is a 'failure', but as a consistent character he is brilliantly successful, so much so that I think we must assume that Shakespeare meant him that way, and that the worrying effect is intentional. Wilson Knight stresses the play's Sonnet affinities which argue a peculiarly 'personal'[11] interest in the story. By developing these suggestions, and noticing the resemblances and verbal echoes between play and poems, I hope to account for much of the 'peculiarity' of *All's Well*, including the effect of its finale, and to suggest the reasons why there is so much intensity and heartbreak—but not 'indifference' or 'cynicism'—and, in the end, perhaps, a curious worrying uncertainty.

II

However the play is interpreted, the centre must surely be Helena's passionate love and the power of its expression. In her speeches there is an extremity of utterance which is so powerful that it goes far beyond conventional compliment in its attempt to express an emotional intensity which is almost inexpressible, as Shakespeare himself so often strives in the Sonnets.

> Better 'twere
> I met the ravin lion when he roar'd
> With sharp constraint of hunger; better 'twere
> That all the miseries which nature owes
> Were mine at once.   (*A.W.*, III, ii, 116–20)

> But in the onset come; so shall I taste
> At first the very worst of fortune's might;
>   And other strains of woe, which now seem woe,
>   Compar'd with loss of thee will not seem so.   (Sonnet 90)

There could be few better mottoes for Helena's love than

> Such is my love, to thee I so belong,
> That for thy right myself will bear all wrong.   (Sonnet 88)

And Wilson Knight[12] notes the same intense suggestion of devotion in Shakespeare's loving his friend 'next my heaven the best' (Sonnet 110) and Helena's loving Bertram 'next unto high heaven' (I, iii, 188). But he takes this as another proof that Shakespeare is examining sainthood in Helena, while I take both as similar attempts to suggest an overwhelming human passion by hyperbolical means—hyperbolical, that is, in the intense, exclusive, serious manner of the tragedies rather than in the witty, half-amused manner of the earlier comedies.

Helena's first soliloquy plunges us into that uncompromising obsession with her beloved that many of the Sonnets show:

>   my imagination
> Carries no favour in't but Bertram's.   (I, i, 80–1)

This is paralleled, in a simple way, by the disturbed rest with which the friend's 'shadow' torments Shakespeare:

>   my soul's imaginary sight
> Presents thy shadow to my sightless view,
> Which, like a jewel hung in ghastly night,
> Makes black night beauteous and her old face new.   (Sonnet 27)

The preoccupation with Bertram has an intensity, in words like 'plague', which is reflected in the Sonnets by the vivid impression of an overpowering obsession, especially in words like 'surfeit' and 'gluttoning', or

> Sometime all full with feasting on your sight,
> And by and by *clean starved* for a look   (Sonnet 75, italics mine)[13]

The desperate fervour of Helena's

> I am undone; there is no living, none,
> If Bertram be away   (I, i, 82–3)

has a very similar ring to the 'You are my all the world' and

> You are so strongly in my purpose bred
> That all the world beside methinks are dead

of Sonnet 112. When Helena says 'my idolatrous fancy/Must sanctify his relics' (I, i, 95–6) she uses an image which aptly describes both her love and Shakespeare's own. Shakespeare's denial, 'Let not my love be call'd idolatry' (Sonnet 105) only serves in fact to stress that element of 'religious adoration' which is so strong in them. Both he and Helena devote the whole of their praises 'To one, of one, still such, and ever so' (105). J. B. Leishman, calling Shakespeare the lover 'indeed a worshipper',[14] says that many of the Sonnets are 'religiously idolatrous'; and though Helena makes only a single comparison, she echoes that particularly Shakespearian idea that the old loves are reincarnated in the friend, as well as the 'holy' tears and image of the beloved.[15] Helena returns to phrases of religion in her next scene:

> Thus, Indian-like,
> Religious in mine error, I adore
> The sun that looks upon his worshipper
> But knows of him no more.   (I, iii, 199–202)

Helena's combination of unhappiness and abject devotion is echoed in the two Sonnets 57 and 58, which perhaps more than any others seem to be very close to Helena's expression of her love:

> Being your slave, what should I do but tend
> Upon the hours and times of your desire?   (Sonnet 57)

Those Sonnets, moreover, in their almost heartbreaking simplicity of statement, remind us that passionate hyperbole is not the only style in the sequence. That simplicity which is so marked a feature of Shakespeare's undeceived lovers in the earlier comedies (the finale of *Love's Labour's Lost*, Beatrice and Benedick in the church, above all Viola's 'sister' speech to Orsino) and which suggests so much emotion and awareness of potential unhappiness makes a powerful impression both here and in Helena's language too. What J. W. Lever calls Shakespeare's 'extreme capacity for self-effacement'[16] in the Sonnets, the simple quietness and lack of self-display, 'painting', or 'ornament' in much of the language, is clearly shown in

> Nor dare I chide the world-without-end hour,
> Whilst I, my sovereign, watch the clock for you,
> Nor think the bitterness of absence sour,
> When you have bid your servant once adieu.   (Sonnet 57)

The same humility which conceals anguish, the same reticence in proclaiming a bond between the beloved and the speaker is evident in all Helena says to Bertram ('I am not worthy of the wealth I owe', 'Sir, I can nothing say But that I am your most obedient servant', 'I shall not break your bidding, good my lord'). There is a marked contrast between the 'ornament' of Parolles's deceitful remarks about Bertram,

> Whose want and whose delay is strew'd with sweets,
> Which they distil now in the curbed time,
> To make the coming hour o'erflow with joy
> And pleasure drown the brim (II, iv, 42–5)

and her utter simplicity ('What's his will else?', 'What more commands he?', 'In everything I wait upon his will'). Her fear of being 'refused' is typical of her humble, fearful approach to Bertram, reflected in her actual words to him:

> I dare not say I take you, but I give
> Me and my service, ever whilst I live,
> Into your guiding power. (II, iii, 102–4)

The statements of service here are closely paralleled, again in Sonnets 57 and 58 ('Being your vassal bound to stay your leisure', 'O, let me suffer, being at your beck') and in Sonnet 87 ('My bonds in thee are all determinate').

Against her own simplicity or intensity is Helena's picture of a more superficial kind of love which Bertram may meet at the court, expressed in the conceited language of flattering Elizabethan love poetry such as is also used by the muddled lovers in *A Midsummer Night's Dream* (cf. II, i, 220–6; III, ii, 58–61, 137–44, etc.):

> His humble ambition, proud humility,
> His jarring-concord, and his discord-dulcet,
> His faith, his sweet disaster; with a world
> Of pretty, fond, adoptious christendoms
> That blinking Cupid gossips. (I, i, 167–71)

The conventional oxymorons and the 'blinking Cupid' are so superficial, so different from Helena's powerful self-expression, that Hunter must be right in taking all this to refer to the courtly lovers: 'Helena's refusal to trade on her virginity leads to the sense that others elsewhere may be less scrupulous, which leads directly to her evocation of the amorous dialect of the court.'[17] And the point of such an evocation is that it leads to a fear about Bertram himself:

> Now shall he—
> I know not what he shall. God send him well!
> The court's a learning-place, and he is one— (I, i, 171–3)

Hunter notes that 'What is suppressed must be something like "all too apt to learn courtly ways"'. This realistic fear, even while she adores Bertram, is very similar to Shakespeare's own saddened awareness that his beloved was by no means a paragon:

> But why thy odour matcheth not thy show,
> The soil is this—that thou dost common grow.　　　(Sonnet 69)

And when Bertram actually justifies Helena's fears, he woos Diana in conventional complimentary phrasing like 'Titled goddess; And worth it, with addition' and 'holy-cruel' which have a very different ring from Helena's statements of her love and service: Bertram will love

> By love's own sweet constraint, and will for ever
> Do thee all rights of service...
> *Diana:* 'Tis not the many oaths that makes the truth,
> But the plain single vow that is vow'd true.　　　(IV, ii, 16–22)

Such a vow is Helena's

> 　　　　　I will be gone,
> That pitiful rumour may report my flight
> To consolate thine ear　　　(III, ii, 126–8)

or Shakespeare's own

> I am to wait, though waiting so be hell.　　　(Sonnet 58)

Helena emphasizes that her love depends upon a real concern for desert; it is this which is proper to a servant:

> Nor would I have him till I do deserve him;
> Yet never know how that desert should be.　　　(I, iii, 194–5)

An exactly similar feeling of unworthiness underlines several of the Sonnets, all of them very sad, as when Shakespeare guards 'Against that time when thou shalt strangely pass':

> Against that time do I ensconce me here
> Within the knowledge of mine own desert,
> And this my hand against myself uprear,
> To guard the lawful reasons on thy part.　　　(Sonnet 49)

The final couplet,

> To leave poor me thou hast the strength of laws,
> Since why to love I can allege no cause,

parallels Helena's strikingly sympathetic use of 'poor' elsewhere ('poor lord', 'poor thief').[18] If the similarities between her language and that of the Sonnets indicate anything, it would seem to be that Shakespeare intends Helena's passion to have an all-consuming, overpowering intensity which makes descriptions like 'cynicism' and 'man-hunting' very unsuitable.

III

The most extraordinary feature of *All's Well*, surely, is the curiously unsympathetic portrait of its hero. Tillyard comments:

The irony and the truth of Helena's situation are that with...so firm a mind she can be possessed by so enslaving a passion for an unformed, rather stupid, morally timid, and very self-centred youth.[19]

As well as the irony, though, Tillyard stresses the 'truth' of the situation. For Shakespeare, the source seems to have provided a story of essential truth: and it seems to have been a peculiarly personal response to it which suggested his notorious alterations to Boccaccio's Beltramo, which, as Bradbrook notes, consistently show 'greater dependence, humility, and enslavement on Helena's part and greater weakness and falsehood on Bertram's'.[20] Bertram stands universally criticized, and what is so interesting is that this criticism corresponds with even the details of the suggested 'fault' of the friend of the Sonnets. Though the friend is praised for his outward show, his 'sensual fault' provokes criticism as well: others

> In other accents do this praise confound
> By seeing farther than the eye hath shown.
> They look into the beauty of thy mind,
> And that, in guess, they measure by thy deeds. (Sonnet 69)

So Bertram's own mother condemns the deeds of this 'rash and unbridled boy', and suggests that his 'well-derived nature' is being corrupted (III, ii, 26–31, 88). Helena herself had feared what Bertram would 'learn' from the court. Bertram is shown sinking lower and lower into unworthiness, and is presented much more harshly than Shakespeare's love will allow him to present his friend. Though the friend lives 'with infection', he *graces* 'impiety' (Sonnet 67).[21]

   Far more central to the play is the constantly emphasized contrast in rank between Helena and Bertram. This is the cause of some of the most harsh utterances in the play and it has a strong parallel with some of the most deeply felt and unhappy Sonnets. Helena's feeling of utter social separation from Bertram:

> My master, my dear lord he is; and I
> His servant live, and will his vassal die (I, iii, 153–4)

is closely paralleled by the 'vassalage' shown to Shakespeare's own 'Lord of my love' (Sonnet 26). The image of the star is used by both:

> 'twere all one
> That I should love a bright particular star
> And think to wed it, he is so above me. (I, i, 83–5)

The 'comfort' sought by Helena from Bertram's 'bright radiance' is echoed in Shakespeare's personal hope for some 'good conceit' of his friend,

> Till whatsoever star that guides my moving
> Points on me graciously with fair aspect,
> And puts apparel on my *tattered* loving,
> To show me *worthy* of thy sweet respect. (Sonnet 26, italics mine)

Bertram emphasizes the social gulf in violently humiliating terms:

> But follows it, my lord, to bring me down
> Must answer for your raising? I know her well:
> She had her breeding at my father's charge—
> A poor physician's daughter my wife! Disdain
> Rather corrupt me ever!   (II, iii, 112–16)

In Sonnet 49, Shakespeare feared that time

> When I shall see thee frown on my defects, ...
> ... that time when thou shalt strangely pass,
> And scarcely greet me with that sun, thine eye.

The insulting aspersion cast on the 'physician's daughter' is paralleled in Shakespeare's emphasis of his 'fault' which seems to depend chiefly on his being 'a motley to the view', an actor who depends on

> public means which public manners breeds.
> Thence comes it that my name receives a brand.   (Sonnet 111)

Shakespeare's saddened awareness of the social gulf leads him to the admission that, love or no love, he cannot be acknowledged in public:

> I may not evermore acknowledge thee,
> Lest my bewailed guilt should do thee shame;
> Nor thou with public kindness honour me,
> Unless thou take that honour from thy name.   (Sonnet 36)

But Shakespeare will not put his lover in this position:

> But do not so; I love thee in such sort,
> As, thou being mine, mine is thy good report.

Similarly, Helena, discovering too late that Bertram cannot show 'public kindness' in any way, tries to save him:

> *Bertram:* I cannot love her nor will strive to do't. ...
> *Helena:* That you are well restor'd, my lord, I'm glad.
> Let the rest go.   (II, iii, 145–8)

Shakespeare's Sonnets stress the unhappiness stemming from the friend's public behaviour, and, especially, some kind of rejection of the poet as is suggested in the near-bitter anguish of Sonnet 87:

> Thy self thou gav'st, thy own worth then not knowing,
> Or me, to whom thou gav'st it, else mistaking;
> So thy great gift, upon misprision growing,
> Comes home again, on better judgement making.

Though there is giving as well as taking back here, the actual suggestion of taking back on a question of legal ('patent') worth is chilling, as is the suggestion of utter deception in the conclusion:

> Thus have I had thee, as a dream doth flatter:
> In sleep a king, but waking no such matter.

The implied rejection of the poet seems to have been a shatteringly humiliating one: and something of the same discomfort is surely felt by any audience as it hears Bertram speak of his 'clog' whom he will not 'bed', or, worse:

> Wars is no strife
> To the dark house and the detested wife. (II, iii, 287–8)

And one of the most disturbing scenes in all Shakespeare (disturbing not because it is horrifying or tragically shattering, but because it is so *coldly* formal) is that in which Bertram refuses Helena a kiss. His clipped language reminds us of such sad phrases in the Sonnets as the suggestion that the friend will 'strangely pass', 'frown on my defects' and speak with 'settled gravity'. If ever there was 'settled gravity' it is in Bertram's denial to Helena of

> The *ministration* and *required office*
> On my *particular*. Prepar'd I was not
> For such a *business*; therefore am I found
> So much unsettl'd. (II, v, 60–3, italics mine)

Those abstract nouns have the coldly legal ring suggested in Sonnet 87 by 'the charter of thy worth', 'my bonds', 'my patent', and 'misprision'. That sonnet touches a bitterness which Shakespeare never shows elsewhere in the sequence, and which Helena does not show in her reply. Indeed, she reaffirms her service—'Sir, I can nothing say But that I am your most obedient servant'—in terms which recall the absolute self-effacement of 'Being your slave, what should I do but tend' (Sonnet 57).[22]

The icy unpleasantness of Bertram's curt 'Come, come; no more of that', 'My haste is very great. Farewell. Hie home' and 'What would you have?' is so unavoidable as to suggest something like the 'wakened hate' which Shakespeare so feared from his own beloved (Sonnet 117). But not even this can destroy Helena's love, though the suffering as well as the passion emerges as she begs the kiss:

> I am not worthy of the wealth I owe,
> Nor dare I say 'tis mine—and yet it is;
> But, like a timorous thief, most fain would steal
> What law doth vouch mine own. (II, v, 79–82)

The verbal echoes of Sonnet 40 serve to underline, not an exact parallel, but a similarity of devotion between Helena and Shakespeare himself:

> I do forgive thy robb'ry, gentle thief,
> Although thou steal thee all my poverty.

Her terror of calling Bertram hers echoes the disenchanted 'The cause of this fair gift in me is wanting' (Sonnet 87) and the simple hesitation of

> Something, and scarce so much; nothing indeed.
> I would not tell you what I would, my lord　　　　　　　　　(II, v, 83–4)

and

> I shall not break your bidding, good my lord　　　　　　　　(II, v, 88)

are closely parallel to the utterly simple, unaccusing misery of

> And patience, tame to sufferance, bide each check,
> Without accusing you of injury.　　　　　　　　　　　　　(Sonnet 58)

And Bertram's heartless refusal, 'I pray you, stay not, but in haste to horse' is the kind of remark which seems sufficiently brutal to provoke such a reaction as Sonnet 58. The scene is a masterly one. It is horrifying in human terms, but it is not cynical or indifferent. There seems a confident, open-eyed realism about the portrayal of both characters that suggests that Shakespeare knew exactly what he was doing. The parallel with the Sonnets is intended to suggest no more than that it was a personal awareness of this *kind* of unequal relationship that made him believe that he could convincingly bring Giletta's story to the stage. Whether he in the end succeeded depends on how the final scene is interpreted; but the kiss scene is so unflinchingly presented, that to play it with Bertram almost giving the kiss until recalled by a 'psst' from Parolles, as happened in two recent productions, is a piece of cheap sentimentalism which only serves to remind us how searingly painful the original writing is.

IV

The complex turns of the finale, both here and in *Measure for Measure*, seem intended to twist the tension so that the key moments—Helena's reconciliation and Isabella's plea for Angelo— may be almost unbearably poignant. Neither case is wholly successful. Though Shakespeare attempts to maintain the unyielding realism of Bertram to the end, there is just too much weight of honesty for the romantic situation to carry. There is, indeed, no other description than Hunter's 'cryptic fustian'[23] for Bertram's

> If she, my liege, can make me know this clearly
> I'll love her dearly, ever, ever dearly.　　　　　　　　　　(v, iii, 309–10)

Determined not to falsify, and to maintain Bertram's shallowness to the end, Shakespeare has imperilled the impression of reconciliation he needs at this point. I believe that his determination stemmed from his conviction that, from his own experience, Bertram's story was a meaningful, possible one.

The mature, melancholy poetry with which the King sets the tone of this scene echoes those images in the Sonnets by which Shakespeare conveys his sense of loss and hence of love,[24] and especially the very intense Sonnets 33 and 34. The King's

> I am not a day of season,
> For thou may'st see a sunshine and a hail
> In me at once. But to the brightest beams
> Distracted clouds give way   (v, iii, 32–5)

strongly recalls the imagery of those two Sonnets of disappointment at—and forgiveness of—the friend's fault: after the glorious sun has flattered the mountain tops, and kissed the meadows, he will

> Anon permit the basest clouds to ride
> With ugly rack on his celestial face   (Sonnet 33)

but then, in the next Sonnet, the 'rotten smoke' of the 'base clouds', as in the King's image, gives way:

> through the cloud thou break
> To dry the rain on my storm-beaten face.   (Sonnet 34)

At first, this is 'not enough' to Shakespeare 'to dry the rain'. In this impressively honest Sonnet, Shakespeare gives his disappointment rein:

> For no man well of such a salve can speak
> That heals the wound, and cures not the disgrace.
> Nor can thy shame give physic to my grief;
> Though thou repent, yet I have still the loss.

Helena never reminds Bertram of her earlier humiliation before the court; but as Bradbrook notes, 'her devotion (is) tinged for the first time with bitterness'[25]:

> O my good lord, when I was like this maid
> I found you wondrous kind.   (v, iii, 303–4)

When she says

> 'Tis but a shadow of a wife you see;
> The name and not the thing   (v, iii, 301–2)

one is reminded of the constant recurrence of the word 'shadow' in Shakespeare's presentation of his relationship with his friend; of the suggestion of deception and uncertainty in 'Thus have I had thee, as a dream doth flatter'; and of implied sexual betrayal:

> For thee watch I, whilst thou doth wake elsewhere,
> From me far off, with others all too near.   (Sonnet 61)

Helena surely refers back to that remarkable speech made after sleeping with Bertram:

> But, O strange men!
> That can such sweet use make of what they hate,
> When saucy trusting of the cozen'd thoughts
> Defiles the pitchy night.   (IV, iv, 21–4)

It is an extraordinary statement of her awareness that this act, 'strange' and 'defiling' the darkness of night in a 'saucy', not a 'tragic' way, is oddly insignificant. It is dismissed ('But more of this hereafter') to give place to her confidence in the future:

> But with the word: 'the time will bring on summer'—
> When briars shall have leaves as well as thorns,
> And be as sweet as sharp. (IV, iv, 31–3)

The freshness of this speech has to be set against the 'pitchy', defiling night: that is over, and in itself has not been intensely important. What Helena relies upon is the power of her own love. In this play, love is a matter *both* of 'pitchy' night and 'sweet' leaves; both thorns and flowers are used to evoke the complex experience of love:

> this thorn
> Doth to our rose of youth rightly belong. (I, iii, 124–5)[26]

Yet, however much his vices may be stressed, it is made clear that Bertram is not wholly beyond redemption,[27] and it is *because* Helena is aware by the end of his *whole* personality that she may redeem him. So, to return to Sonnet 34, after Shakespeare has given full vent to his 'wound', as Helena does less sharply, he concludes on a totally forgiving note:

> Ah! but those tears are pearl which thy love sheds,
> And they are rich, and ransom all ill deeds.

So Bertram's direct 'Both, both. O pardon!' gives hope. That, at least, is not 'cryptic fustian': yet perhaps it is even more convincing because *combined* with the fustian, suggesting that the direct outburst is real because he speaks like his former self as well. If Helena had a speech at this point like her Rossillion one in III, ii, we might be fully convinced that her love is enough to make the marriage work; but the problem is that in front of the court this just cannot be said. M. C. Bradbrook is quite right: the emotional situation does require 'another mode of expression than the last dozen lines allow',[28] something like that final couplet of Sonnet 34. But such intensely personal feeling *cannot* be spoken in public. What we long for her to say she cannot say—but not because Shakespeare did not know how to say it; the Rossillion soliloquy expressed her love perfectly. But in this formal finale the situation is too intense for Helena's (as opposed to Bertram's) emotion to be made clear. To this extent, the King's cautious, slightly uneasy 'All yet *seems* well' and his wistful epilogue have to close the play, and leave us dissatisfied. We have to refer back to Helena's earlier speeches, and though this does not excuse flawed stagecraft, it explains, I think, why Shakespeare felt that it ended well. Sonnet 34, because it states grievance as well as passion, convinces in its reconciling couplet. If the Sonnets in general state anything, it is surely Shakespeare's conviction that to love, and to forgive, is what is important, not necessarily to receive. For, as Leishman says,

nowhere...is there unmistakable evidence that Shakespeare really believed that his friend, in any deep and meaningful sense of the word, loved him at all. At most, perhaps, his friend 'quite liked him'. Saddest of all...are those sonnets where Shakespeare speaks of their difference in rank...as an insuperable barrier between them, for they suggest that he may actually have had to endure (and to forgive)...slights and insults.[29]

And the poignant unhappiness of such a relationship is the basic situation Shakespeare found in the story of Giletta of Narbonne.

Shakespeare's problem was to transform Boccaccio's wit into serious emotion, presumably because he did not want to tell Helena's story wittily, since it contained emotions he understood and could express in powerful poetic terms. Helena, in the end, survives her humiliations, not through resilient, witty gaiety, but through a completely clear-eyed view of herself and Bertram. Shakespeare invests her with a near-desperate fervour to communicate unmistakably that her love is sufficiently powerful to enable her to overcome all humiliations: and the key is the 'Rossillion' soliloquy. The most impressive writing occurs at the most crucial moment of the play when the strength of Helena's love must be made unforgettable. And unforgettable it is. The tone of mingled sadness and tenderness in

> *Poor* lord, is't I
> That chase thee from thy country, and expose
> Those *tender* limbs of thine to the event
> Of the none-sparing war?   (III, ii, 102–5, italics mine)

recalls the self-effacement of

> That god forbid that made me first your slave
> I should in thought control your times of pleasure.   (Sonnet 58)

Helena's sad, simply-expressed resolve,

> I will be gone,
> That pitiful rumour may report my flight
> To consolate thine ear. Come, night; end, day;
> For with the dark, poor thief, I'll steal away   (III, ii, 126–9)

has the same immensely quiet but immensely unhappy note as

> I'll myself disgrace, knowing thy will...
> Be absent from thy walks.   (Sonnet 89)

The whole speech is crowned by the memorably intense hyperbole of

> Shall I stay here to do't? No, no, although
> The air of paradise did fan the house
> And angels offic'd all   (III, ii, 124–6)

which has an eloquent grandeur similar to Shakespeare's great manifesto of what he understood by 'love':

> Love is not love
> Which alters when it alteration finds,
> Or bends with the remover to remove.
> O! no! it is an ever-fixed mark,
> That looks on tempests and is never shaken.   (Sonnet 116)

Helena's love is sorely tried; her suffering and her hint of reproach, though it is barely perceptible, in the finale, do not however destroy it. Shakespeare's love in the Sonnets seems to have undergone similar trials and overcome them. He seems to convey both Bertram's cruelty and Helena's ecstasy and anguish in the kind of language which he had used to express his own passion and his friend's behaviour. If in the finale he failed to provide a powerful and reassuring speech for her, he may have felt that it was not necessary; that what he had already given her to say would convince his audience that despite—maybe because of—everything, her single-minded love would ensure that all ended well.

All's Well, it must be admitted, is not a complete success; if it were, it would not have worried so many, nor have taken so many words here. But since so much of it is very impressively written, it can tease the mind. The uncompromising power with which Bertram is drawn and the memorable intensity of Helena compel attention and, because of the last scene, explanation. In suggesting that the Sonnets cast a revealing light on Shakespeare's attitude to Helena and her story, I have tried not to excuse dramatic weaknesses. The play remains a 'peculiar' one; but Helena's passion, which always emerges as the centre-piece in performance, has so much in common with the Sonnets that this may indicate why Shakespeare chose the story. I think that he made Helena so intense, and presented her beloved with such relentless honesty, because he had something especially personal to say about the power of love to prevail over all 'altera-tion' and humiliation, even if it proved less easy to show matters ending well in dramatic than in non-dramatic terms.

© ROGER WARREN 1969

NOTES

1. *Leamington Spa Courier*, 24 April 1959.
2. *All's Well That Ends Well*, The Arden Shakespeare (1959), pp. xxix, liii. All quotations from *All's Well* are from this edition; those from the Sonnets are from Peter Alexander's 1951 edition of the *Complete Works*.
3. *Shakespeare's Problem Plays* (1951), p. 104.
4. 'Virtue Is the True Nobility', *R.E.S.*, XXVI (1950), p. 301.
5. *Ibid.* p. 290.
6. *The Sovereign Flower* (1958), pp. 146, 154.
7. Hunter, *op. cit.* p. xlvii.
8. Tillyard, *op. cit.* p. 106.
9. *Shakespeare and Elizabethan Poetry* (1951), pp. 169–70.
10. *R.E.S.*, XXVI (1950), p. 290.
11. Wilson Knight, *op. cit.* p. 132.
12. Wilson Knight, *op. cit.* p. 136. Cf. also *A.W.*, I, i, 89–90, and Sonnet 92, lines 2–4.
13. Cf. *A.W.*, I, i, 93–4, and Sonnet 113, lines 9–12.
14. *Themes and Variations in Shakespeare's Sonnets*, 2nd edn. (1963), p. 133.
15. Cf. *A.W.*, I, i, 77–81, and Sonnet 31, lines 5–8.
16. *The Elizabethan Love Sonnet* (1956), p. 185.
17. Hunter, *op. cit.* pp. 13–14.
18. Cf. also *A.W.*, I, iii, 196–9, and Sonnet 87, lines 4–8.
19. Tillyard, *op. cit.* p. 112.
20. *R.E.S.*, XXVI (1950), p. 291.
21. But cf. *A.W.*, I, i, 97–103.
22. Cf. also *A.W.*, II, v, 73–6, and Sonnet 58, lines 9–12.
23. Hunter, *op. cit.* p. lv.
24. Cf. *A.W.*, V, iii, 38–42, and Sonnets 77, line 8, and 65, lines 11–12.
25. *R.E.S.*, XXVI (1950), p. 301.
26. Cf. Sonnet 35, lines 1–4.
27. Cf. *A.W.*, IV, iii, 68–71, and Sonnet 35, line 5.
28. *R.E.S.*, XXVI (1950), p. 301.
29. Leishman, *op. cit.* p. 226.

SOME DRAMATIC TECHNIQUES IN 'THE WINTER'S TALE'

BY

WILLIAM H. MATCHETT

This discussion might well be entitled 'Three Points of Stage-Craft in *The Winter's Tale*', were I not anxious to avoid the implication that it offers only half the value already provided by Nevill Coghill in *Shakespeare Survey 11*.[1] I hope instead to offer an analysis which, building upon Coghill's insights, goes beyond them to call particular attention to the way in which Shakespeare, thus late in his career, had learned both to trust his actors and to manipulate audience response.

A beginning playwright is apt to think almost entirely in terms of putting necessary information into his lines. In setting the bare Elizabethan stage, no other course is open to him:

> These are the city gates, the gates of Roan... (1 *Henry VI*, III, ii, 1)

> Under this thick-grown brake we'll shroud ourselves... (3 *Henry VI*, III, i, 1)

His maturing as a playwright—as far as setting the stage is concerned—is primarily a matter of his moving away from such blunt announcements in the first lines of scenes and finding subtler ways of inserting the necessary information as the scenes proceed:

> How sweet the moonlight sleeps upon this bank!
> ...Look how the floor of heaven
> Is thick inlaid with patines of bright gold...
> (*The Merchant of Venice*, v, i, 54–9)

I think this be the most villainous house in all London road for fleas; I am stung like a tench...Why they will allow us ne'er a jordan; and then we leak in your chimney; and your chimney-lye breeds fleas like a loach. (1 *Henry IV*, II, i, 13–21)

Stage action is a different matter. Eager to control the action and to make his meaning clear to actor and audience alike, the beginning playwright will produce lines like these:

> My lord, you are unjust, and more than so:
> In wrongful quarrel you have slain your son.
> (*Titus Andronicus*, I, i, 292–3)

> Why droops my lord, like over-ripen'd corn
> Hanging the head at Ceres' plenteous load?
> Why doth the great Duke Humphrey knit his brows,
> As frowning at the favours of the world?
> Why are thine eyes fix'd to the sullen earth,
> Gazing on that which seems to dim thy sight? (2 *Henry VI*, I, ii, 1–6)

In terms of stage action, such lines are redundant. The audience has just seen Titus kill his son and has judged for itself that the quarrel was 'wrongful', Titus 'unjust'. It does not need to be told. Even the name is not necessary information in the second scene of *2 Henry VI*; Duke Humphrey has been on stage and sufficiently identified in the first scene. The audience will recognize him when he reappears. The speech indeed instructs the actor playing the role exactly what gestures he must make, but the audience in the meantime has the information twice, in the lines and in the acting.

For Shakespeare to learn that his lines are not the whole play and need not carry the whole meaning is hardly surprising. He naturally learned to handle his stage more effectively as he matured in his art, but the subtlety he achieved is often lost to us through the historical accident of his not providing full stage directions. That he came to trust his actors, that his scripts were prepared for them and not for readers, that he was a member of the company and could answer any questions put to him—all these factors have meant that we have inevitably lost many of the stage-effects upon which he may have counted. We have only to remember the slight stammer which Olivier and others built into their characterizations of Hotspur, the speech impediment adding immeasurably to the sense of impetuosity as Hotspur stumbles over his words in pouring them out, to recognize the situation. The detail, his 'speaking thick, which nature made his blemish' (*2 Henry IV*, II, iii, 24), is not mentioned in the play in which Hotspur appears; it is preserved only through the lucky accident of his being mentioned in the sequel. There may well be thousands of such details which have not been preserved, conceptions of his characters passed verbally by the author to his fellow actors, moulding their presentation and therefore needing no redundant place in the script.

This is, of course, where the director comes in. To be honest, one must admit that there is gain as well as loss in not having full stage directions. There is gain in the fact that a director has the greater freedom to go at a script afresh, revealing it from a new perspective, infusing it with his own insight and not held to each detail of action and inflexion by the traditions of some Global D'Oyly Carte. I would take it that the Shakespeare critic needs also to think as a director, not considering lines alone but lines in a stage context. The difference is that the director must invent business to carry every moment of an entire production while the scholar–critic will seek to avoid invention, attempting to hold himself to what is clearly implied by the evidence. The director must reach a decision; the critic may admit to his ignorance.

I want, then, to discuss again the three most 'difficult' scenes in *The Winter's Tale*—the jealousy of Leontes (I, ii), the death of Antigonus (III, iii), and the statue scene (v, iii)—in an attempt to indicate what seems to me the range of Shakespeare's final control over audience response. If I can make no other claim for comprehensiveness, I am at least looking at the beginning, the middle and the end.

1. Coghill is of course right that Camillo and Archidamus, in the first scene in the play, prepare the audience 'for what it is about *not* to see' (p. 32); the friendship they describe is destroyed by Leontes' jealousy. But even Coghill's 'little miracle of stage-craft' (p. 33) consists in bringing an already jealous Leontes onto the stage and showing that he has sufficient motive for his jealousy. This is not, I would suggest, the way the scene has been constructed.

Shakespeare's problem in *The Winter's Tale* is that of compressing a complete tragedy into the first half in order to pass through and beyond it in the second. He has to work fast, but he does work. He not only gives the audience everything it needs; he leads it precisely where he wants it. We are asked to believe that Leontes has been a good friend to Polixenes and a good husband to Hermione, but how apt are we to be convinced of this if we are shown him jealous from the first? Even a sufficient motive is no substitute for an initial image of stability. Shakespeare sets out to show us Leontes becoming jealous; his short-hand method is that of making his audience suspicious first so that Leontes' jealousy comes less as a surprise than as a confirmation. The dramatic surprise should come later, in fact, when we discover that he and we were wrong. As is so often the situation, we are misled in our understanding of the play because we know the story too well and therefore know all along that Hermione is innocent. Whether anyone is guilty should, at the beginning of the play, be an open question.

First, then, enter with others a visibly pregnant Hermione.[2] May we expect such 'realism' in Shakespeare's theatre? Indeed we may. We may confirm it in a number of places. As early as 2 Henry IV, Doll Tearsheet claims pregnancy in an attempt to avoid prison, and the Beadle, with some appropriate but unspecified action, demonstrates that her swelling is nothing but a cushion (v, iv). We may confirm the effect, closer to The Winter's Tale, in the stage direction for the dumb show at the beginning of the third act of Pericles: 'enter Thaisa, with child'. The unborn child will be Marina, to be born on shipboard during the storm. And there may be other instances, though these are less certain. Helena is pregnant, and very likely visibly so, when she claims, in the final scene of All's Well, to have fulfilled the conditions Bertram laid upon her. Though there is no specific evidence, one has to admit that it adds immensely to the mixture of ironies in Henry VIII if the glorious procession leading from her coronation and probable marriage accompanies an Anne Bullen not only, as the stage direction for the pageant says, 'in her hair'—which is to say, with her hair down like a bride[3]—but also visibly pregnant. She has indeed, as one of the observant gentlemen says, 'had all the royal makings of a queen' (IV, i, 87).

But these instances have moved from certainty to conjecture. Most important, of course, is the fact that the visible pregnancy of Hermione can be confirmed later in The Winter's Tale itself. 'The Queen your mother rounds apace', says a Lady in Waiting, speaking to Mamillius at the beginning of the second act (II, i, 16) after a supposed lapse of not more than a few hours, and another Lady adds, 'She is spread of late / Into a goodly bulk' (lines 19–20). When Leontes first denounces his wife, he says ' 'tis Polixenes / Has made thee swell thus' (lines 61–2), while Hermione, in asking for women to accompany her to prison, appeals to the obvious, saying 'you see / My plight requires it' (lines 117–18).

If, then, we set aside our extraneous knowledge of Hermione's innocence and recognize that she enters the scene visibly pregnant, what follows? One of the kings speaks—in staging, as opposed to reading, we don't yet know which he is:

> Nine changes of the wat'ry star hath been
> The shepherd's note since we have left our throne
> Without a burden. Time as long again
> Would be fill'd up, my brother, with our thanks;
> And yet we should for perpetuity
> Go hence in debt. And therefore, like a cipher,
> Yet standing in rich place, I multiply

With one 'We thank you' many thousands moe
That go before it.   (I, ii, 1-9)

We quickly recognize that this is the visitor from Bohemia—the first scene has clarified the general situation for us—and what phrases leap out at us from what he is saying? 'Nine' months, 'burden', 'fill'd up', 'Go hence in debt', 'standing in rich place, I multiply'. Shakespeare has filled this speech with the diction of conception, fertility and gratitude. We have come to the theatre expecting drama, which means plot complication, and we have already found it. We see the pregnant woman and we hear apparent allusions to adultery.

And these references continue. Listen to Polixenes' second speech:

I am question'd by my fears of what may chance
Or breed upon our absence that may blow
No sneaping winds at home, to make us say
'This is put forth too truly'. Besides, I have stay'd
To tire your royalty.   (lines 11-15)

True, he is speaking of what may be going on in Bohemia, but we expect, in the theatre to which Shakespeare has trained us, to hear things with metaphoric reference, and we hear him simultaneously speaking of what is apparently going on in Sicilia: 'my fears of what may chance / Or breed', 'put forth too truly', and 'blow', with its suggestions of 'fly-blown' or the engendering of flies and 'by-blow' or illegitimate child. Finally, then, the vintage Shakespearian pun of 'Besides, I have stay'd / To tire your royalty'. I have overstayed my welcome. To 'tire' is to 'fatigue'. And this, it turns out, is all Polixenes was saying. But we hear more. To 'tire' is also to 'adorn', to *attire*. I have stayed to add this ornament to your royal line. And to 'tire' is also to 'prey upon', a term from falconry, as in the lines of *3 Henry VI* in which Henry speaks of his enemy the Duke of York, 'that hateful Duke / Whose haughty spirit, winged with desire, / Will cost my crown, and like an empty eagle / Tire on the flesh of me and of my son!' (I, i, 266-9). The language, no less than Hermione, is pregnant. If we are alert to the situation before us, we hear Polixenes saying that he is fatiguing and adorning and preying upon Leontes.

And in his next speech we find him calling his further stay at court 'a charge and trouble' to Leontes. 'To save both, / Farewell, our brother' (lines 26-7). And Hermione, asked by the as yet unsuspicious Leontes to intervene, boasts of her power:

I had thought, sir, to have held my peace until
You had drawn oaths from him not to stay. You, sir,
Charge him too coldly.   (lines 28-30)

She, we are by now convinced, is accustomed to using more warmth with Polixenes. It is true that we must later discover that we were wrong, that all this was innocent. But Shakespeare's dramatic method here is first to mislead *us* in order to hasten the process of misleading Leontes. He has in fact misled us twice: first in Scene i by preparing us for innocent friendship and now in Scene ii by presenting an image of guilt where there is in fact innocence. That Scene ii should deny what we were led to expect in Scene i is a fairly common dramatic technique, one which we are quite prepared to accept with a somewhat smug awareness that this is how drama goes. Our very acceptance of this reversal, however, our sense that we are on top of what the playwright is doing, makes it easier for him to fool us the second time.

At any rate, what turns out to have been Hermione's innocent playfulness comes to us double-edged when she speaks of Polixenes' 'limber vows' (line 47), calls 'a lady's "verily"', her vow, 'as potent as a lord's' (lines 50–51), tells him that, if he won't be her guest, he will be her prisoner —'so you shall pay your fees / When you depart, and save your thanks' (lines 53–4).

We, as audience, are thus led into the trap of reading a guilty meaning into all that we hear. When Polixenes speaks of his boyhood with Leontes, he says:

> We were as twinn'd lambs that did frisk i' th' sun
> And bleat the one at th' other. What we chang'd
> Was innocence for innocence; we knew not
> The doctrine of ill-doing, nor dream'd
> That any did. Had we pursu'd that life,
> And our weak spirits ne'er been higher rear'd
> With stronger blood, we should have answer'd heaven
> Boldly 'Not guilty'...   (lines 67–74)

He is speaking of general human guilt; we take him, however, as speaking of the specific guilt into which we consider him, as an adult with 'stronger blood', to have fallen. His generalized comment, 'Temptations have since been born to 's' (line 77), we hear as a sophisticated understatement shared with Hermione and the audience behind Leontes' back. By this time we should be wondering when Leontes will face what is going on.

Similarly, when Hermione responds, 'Th' offences we have made you do we'll answer, / If you first sinn'd with us' (lines 83–4), she is in fact saying, 'You have not sinned with me'. And so ultimately we come to realize. But if we are clinging firmly here to our ultimate knowledge of her innocence, we miss the whole point of Shakespeare's masterful manipulation. What we are led to hear, at this point in the play, is not 'You have not sinned with me', but 'I am well aware that I am not the first with whom you have sinned'.

And all this time Leontes remains unsuspicious. We are far ahead of him. 'Is he won yet?' he asks (line 86), and again we wince at what we take to be dramatic irony. 'He'll stay, my lord'. 'At my request he would not' (line 87). It is simply a statement of fact. Even yet he need not be suspicious, though the fact serves to confirm our suspicions and may indicate the beginning of his. Hermione's very playfulness with her husband should be striking us as shameless, so that his 'Too hot, too hot!' when it finally comes (line 108), is a relief. Far from feeling that Leontes is too rapidly jealous, we should feel that he has been very slow about it.

Shakespeare has taken only 108 lines to reach this point in the scene. In *Othello* 180 lines intervene, in Act III, Scene iii, between 'Excellent wretch! Perdition catch my soul / But I do love thee' and 'I am abus'd; and my relief / Must be to loathe her'. And the Moor, of course, is worked upon by Iago. *Othello* is clearly, and understandably, in the back of Shakespeare's mind as he writes *The Winter's Tale*; it shows up in such perhaps unconscious details as Hermione's having, like Desdemona, an attendant named Emilia. We cannot but think of *Othello* ourselves when Antigonus faces the raging Leontes in the second act to say, 'You are abus'd, and by some putter-on / That will be damned for't. Would I knew the villain!' (II, i, 141–2). There has been no putter-on; Leontes is his own Iago. But we should not feel free to scorn him for his blindness. Shakespeare has accomplished the compression of this remarkable scene by letting his audience participate directly in the fall of Leontes, by leading us to mistake innocence for guilt. We watch Othello fall before the machinations of a clever villain; in *The Winter's Tale* we should ourselves fall before the machinations of a clever Shakespeare. How, then, can we entirely blame Leontes?

If only we will follow what is happening and being said, setting aside our knowledge of the outcome, we will find that Shakespeare has never written with firmer control of his stage or his language. 'Gone already!' Leontes says as Hermione leaves the stage with Polixenes. 'Inch-thick, knee-deep, o'er head and ears a fork'd one!' (I, ii, 185–6). And then, to his son, 'Go, play, boy, play; thy mother plays, and I / Play too; but so disgrac'd a part, whose issue / Will hiss me to my grave' (lines 187–9). We hear all the playing with 'play', as child's play for Mamillius, amorous play for Hermione, acting a part for Leontes, deception for both the adults. Knowing the end, we hear also the dramatic irony of the 'issue' which will hiss him to his grave—the illegitimate issue of Hermione's pregnancy, as he intends; the end of his proceedings against his innocent wife, as we see it in Act III. But listen also to what we should hear in that 'Gone already!' 'Gone'—from the scene; she has left the stage. 'Gone'—from me; my wife has left me. 'Gone'—pregnant; she has conceived. 'Gone'—into sin; she has fallen. 'Gone'—come to climax with Polixenes, as when Charmian, in *Antony and Cleopatra*, would have her revenge upon Alexas by praying 'O, let him marry a woman that cannot go, sweet Isis, I beseech thee!' (I, ii, 59–60). All these meanings are implicit in the single word; all of them fit what Leontes is saying. But there is yet another which he overlooks, until it is brought home to him in the third act: 'The Prince your son, with mere conceit and fear / Of the Queen's speed, is gone.' 'How Gone?' 'Is dead' (III, ii, 41–2). Then Hermione herself falls and Paulina confirms it all with her later reference to 'her that's gone' (V, i, 35).

It is sometimes assumed that there has been a relaxation of dramatic intensity in the late romances. I would not think that the scene we have been considering suggests any such relaxation. If there is anything new here, it is that Shakespeare is working more directly than ever with audience response, not merely presenting an action for our consideration, but directly manipulating our response in order to bring us out where he wants us. As dramatic action goes, however, the scene does not ask us to respond to the stage in any particularly new way. It conveys still the illusion of human beings engaged in a possible human situation; it is the dramatic illusion of ongoing life. The other two scenes to which we now turn function, I would maintain, in a quite different way.

2. A good deal of attention has been given to the stage direction for Antigonus' departure: 'Exit, pursued by a bear'. As a stage direction, it is one of the funnier in Shakespeare, in a class with 'Enter Ariel, invisible' (*The Tempest*, III, ii, 39), and 'Enter Pericles, wet' (*Pericles*, II, i, 1). The discussion has tended to go back and forth among those who think that the scene was originally staged with an actor on all fours in a bear suit, those who think he would do better on his hind legs, and those who argue for the realism of the company's having borrowed a tame bear from their neighbours in The Bear Garden. There has been divided opinion as to whether The Bear Garden could be expected to have any tame bears. Coghill comes out for the bear

suit: 'Real bears are neither so reliable, so funny, nor so alarming as a man disguised as a bear can be' (p. 34).

That the effect was both 'funny' and 'alarming'—'terrifying and pitiful' and also 'wildly comic' (pp. 34–5)—I quite agree, though I have no idea whether it was staged with man or bear. I would direct attention to something else: whichever way it is staged, it cannot but call attention to the mechanics of the staging; it cannot but break any illusion of ongoing life.

It is one of the paradoxes of the theatre that the more realistic one tries to be, the less one succeeds. There was, for example, the revival of *Sherlock Holmes* some years ago which boasted a last act with a real waterfall on stage. Holmes, you remember, struggles with Moriarty at the top of the waterfall, and is killed, or not killed, as the case may be. At any rate, there it was with real water falling amidst real rocks and ferns and birches. But did this increase audience faith in the reality of the illusion? Of course not. The audience thought of plumbing, and of how ingenious the designer was to manufacture a real waterfall on stage. Too much reality destroys itself. It is notorious how disastrous it can be to introduce real horses on stage. At best, the audience is always nervously aware of the men with shovels waiting in the wings.

I am arguing that Shakespeare's bear—whether man or bear—is not a way of increasing the realistic effect; it is a way of making the audience aware of the medium, like Rodin's 'Hand of God' emerging from the rock of which it is a part, so that one must experience not only the realized form but its relationship to the inchoate rock, or like those canvases of Van Gogh which remind us constantly that whatever has been achieved has been achieved with paint—not with magic but with material. The bear here inevitably reminds us of drama as pretence, insists that a tale is not life but an image of life. It is part of the scene modulating from the first half of *The Winter's Tale* to the second, a scene with one of the strangest mixtures of tones in all Shakespeare, a transition from the mode of tragedy to the mode of—what?—of comedy? Yes, comedy, but what an unsatisfactory word that is for what we find at the end of this play.

We are used to the idea of an alternation of comedy with tragedy—the porter at the gate who interrupts and thereby heightens the suspense following the murder of Duncan in *Macbeth* is the obvious example. But an alternation of scenes is not a mixture. We sometimes have a mixture of the two styles in one scene at points of minimum dramatic success. I think particularly here of the unfortunate conspiracy of Aumerle in the latter part of *Richard II*, when the Duke of York comes to accuse his son before Bolingbroke, followed, buckety-buckety, by the Duchess, come to excuse her son and blame her husband (v, iii). The action starts as a serious dealing with a tragic political issue of central importance to the play, but it degenerates into something close to farce, and one cannot but feel that the playwright has lost control of his tone. We sometimes have a successful intrusion of one style into the other, as when the news of the King's death casts its chill over the festivities at the end of *Love's Labour's Lost*. But this also is not a simultaneous mixture.

Toward the end of his career, Shakespeare appears to have been conducting a series of experiments with mixtures of tone far beyond anything one encounters earlier. There are forays in this direction of course in the storm scenes in *Lear*, but these are all under the control of the suffering of the King. We are moved in a number of directions, but we respond primarily to that suffering. In *Cymbeline*, however and for example, we find something quite different, a mixture which conveys no sense of loss of control and yet refuses to guide us to a particular response. I speak of the scene (IV, ii, 290 ff.) in which Imogen awakens beside the headless torso of, as she supposes, her husband—it is, after all, clothed in her husband's garments. We know, however, that the body is that of Cloten, the lubberly villain who wore the clothing of Post-humus as part of his scheme to rape Imogen. Imogen suffers, but we are more aloof than we are from Lear's suffering for we know she suffers as the result of a mistake which can be cor-rected. This does not free our response to the humour of the scene, however, for how *should* we respond to the wry fact that her praise for the physical attributes of this body is praise for the body of the disgusting Cloten? The situation is more complex than I wish to take space here to indicate, but this is enough to make the point.

What, then, is happening in the transition scene in *The Winter's Tale*? We must recognize first that we have been shaken by tragedy. Hermione is dead. We have been allowed no other possibility. We have seen her collapse on stage; she has been carried out; Paulina has returned to announce her death in no uncertain terms: 'I say she's dead; I'll swear it. If word nor oath / Prevail not, go and see' (III, ii, 200–1). Again we must rule out our knowledge of the outcome and recognize that, at this point in the play, it should not occur to us to doubt Hermione's death. Antigonus has even seen her ghost.

Nor, indeed, is Hermione's death all that has shaken us, though it has been the climax. Paulina has summarized for us both Leontes' guilt and the emotional priority of the various offences:

> That thou betray'dst Polixenes, 'twas nothing;
> That did but show thee, of a fool, inconstant,
> And damnable ingrateful. Nor was't much
> Thou wouldst have poison'd good Camillo's honour,
> To have him kill a king—poor trespasses,
> More monstrous standing by; whereof I reckon
> The casting forth to crows thy baby daughter
> To be none or little, though a devil
> Would have shed water out of fire ere done't;
> Nor is't directly laid to thee, the death
> Of the young Prince, whose honourable thoughts—
> Thoughts high for one so tender—cleft the heart
> That could conceive a gross and foolish sire
> Blemish'd his gracious dam. This is not, no,
> Laid to thy answer; but the last—O lords,
> When I have said, cry 'Woe!'—the Queen, the Queen,
> The sweet'st, dear'st creature's dead; and vengeance for't
> Not dropped down yet.   (III, ii, 182–99)

It is upon this catalogue of guilt and tragic loss that Shakespeare, in *The Winter's Tale*, sets out to build an image of forgiveness and reconciliation. 'O thou tyrant!' Paulina adds,

> betake thee
> To nothing but despair. A thousand knees

> Ten thousand years together, naked, fasting,
> Upon a barren mountain, and still winter
> In storm perpetual, could not move the gods
> To look that way thou wert. (lines 204–10)

This, we are willing to believe, is what Leontes deserves; it is, however, what the play ultimately denies. Life does sometimes offer second chances; forgiveness is possible. It is of this that Shakespeare will give us an image, and he approaches it not only via Time, the Chorus, who will carry us over sixteen years, but, even before that, by following his tragic impact with a quite disorienting mixture.

Perdita is being abandoned. The very fact that this scene is staged alerts us to the possibility of continuance and change in the plot, for not only is the play obviously not over, but the baby's being brought to 'The deserts of Bohemia' (III, iii, 2) tells us that further connexions are being made. Now if Shakespeare simply wanted to continue his story in the same realistic vein, and wanted Antigonus killed by a bear, there is no reason why the whole action could not take place off stage to be reported by the younger shepherd, as is the death itself. But Shakespeare chooses to bring the bear on stage and thereby cuts in upon audience response with an inevitable reminder that this is art, not life. Why? I don't, of course, know what went on in his mind. I can only report what I think is the effect of his choice. We are wrenched from our response to the plot and the action to a wider perspective which lifts us out of the action as life and forces us to see it as a created image of life. All drama is, of course, such an image, with more or less directness; the gain in calling attention to the fact is that breaking in upon the illusion allows a fuller comprehension. Challenging our awareness, it opens us to fresh experience.

Nor is this wider perspective dependent only upon the bear, for we find ourselves entirely disoriented from any appropriate response as we listen to the shepherds. The old man enters condemning the follies of youth—'getting wenches with child, wronging the ancientry, stealing, fighting'—and finds the baby, whom he immediately takes as 'some stair-work, some trunk-work, some behind-door-work; they were warmer that got this than the poor thing is here' (III, iii, 61–75). We are moved, that is, from our immediate story to the larger perspective of, first, the gulf between youth and age in general and, second, an easy acceptance of perpetual sexuality as an inherent fact. We are ready to take this as interrupting humour—'If thou'lt see a thing to talk on when thou art dead and rotten, come hither' (78–9)—but we are jarred from this response when the younger shepherd begins describing 'the most piteous cry of the poor souls' (line 88) on the ship, and we are disoriented still further when he describes 'how the bear tore out his shoulder-bone' (line 93), for Antigonus is a character with whom we have had some sympathy. But the style remains that of the rustic at whom we were prepared to laugh. We may recognize it as the style of Launcelot Gobbo: ' "Budge", says the fiend. "Budge not", says my conscience. "Conscience", say I, "you counsel well". "Fiend", say I, "you counsel well" ' (*The Merchant of Venice*, II, ii). For this is the manner in which the younger shepherd describes the simultaneous losses: 'but first, how the poor souls roared, and the sea mock'd them; and how the poor gentleman roared, and the bear mock'd him, both roaring louder than the sea or weather' (lines 96–9).

Nor will Shakespeare allow us to distance our response. 'Name of mercy, when was this, boy?' 'Now, now; I have not wink'd since I saw these sights; the men are not yet cold under water, nor the bear half din'd on the gentleman; he's at it now' (lines 100–3).

Are we to feel terror? Are we to laugh? We feel unsure. 'Exit, pursued by a bear.'

The summary statement of course is the old man's 'thou met'st with things dying, I with things new-born' (line 110). Here is the eternal mixture. But how is one supposed to feel about it? We have not forgotten the dead Hermione or the suffering Leontes when Perdita is found; we are not allowed to forget the mangled Antigonus—'I'll go see if the bear be gone from the gentleman, and how much he hath eaten' (lines 122–3)—when the old shepherd offers his personal summary: ' 'Tis a lucky day, boy; and we'll do good deeds on't' (line 131).

It is easy enough to say simply, 'This is romance and in romance any extravagance goes', but that does not really answer any questions. What is the result of such extravagance? What precisely does Shakespeare accomplish within the form? Through almost three acts we have had tragic drama in the usual mode of tragedy; now suddenly Shakespeare cuts across this with—what? Not just comedy, but with continuing tragedy in the mode of comedy. And not just that either, for we recognize the possibility of a new beginning, a new generation, though it has not yet been suggested that the new might redeem the old. What I am calling attention to primarily in this scene, however, is the insistent way in which Shakespeare forces us out of mere passive participation in an ongoing story into an active disorientation which leaves us no choice but to question our own responses. No simple response is adequate and we are left shaken not only by tragedy but by the necessity of continuing to respond after that pattern had appeared complete.

3. What do we expect as we approach the final scenes? Remember that we still have no inkling that Hermione is alive. Coming to the end of the play knowing that Hermione is alive dulls our response to Shakespeare's artistry here, just as coming to the beginning knowing that she is innocent dulls our response to the skill with which he builds his grounds for Leontes' jealousy. We expect nevertheless a number of reunions at the end of the play: Leontes with Perdita—this should be the main one—but also Leontes with Polixenes, Polixenes with Florizel, and Camillo with Leontes. We expect not only reunions, but forgiveness, and young love overcoming the objections of Polixenes, since the shepherdess is, after all, a princess. This is the ending we expect. It is the usual ending for comedy. Shakespeare, of course, has his surprise up his sleeve and, in addition to all that we expect, he will give us also the reunions of Leontes, Perdita, and, indeed, Polixenes with Hermione. Of all the reunions, that of Leontes with Hermione is his climax—it is the forgiveness beyond all deserving and hope which is the point of this play. There are two major features in the staging of it to which I wish to direct attention.

First, the statue, like the bear, reminds us immediately of the dramatic medium. We no sooner see the statue than we recognize the actress—or in Elizabethan times the actor—in the costume of Hermione. But note that this very recognition of the dramatic pretence prevents our being certain how we should respond. Hermione is still dead—or is she? If the wild bear has been played by a tame bear, or a man in a bear suit, how else would we stage a statue but to have it represented by the actor who played the character the statue itself represents? The presence of Hermione on stage, then, does *not* immediately tell us that Hermione is alive. Even if we catch the statue breathing, we have no clue—for we know the actor has to breathe. Shakespeare plays upon our uncertainty. 'The fixure of her eye has motion in't', says Leontes,

'As we are mock'd with art' (v, iii, 67–8)—a line which cuts much deeper than the superficial use I am now making of it. For more than eighty lines the statue stands on the stage as our hopes are alternately raised and then dashed until, somewhere along the line, the very game of suspense gives its end away.

I could not pick the exact point at which an audience should decide that Hermione is, after all, alive. But Shakespeare does his utmost to hold it off as long as possible. Just as he has insisted originally that Hermione is dead, so he insists that the statue is a statue, carved by 'that rare Italian master, Julio Romano, who, had he himself eternity and could put breath into his work, would beguile nature of her custom, so perfectly is he her ape' (v, ii, 93–5). Critics argue over the origin of the name Julio Romano. That seems to me less important than why it has been brought in at all. Surely it is here as part of the general insistence that we not suspect the statue of being anything more than a statue. And then, when we see it, hope after hope is raised, to be explained away or withheld from proof. The statue is wrinkled, unlike the Hermione of sixteen years ago: 'So much the more our carver's excellence, / Which...makes her / As she liv'd now' (v, iii, 30–2). Perdita will kiss her hand: 'O patience! / The statue is but newly fix'd, the colour's / Not dry' (lines 46–8). 'Would you not deem it breath'd, and that those veins / Did verily bear blood?': 'Masterly done! / The very life seems warm upon her lips' (lines 64–6). Leontes will kiss her: 'Good my lord, forbear. / The ruddiness upon her lip is wet; / You'll mar it if you kiss it; stain your own / With oily painting. Shall I draw the curtain?' (lines 80–3).

No. Do not draw the curtain. We must resolve *our* doubts. Once again, notice how closely Shakespeare has involved us, the audience, in the ongoing dramatic process. We suspected Hermione before Leontes became jealous; similarly here, we are not simply watching to see how Leontes will take the living Hermione—we are forced through the process of ourselves coming to recognize that Hermione is alive. It is not something we knew all the time; it is not even a miracle which is reported to us or staged for us: it is a miracle in the full effect of which we participate.

The other point, the final point to which I would call attention, is Shakespeare's complete faith in his actors at this emotional climax of his play. Shakespeare has so many reunions to arrange here at the end of the play that the result could be emotionally incoherent. He even introduces an unnecessary reunion in coupling Paulina with Camillo. How then does he centre our attention upon the reunion of Leontes and Hermione?

He begins, of course, by playing down the others: they are all kept off stage. First Autolycus hears from a court gentleman how Polixenes and Camillo have learned from the shepherds that Perdita is Leontes' daughter.[4] Then another gentleman reports upon the meeting of Leontes and Polixenes, and Shakespeare invites the audience to wonder why it has not been allowed to witness this important reunion: 'Did you see the meeting of the two kings?' 'No.' 'Then you have lost a sight which was to be seen, cannot be spoken of' (lines 39–41). This being the case, it naturally occurs to us that the least he could have done would have been to show it to us—but we must be content with hearing it described, and the play moves on, leaving us feeling somewhat cheated. Even the reunion of Perdita with her father is kept off stage and merely reported. All this, we realize later, is Shakespeare's method of keeping the emotional focus on the reunion of Leontes and Hermione. This he stages. Here, then, at least, we would expect his poetry to reach an emotional climax.

And what do we have? We have silence.

After the long indecision as to whether or not the statue is an actor playing a statue, or an actor playing Hermione playing a statue, after the long suspense, we find the dramatic climax not in a burst of impassioned verse, but in a silent embrace. Nor is this just a curious circumstance; it is a carefully constructed thematic triumph. I cannot take the space here for a full coverage of this play's attention to the limitations of language as a medium, but let me point to enough instances to establish the theme's presence and let me suggest merely that it is related also to Shakespeare's calling his audience's attention at key points to drama itself as a limited medium.

In the first lines of the play, when the two courtiers are providing the necessary exposition about the two kings and the visit of Bohemia to Sicilia, one of them is already having trouble with the inexpressible. 'Verily', he says, 'I speak it in the freedom of my knowledge: we cannot with such magnificence, in so rare—I know not what to say' (I, i, 11-12).

'I know not what to say.' That is one problem in communication, but it is not the only one. There is the opposite problem caused by knowing too readily what to say, the problem into which we fell ourselves in first misjudging Hermione. It is central to the blasphemy of Leontes, which builds from his denial of Camillo's insight—'you lie, you lie. / I say thou liest, Camillo' (I, ii, 299-300)—through his denial of Paulina and the entire court—'You're liars all' (II, iii, 145)—to its climactic denial of the truth of Divinity itself—'There is no truth at all i' the oracle./ The sessions shall proceed' (III, ii, 137-8).

Discourse breaks down for Leontes when he is trying to explain his vision of Hermione's guilt. Listen to the tortuous twistings of this speech, almost unintelligible to a theatre audience until it reaches the thundering clarity of its false conclusion:

> Praise her for this her without-door form,
> Which on my faith deserves high speech, and straight
> The shrug, the hum or ha, these petty brands
> That calumny doth use—O, I am out!—
> That mercy does, for calumny will sear
> Virtue itself—these shrugs, these hum's and ha's,
> When you have said she's goodly, come between,
> Ere you can say she's honest. But be't known,
> From him that has most cause to grieve it should be,
> She's an adultress. (II, i, 69-78)

The last words ring out after the syntactical maze—and they are false.

'Sir', says Hermione to her accuser during the trial, 'You speak a language that I understand not' (III, ii, 78).

Silence, then, becomes the final language, the language of love and forgiveness which all can understand, the wordless communion in which the exchange is most complete. Nor am I creating something from nothing here. Shakespeare points in various ways to the meaning of this final scene. 'The silence often of pure innocence', Paulina has said, 'Persuades, when speaking fails' (II, ii, 41-2). The gentleman who reports the response of Polixenes and Camillo to the information as to Perdita's identity, says, 'there was speech in their dumbness, language in their very gesture' (v, ii, 15). And silence is the emphasized response from the moment Paulina first draws the curtain revealing the statue. 'I like your silence' (v, iii, 21), she says, and she can only say it if there has been a preceding silence for her to like. The rapt attention of the viewers is both their appropriate response and a chance for us in the audience to begin trying to sort out our own responses.

Finally, Paulina demands that Leontes put his thoughts into words, and he speaks both of the likeness and the unlikeness, of the statue's having aged Hermione, and then of the rebuke of this cold stone representing warm life to him who was more stone than it. All this time the others remain rapt, and Leontes calls our attention to Perdita 'Standing like stone' (line 42). When Perdita kneels before the statue, Leontes falls again into silent wonder, from which neither Camillo nor Polixenes can rouse him. Only Paulina's move to draw the curtain again forces him into speech.

At last Paulina calls the statue to life and Leontes draws back: 'Do not shun her...Nay, present your hand' (lines 105–7). It is Hermione who comes to Leontes. He has only one brief exclamation when they touch—'O she's warm! / If this be magic, let it be an art / Lawful as eating' (lines 109–11)—and Hermione says not one word. 'She embraces him', says Polixenes. 'She hangs about his neck', adds Camillo (lines 111–12), and if the stage method is reminiscent of the redundant description of Duke Humphrey's actions quoted earlier from *2 Henry VI*, there is, I would say, a vast difference in effect. There, the lines seek to embellish the meaning of the action through description of it and, in pace, the speech dominates the actions described. Here, the descriptions of action are perfectly simple, unembellished. They do not tell the audience what to see but express the emotion of wonder at the miracle of what the characters and the audience see. The action, slow-paced and deeply moving, will quite dominate these expressions of awe.

Camillo continues, 'If she pertain to life, let her speak too', to which Paulina answers, 'That she is living, / Were it but told you, should be hooted at / Like an old tale; but it appears she lives / Though yet she speak not' (lines 113–18). And Hermione's only words, when they come, are for Perdita.

Why does she not speak to Leontes? The point is, of course, that she does. She speaks the common language they both now understand. Her forgiveness is acted, not spoken; her forgiveness is clear in her coming to Leontes and their reunion is clear in their embrace. 'It appears she lives.' What more could possibly be said that would enrich—that would not detract from—this meaningful stage image?

Yet Shakespeare cannot simply stop at this point. There is no curtain for him to close and he must both move his actors from the stage and modulate away from this emotional climax for his audience. In the few remaining lines he provides, in fact, three further reunions, each very different from the others. First there is the reunion of Hermione and her lost daughter, with its prayer helping to define the enveloping emotional aura of the reunion of husband and wife: 'You gods, look down, / And from your sacred vials pour your graces / Upon my daughter's head!' (lines 121–3). Then Paulina, lamenting her husband, Antigonus, is abruptly handed to Camillo by Leontes. This hastily arranged marriage is something of a jolt. It is, after the profound effect of the meaningful reunions, a mere mechanical alignment for the apparent sake of plot neatness. Symbolically, the point, one can see, is that the two most faithful counsellors are being paired. Naked of any preparation, however, this is just what it is—a coldly symbolic arrangement. Because they are so immediately juxtaposed, we must perforce compare the union of Camillo and Paulina with the moving image of meaningful reunion preceding it. I would suggest that the point may lie in the juxtaposition, that Shakespeare once again gives us an insistent reminder of his medium, this time through the formal balance of multiple marriages—for the reunion of Leontes and Hermione serves almost as a marriage and Perdita and Florizel are of course here also—the appropriate end for comedy. It is, I would suggest, the very inappropriateness of this literary neatness to the living experience of the preceding moments which serves to bring us back to the stage. The usual device for enabling a comedy to conclude, this tidy arrangement serves here to reveal the chasm, the strangely bridgeable chasm, between art and life.

And there remains one further reunion, that of Hermione and Polixenes, for the wrong Leontes did each of them cannot but have raised a barrier of embarrassment between them as they meet again. 'Let's from this place', says Leontes, and then 'What! look upon my brother', after which he offers his brief apology: 'Both your pardons, / That e'er I put between your holy looks / My ill suspicions' (lines 145–8). 'What! look upon my brother.' He must speak this line to Hermione, but how does he say it? I see two possibilities: he might pretend to mock jealousy as they once more greet each other—and such a mock jealousy would highlight the depth of his faith in her forgiveness. Or he might be telling Hermione not to be shy of Polixenes but to look up and greet him, for no suspicion is possible.

At any rate, these additional endings following the emotional climax help us to recognize that the reunion is not an easy 'they lived happily ever after' tacked awkwardly onto the end of an aborted tragedy. We have been made aware of how short an 'ever after' is left to them, and of what a price in time and suffering they have had to pay. Mamillius and Antigonus are dead. Hermione has lived in seclusion and Leontes on his knees for sixteen years. The cost has not been denied, but out of the mixture of styles has emerged a stage image of a human truth for which the tragic genre leaves no room, the truth that men sometimes *do*, against all the odds, have a second chance. If we count upon a second chance, we are no doubt going to be disappointed one way or the other. We will probably be disappointed because it will not come; but, even if it should come, we will have cheapened it in counting upon it. This is not the image Shakespeare gives us. He gives us instead an image of undeserved and unexpected forgiveness.[5] He gives us the experience of restoration after total loss. We have participated directly in the guilt; we participate in the loss and we participate in the miracle of restoration. Shakespeare manipulates the response of his audience more directly here, I believe, than in any other of his plays.

Life can indeed be 'mock'd with art'. Art constantly reminds us that it is both longer-lasting and closer to perfection than we are. But it has this seeming permanence and near-perfection only as it keeps contact with life as we believe we can experience it. The theatre, drama, feeds on life and, miraculously, with its trappings and falsifications and pretences, can nevertheless in turn feed life. Here, by keeping us aware in the second half of his play that he is creating an image, not life itself, Shakespeare performs this miracle in which art and life appear to coalesce. The statue *is* Hermione; art becomes life and life is not mocked. 'It appears she lives.' Forgiveness is sometimes possible this side of the grave—given time and suffering, the cycle of the generations, and love. The poet–playwright creates here one of his supreme moments—not magic, but 'an art / Lawful as eating'. In complete control of his stage, he so trusts his dramatic art that he divests himself of words and speaks directly with the eloquence of silence.

NOTES

1. 'Six Points of Stage-Craft in *The Winter's Tale*', *Shakespeare Survey 11* (Cambridge, 1958), pp. 31–41.

2. This point, accepted by Coghill and others, was apparently first made by M. M. Mahood, *Shakespeare's Wordplay* (1957), p. 147.

3. See the note on this stage direction in The Arden Shakespeare *King Henry VIII*, ed. R. A. Foakes (1957), p. 129.

4. Once again there is insistence upon the mixture of emotions—here as visually indistinguishable: 'A notable passion of wonder appeared in them; but the wisest beholder that knew no more but seeing could not say if th' importance were joy or sorrow' (v, ii, 17–19).

5. The word 'grace', or a derivative, occurs some two dozen times in the play, not as a mere title, 'His Grace', but with its theological overtones.

CLEMENCY, WILL, AND JUST CAUSE IN 'JULIUS CAESAR'

BY

JOHN W. VELZ

A passage in Seneca's *De Clementia* throws light on the celebrated 'just cause' crux in *Julius Caesar* and offers a vantage point from which to make a reading of the play.

Shortly before the conspirators assault him in III, i, Caesar protests that his harshness in maintaining the banishment of Publius Cimber is not wrong and that the importunate suppliants have not given him sufficient reason to alter his determination in the matter:

> Know, Caesar doth not wrong, nor without cause
> Will he be satisfied.[1]

Ben Jonson twice alluded to this passage, but both times he cited it in wording quite different from that of the Folio text. In *Discoveries* he gave as an example of Shakespeare's unbridled pen Caesar's supposed statement: '*Caesar did never wrong, but with just cause*'; Jonson labelled this line 'ridiculous'.[2] In 1626, in the Induction to *A Staple of News*, Jonson had one character exclaim facetiously, '*Cry you mercy, you neuer did wrong, but with iust cause*'.[3]

The difference between what Jonson twice said Shakespeare wrote and what appears in the Folio has elicited much speculation.[4] The explanations that Jonson (who was known for his excellent memory) remembered inaccurately or that he deliberately misquoted in order to malign Shakespeare have both been generally rejected in this century. A consensus has evolved that Shakespeare may well have written what Jonson said he wrote—the reading in F$_1$ then becomes an emendation of the playhouse text.[5] Most of the scholars cited in note 5 regard the line Jonson gave as more appropriate to the character of Shakespeare's Caesar than the Folio lines. Two of them, Miss Proestler and Starr, have pointed out that according to both Suetonius ('Deified Julius' xxx, 5) and Cicero (*De Officiis*, III, xxi) the historical Julius was fond of quoting a distich from Euripides' *Phoenissae* to the effect that wrong done to seize a throne is not wrong—in all else, however, a man should be upright in the eyes of the gods:

> Nam si violandum est ius, regnandi gratia
> Violandum est; aliis rebus pietatem colas.[6]

If Shakespeare did write a statement of ethical expediency for his Caesar, they argue, he was conveying the same deviousness that Cicero and Suetonius had found in the man.[7]

An analogue of a different implication for the character of Caesar can be found in Seneca's *De Clementia*. At I, xi, 4 Seneca distinguishes for Nero between kings and tyrants in these words:

Quid interest inter tyrannum ac regem (species enim ipsa fortunae ac licentia par est), nisi quod tyranni in voluptatem saeviunt, reges non nisi ex causa ac necessitate?[8]

Seneca is speaking in this passage of clemency for political offenders; clemency for Publius Cimber is the question at issue in III, i of *Julius Caesar*. The phrase *non nisi ex causa* is reminiscent of Ben Jonson's '*never...but with just cause*'.[9] Moreover, Seneca, like Shakespeare, is specifically concerned with the wrong of harshness (*saevitia*), while Cicero and his descendants allude more generally to *ius violandum*.

The analogue takes on further interest in the face of the tension in the first three acts of *Julius Caesar* between tyranny and kingship. Caesar is consistently regarded by the conspirators as a tyrant. Cassius introduces the matter when he generalizes about the benefit of suicide as an escape from tyrants (I, iii, 92, 99–100), and a moment later he openly stigmatizes Caesar: 'And why should Caesar be a tyrant then?' (103). Brutus, too, thinks of Rome under Caesar as a world where 'high-sighted tyranny range[s]' (II, i, 118), and the moment Caesar falls Cinna cries out that 'Tyranny is dead!' (III, i, 78). The First and Third Plebeians temporarily catch the mood of the conspirators and agree that 'this Caesar was a tyrant' (III, ii, 71). A delayed echo comes from Young Cato, fighting against Caesar's inheritors, who announces that he is 'a foe to tyrants' (V, iv, 5).

Caesar, of course, has no such view of himself. Shortly after these crucial lines about 'cause' he speaks of himself in an extended simile which for Elizabethans would have unmistakable connotations of kingship:

> I am constant as the northern star.
>
> .   .   .   .
>
> The skies are painted with unnumber'd sparks,
> They are all fire, and every one doth shine;
> But there's but one in all doth hold his place.
> So in the world: 'tis furnish'd well with men,
>
> .   .   .   .
>
> Yet in the number I do know but one
> That unassailable holds on his rank,
> Unshak'd of motion; and that I am he,
> Let me a little show it...[10]

Caesar's self-apotheosis in these lines probably derives from Ovid;[11] Shakespeare refers to Ovid's stellification of Julius Caesar (*Meta.*, XV, 843–52) in *The First Part of King Henry VI* where apotheosis also is associated with royalty.[12] The six allusions to lions in *Julius Caesar* also contribute connotations of kingship which underline Caesar's self-image and his aspirations. Shakespeare apparently injected them quite deliberately: the two portentous lions—the one which 'glaz'd upon' Casca 'and went surly by' (I, iii, 21) and the lioness that Calphurnia heard had 'whelped in the streets' of Rome (II, ii, 17)—are not mentioned in Plutarch. As he pours out to Casca his bitterness at the political situation in Rome, Cassius twice pejoratively associates the lion with Caesarism (I, iii, 72–5, 106). The pattern moves to a climax in which Caesar hyperbolically characterizes himself as a brother to danger: 'We are two lions litter'd in one day' (II, ii, 46). All of the allusions appear in the first and second acts when Caesar is aspiring to the crown: in the light of these associations of Caesar with the royal lion, Decius Brutus' reference to catching lions in toils (II, i, 206) takes on ironic significance; the net of flattery is being prepared for the would-be king.

Caesar, then, has a radically different picture of himself from that the conspirators hold. If he did indeed say on the stage what Jonson claimed that he said, and if we were to consider the passage from *De Clementia* as a source, rather than as an analogue, we might have a clue to the difference between Caesar as he is seen and Caesar as he sees himself. Caesar thinks of himself as a man who is cruel only *ex causa ac necessitate*—as a king.

But, according to renaissance political reasoning, Caesar is not a king, nor can he be anything but a tyrant, no matter how he dresses himself in imagery—even should he adhere royally to the Senecan precept about cause and clemency. The renaissance distinction between kings and tyrants went beyond the difference Seneca posits. A man who sought a throne which did not come to him by inheritance was the worst sort of tyrant; no matter how benevolent or just his rule, he was tyrannical by definition.[13] Pierre Charron puts it clearly:

The prince is a tyrant and wicked either in the entrance, or execution of his gouernmēt. If in the entrance, that is to say, that he treacherouslie inuadeth, and by his owne force and powerfull authoritie gaines the soueraigntie without any right, be he otherwise good or euill (for this cause he ought to be accounted a tyrant) without all doubt we ought to resist him either by way of iustice, if there be opportunitie & place, or by surprise: and the Grecians, saith *Cicero*, ordeined in former times rewards and honors for those that deliuered the common-wealth from seruitude and oppression. Neither can it be said to be a resisting of the prince, either by iustice or surprise, since he is neither receiued, nor acknowledged to be a prince.[14]

By Charron's standards, Caesar can never be a king, and the conspirators have a moral right—even an obligation—to strike him down. Their ethic is underlined as they assassinate him in the Senate chamber to which he comes expecting to be crowned.[15]

The usual assumption was that a tyrant 'in the entrance' would prove also to be a tyrant 'in the execution'.[16] To support the conspirators' view of Caesar as a tyrannical usurper of sovereignty, Shakespeare also portrays in him the kind of tyrant Seneca is concerned with in *De Clementia*. Seneca's tyrant acts *in voluptatem*, feeding the pleasure of his own will, without regard for just cause.[17] Despite his protestations of constancy in the moments before his death, Caesar is a man of arbitrary and changeable will. He moves rapidly in II, ii from an adamant determination to 'go forth', to concession to Calphurnia's plea that he stay at home, and finally to a new determination to go, as Decius tempts him with the prospect of a crown. And, as Bernard Breyer has pointed out, all this time he talks of his 'will'.[18] After three imperious announcements to Calphurnia that 'Caesar shall go forth' (lines 10, 28, 48), he changes his mind and orders Decius to

> bear my greeting to the senators,
> And tell them that I will not come to-day;
> Cannot, is false; and that I dare not, falser;
> I will not come to-day. Tell them so, Decius. (lines 61–4)

Having a moment before promised Calphurnia to send the message that he is sick, he arbitrarily breaks his word to her and pompously protests that he will tell the truth: 'Decius, go tell them Caesar will not come' (line 68). Decius points out that such arbitrariness is perhaps laughable, antithetical as it is to logic: 'Caesar, let me know some cause'. Caesar's reply is a flat insistence that cause and will are the same thing:

> The cause is in my will: I will not come;
> That is enough to satisfy the Senate. (lines 71–2)

The legislative body of the state, seeking cause, must be satisfied with the mere will of the ruler. Small wonder if Decius and the other conspirators regard Caesar as a tyrant.[19]

Shakespeare's audience would be likely to agree with the conspirators if they had read much political philosophy. La Primaudaye typifies the numerous commentators in the sixteenth and seventeenth centuries who contrasted kings with tyrants in the manner of Seneca's *De Clementia*:

As it properly belongeth to a royall estate to governe and to rule subjects, not according to the sensual appetite, and disordered will of the Prince, but by maturity of counsell, and by observation of lawes and of justice: so it agreeth with a tyrant to raigne by his absolute will, without all regard either of lawes, or of the precepts of justice.[20]

Nicholas Breton, defining 'An Vnworthy King', puts it more succinctly: 'his care is but his will'.[21] Erasmus, in *The Education of a Christian Prince*, agrees with Seneca that 'it is the character, not the title, that marks the king', and he later brackets Julius Caesar with Achilles, Alexander the Great, and Xerxes as tyrants.[22] The pseudo-Plutarchian comparison between Caesar and Alexander the Great, first printed in the 1603 edition of North's Plutarch, says of Caesar exactly what Shakespeare's play dramatizes:

Caesar pricked forward by his naturall wit, and tyrannicall manners of his time, was possessed (in an vnluckie hower for him and his countrey) with the intollerable vice of selfe-will and ambition, which was cause of his death. (Sig. Rrr 6ᵛ)

In the context of renaissance political thought, then, Brutus is neither hypocrite nor self-deceiver when he reasons that to make Caesar a tyrant 'in the entrance' is almost certainly to make him a wilful tyrant 'in the execution'.[23] Brutus has not known in the past that Caesar's 'affections [i.e., his will] sway'd / More than his reason' (II, i, 20–1), but he knows that ambition for a crown leads on to 'the intollerable vice of selfe-will':

> Crown him?—that;—
> And then, I grant, we put a sting in him,
> That at his will he may do danger with. (II, i, 15–17)

It is 'a common proof' (line 21), and Caesar's imperious insistence on will at the expense of reasonable cause in the next scene vindicates this generalization.

It is possible that Shakespeare had the passage from *De Clementia* in mind when he characterized Caesar as a wilful tyrant, for immediately after speaking of the danger that Caesar might do 'at his will' if crowned, Brutus goes on to reflect that

> Th'abuse of greatness is when it disjoins
> Remorse from power. (lines 18–19)

This is precisely the thesis of *De Clementia*.[24] Seneca adduces a great many arguments and *exempla* to show Nero that true greatness is clement, while spurious greatness, tyranny, is vindictive. Seneca knew the Emperor well enough to realize that pragmatism would be his best appeal, and accordingly he emphasized that the merciful ruler wins the loyalty of his subjects and sits secure on his throne, while the tyrant lives in constant fear of assassination.[25] Just before making the distinction between kings and tyrants which is at issue here, Seneca recounts at length and in detail the story of Lucius Cinna, who conspired against Augustus despite the latter's many benefactions to him. Having discovered the conspiracy, Augustus showed full clemency to his would-be assassin and later even appointed him Consul; he thus won Cinna's friendship—and his own security as well: 'No one plotted against him further'.[26] If Shakespeare had read *De Clementia*, he might well recall it while working on *Julius Caesar*, in which a tyrant's refusal of clemency immediately precedes his assassination.[27]

T. W. Baldwin does not include *De Clementia* among the works prescribed for the sixteenth-century grammar school,[28] and he argues with some cogency that Portia's sentiments on mercy in *The Merchant of Venice* derive from *Ecclesiasticus*, not from Seneca.[29] Certainly, however, whether he knew *De Clementia* or not, Shakespeare repeatedly advanced ideas which appear in that work:

> Wilt thou draw near the nature of the gods?
> Draw near them then in being merciful;
> Sweet mercy is nobility's true badge.   (*Titus Andronicus*, I, i, 117-19)[3]

> Say 'pardon', king, let pity teach thee how;
> The word is short, but not so short as sweet;
> No word like 'pardon' for kings' mouths so meet.
>   (*Richard II*, v, iii, 114–16)[31]

> We are no tyrant, but a Christian king;
> Unto whose grace our passion is as subject
> As is our wretches fetter'd in our prisons.   (*Henry V*, I, ii, 241–3)[32]

Without concluding for or against Seneca as Shakespeare's source, we can discern in *Julius Caesar* a Senecan antithesis between the clement king who is motivated by just cause and the tyrant with his 'intollerable vice of selfe-will'. Caesar believes that he is the former;[33] the conspirators find in him the latter. The renaissance audience, seeing that Caesar is a tyrant not only 'in the entrance' but 'in the execution' as well, would be expected to invest their sympathies on the ethical side of the conspiracy.

Yet the conspiracy fails the moment it has succeeded; Brutus and Cassius are forced to ride 'like madmen through the gates of Rome' toward their deaths at Philippi. A number of explanations can be offered for this evident reversal of poetic justice in the play. First, it is not divine Providence which punishes the assassins, but 'Caesar's spirit, ranging for revenge'; Plutarch concluded that Caesar's 'great prosperitie and good fortune that favored him all his life time, did continue afterwards in the revenge of his death, pursuing the murtherers both by sea and land, till they had not left a man more to be executed, of al them that were actors or counsellors in the conspiracy of his death' ('The Life of Julius Caesar'). Whatever suggestion of Providential intervention is implicit in this statement Shakespeare minimizes by bringing Caesar's ghost itself on stage to supervise a personal revenge.[34] Secondly, if we agree with Brutus that the conspirators should be called 'purgers, not murderers' (II, i, 180), we will find in their fate the common tragic paradox that those who cleanse the body politic themselves go under in the holocaust—as, for example, Hamlet does. Beaumont and Fletcher put the paradox forcefully at the end of *The Maid's Tragedy*:

> on lustful kings
> Unlook'd-for sudden deaths from God are sent;
> But curs'd is he that is their instrument. (v, iii, 296–8)

Another relevant paradox is that of the guilty founder of a praiseworthy dynasty. Caesar, as a usurper of sovereignty, is in a position like that of Henry Bolingbroke in the Henriad; tyrannical Caesar is to Augustus, the great Emperor, as usurping Bolingbroke is to Henry V, the ideal king. In the final analysis, however, we might prefer to take the approach of Ernest Schanzer, Mildred Hartsock, and others who have argued recently that there can be no resolution of the inconsistencies, that this is a problem play in which the conspirators and their victim both are tainted—that, like the great tragedies which follow in the canon, *Julius Caesar* is rooted in moral ambiguity.[35]

Two Postscripts

I

If we assume that Shakespeare's Caesar did originally go to his death with a claim about just cause on his lips, we can also reason that the emendation of the text was made by deletion, not by substitution. T. S. Dorsch has suggested this original reading:

> *Caes.* ...I spurn thee like a cur out of my way.
> *Met.* Caesar, thou dost me wrong.
> *Caes.* Know, Caesar doth not wrong but with just cause,
> Nor without cause will he be satisfied.

'From this the Folio version would be produced by deleting [Metellus' speech and] *but with just cause*, and filling out the line [III, i, 47] from that which follows' (Arden edition, *loc. cit.*). This hypothesis is the more appealing in that it provides a repetition of the key word *cause* in a play in which there are many formal repetitions—Antony uses this same verbal echo in his oration:

> You all did love him once, not without cause;
> What cause withholds you then to mourn for him? (III, ii, 104–5)[36]

Moreover, the integrity of the line 'Nor without cause will he be satisfied' can be defended on the ground that it harmonizes with a pattern of satisfactions that are offered or demanded elsewhere in the play. The word *satisfy* and its cognates appear in six other contexts in *Julius Caesar*. For Decius' 'private satisfaction' (II, ii, 73) Caesar explains the real reason why he prefers to remain at home. After Caesar's death the excited crowd insists 'We will be satisfied: let us be satisfied' (III, ii, 1), and Brutus defends the assassination with the claim

> That were you, Antony, the son of Caesar,
> You should be satisfied. (III, i, 224–6)[37]

II

Ironically enough, further on in *Discoveries* (in a passage attacking Machiavelli) Jonson himself turned to *De Clementia* for precepts about royal clemency:

No virtue is a Prince's own, or becomes him more than clemency, and no glory is greater than to be able to save with his power...The state of things is secured by clemency: severity represseth a few, but it irritates more...the merciful Prince is safe in love, not in fear...He is guarded with his own benefits.[38]

If Shakespeare's Caesar did originally make a protestation about doing wrong only with just cause, he was, like Jonson, appealing to a view of clemency which can be found in *De Clementia*. Caesar's appeal to the doctrine of just cause is, however, a tragic self-delusion: posture as he will with Senecan claims to kingly virtue, Caesar is a tyrant, both 'in the entrance' and 'in the execution'.

NOTES

1. III, i, 47–8. All quotations from *Julius Caesar* in this article are from the Arden edition, ed. T. S. Dorsch (1955).

2. *Ben Jonson*, ed. C. H. Herford and Percy and Evelyn Simpson (Oxford, 1925–52), VIII, 584.

3. *Ibid.* VI, 280. As Dorsch points out in the Arden edition, the altered type here suggests that Jonson was consciously quoting.

4. For summaries and discussion, see H. H. Furness, Jr., in the Variorum edition (1913), Commentary on III, i, 47–8; J. Dover Wilson, 'Ben Jonson and *Julius Caesar*', *Shakespeare Survey 2* (Cambridge, 1949), 36–43; Dorsch, *op. cit.*, Commentary on III, i, 47–8.

5. An emendation, however, which the players were ignoring as late as 1626; the point of Jonson's parody would be lost unless his audience recognized the prototype (as Dorsch and Wilson both point out— see references above). Among those who have suggested that Jonson was recalling what Shakespeare actually wrote are Michael Macmillan, Arden edition (1902), p. 171; Mary Proestler, 'Caesar Did Never Wrong But With Just Cause', *Philological Quarterly*, VII (1928), 91–2; John Palmer, *Political Characters of Shakespeare* (1945), pp. 44–6; Alfred Harbage, *As They Liked It: An Essay on Shakespeare and Morality* (New York, 1947), p. 83; Dover Wilson, *op. cit.*; Dorsch, *op. cit.*; G. A. Starr, 'Caesar's Just Cause', *Shakespeare Quarterly*, XVII (1966), 77–9.

6. The wording is Cicero's.

7. The Euripidean aphorism and variations on it became a political commonplace in the renaissance. Starr mentions English translations or paraphrases in Grimald's Cicero, Whytinton's Cicero, Lyly's *Euphues*, Udall's translation of Erasmus's *Apophthegmata*, and the Gascoigne–Kinwelmarsh translation of the *Phoenissae*. (He finds none of these as likely a source as *De Officiis*, which it seems probable Shakespeare had studied in Stratford grammar school.) To these can be added a number of analogues:

for a kingdom any oath may be broken:
I would break a thousand oaths to reign one year.
(*3 Henry VI*, I, ii, 16–17)

(In notes on this passage, H. C. Hart [Arden edition, 1910] and J. O. Halliwell [Shakespeare Society edition of *The First Sketches of the Second and Third Parts of King Henry VI*, 1843, p. 194] both quote Cicero's words as a precedent to Edward's thought.)

since a wrong must be, then it excels,
When 'tis to gaine a Crowne.
(*Misfortunes of Arthur*, I, iv, 111–12)

thy flatterers
Perswade thee, that...what pleases *Caesar*
Though neuer so vniust is right, and lawfull.
(Massinger, *The Roman Actor*, v, i, 39–42—cited by Macmillan, p. 171)

if Right (say Ambitious men) may be violated, it is to be violated for a kingdom.
(Pierre de La Primaudaye, *L'Academie Françoise*, trans. T.B. (1586). Sig. Q 3ᵛ)

Si violandum est ius, regnandi causa violandum est, in caeteris pietatem colas.
(Pierre Charron, *De La Sagesse* (1604), Sig. H 4ᵛ)

Finally there is Queen Elizabeth herself, who wrote to Sir Henry Sidney, her Governor in Ireland, 'Si violandum jus regnandi causa' (quoted by Frederick Chamberlin in *The Sayings of Queen Elizabeth*, London, 1923, p. 152). Some of these analogues are discussed by W. A. Armstrong in 'The Elizabethan Conception of the Tyrant', *Review of English Studies*, XXII (1946), 161–81; see also Ruth L. Anderson, 'Kingship in Renaissance Drama', *Studies in Philology*, XLI (1944), 136–55. Neither of these articles discusses the 'just cause' crux in *Julius Caesar*, nor does either of them point to Cicero as the source of infection for the concept.

8. For the suggestion that first sent me to Seneca's prose works in quest of 'just cause' I am grateful to my fellow reader at the Folger Shakespeare Library, E. L. Dachslager.

9. The concept *ex causa* also appears in the variations on Cicero by Charron (first ed., 1601) and Queen Elizabeth (see note 7).

10. III, i, 60–71. In 'The Northern Star: An Essay on the Roman Plays', *Shakespeare Quarterly*, II (1951), 287–93, Roy Walker points out that the cosmic references in *Julius Caesar* (the supernatural portents as well as this simile) are just those which Shakespeare used to give stature to English royalty.

11. Martha Hale Shackford, '*Julius Caesar* and Ovid', *Modern Language Notes*, XLI (1926), 172–4.

12. I, i, 55–6. Bedford invokes the ghost of King

Henry V with the praise: 'A far more glorious star thy soul will make / Than Julius Caesar...'

13. For a discussion of the usurper as a tyrant *ipso facto*, see Armstrong *op. cit*. See also Irving Ribner, 'Political Issues in *Julius Caesar*', *Journal of English and Germanic Philology*, LVI (1957), 10–22: 'An ordinary man, no matter how great, could not aspire to kingship; he could only aspire to tyranny' (p. 13).

14. *Of Wisdome*, trans. Samson Lennard (1612), sig. Ii 8. The marginalium reads: '*Whether it be lawfull to lay violēt hands vpon the person of a tyrant. A double tyrant. The entrāce.*'

15. Shakespeare calls repeated attention to the crown in *Julius Caesar*. In their interrogation of Casca, Brutus and Cassius make a kind of tricolon of the three-times-offered crown (I, ii, 217–23), and Brutus follows by asking a question that has just been answered: 'Was the crown offer'd him thrice?' A moment later Casca makes a pedantic distinction between crowns and coronets which again enforces the symbol of royalty. That Caesar is to be crowned on the Ides of March is mentioned twice—by Casca (I, iii, 85–8) and by Decius, who lures the victim to his death with the claim that

> The Senate have concluded
> To give this day a crown to mighty Caesar.
> (II, ii, 93–4)

16. Macbeth and Richard III are typical instances; see Armstrong, *op. cit*.

17. The association in the renaissance between *voluptas* and *voluntas* is common. See *NED* s.v. *will* sb. sense 2, for a specifically carnal denotation. Shakespeare quibbles with the *voluptas/voluntas* meanings of *will* at *Measure for Measure* II, iv, 163: 'Redeem thy brother / By yielding up thy body to my will' and at *Lucrece* 247: 'Thus graceless holds he [Tarquin] disputation / 'Tween frozen conscience and hot-burning will' (both passages are cited in *NED*). In *Antony and Cleopatra*, Antony, the slave of *voluptas*, is also the slave of his changeable will, as he is unable to commit himself fully either to Rome or to Egypt until all is already lost.

18. 'A New Look at *Julius Caesar*', in *Essays in Honor of Walter Clyde Curry*, Vanderbilt Studies in the Humanities, II (Vanderbilt University Press, 1954), pp. 161–80 (esp. 175–6).

19. Breyer quotes Erasmus's *Education of a Christian Prince* to show that Caesar is behaving tyranically here: 'Those expressions of a tyrant, "Such is my will", "This is my bidding", "Let will replace reason", should

be far removed from the mind of the prince.' [B 451]—trans. L. K. Born (see note 22), p. 189.

20. *The French Academie*, trans. T.B. (1586), sig. Qq 6ᵛ–Qq 7ʳ. Cf. *ibid*. sig. Rr 3 'the one [i.e., 'a good king'] burdeneth his [subjects] as little as may be, and then upon publike necessitie, the other [i.e., a tyrant] suppeth up their blood, gnaweth their bones, and sucketh the marrow of his subjects to satisfie his desires'.

21. *The Good and the Badde, or Descriptions of the Worthies, and Vnworthies of this Age. Where The Best may see their Graces, and the Worst discerne their Basenesse* (1616), sig. Bᵛ.

22. Trans. L. K. Born. *Records of Civilization: Sources and Studies*, XXVII (Columbia University Press, 1936), pp. 169, 200. In his introduction, p. 67, Born paraphrases *De Clementia*, I, xi, 4 as part of the tradition behind Erasmus's distinction between kings and tyrants. See also Breyer for a discussion of Erasmus and the traditional writings on tyranny.

23. See Breyer (note 18) for a discussion of Brutus's soliloquy as a definition of tyranny.

24. For *remorse* as *clemency*, see also the Duke's speech to Shylock in *The Merchant of Venice*, IV, i, 19–21:

> 'tis thought
> Thou'lt show thy mercy and remorse more strange
> Than is thy strange apparent cruelty.

25. Cf. *Octavia*, 442, where the Seneca of the play makes the same point to *Nero*: 'Magnum timoris remedium clementia est'.

26. *De Clementia*, I, ix, 1–12 (John W. Basore's Loeb trans.).

27. The appearance of a man named Cinna in each assassination plot adds colour to the possibility that Shakespeare associated the Senecan thesis with the character of Caesar and with the conspiracy against him. Cinna might stand out among the conspirators in Shakespeare's mind because his attention was caught by Plutarch's account of the mistaken identity which caused the crowd's outrage against the poet Cinna.

28. *William Shakspere's Small Latine & Lesse Greeke* (Urbana, 1944), II, 611: '...the sixteenth-century schoolmaster used Cicero, not Seneca, for moral philosophy'.

29. *Ibid*. II, 611–16. E. A. Sonnenschein had pointed to numerous parallels between *The Merchant of Venice*, IV, i and *De Clementia*; see 'Shakspere and Stoicism', *The University Review*, I (1905), 23–41; 'Latin as an Intellectual Force in Civilisation', *National Review*, XLVII (1906), 670–83; 'Shakespeare's Knowledge of

Latin', *Times Literary Supplement*, 17 March 1921, pp. 179–80.

30. Arden edition. Cf. *De Clementia*, I, xix, 9: 'Non proximum illis locum tenet is, qui se ex deorum natura gerit, beneficus ac largus et in melius potens?'

31. Arden edition. Cf. *De Clementia*, I, iii, 3: 'Nullum tamen clementia ex omnibus magis quam regem aut principem decet'. The passage is paraphrased in the *Polyanthea* of Domenico Nani Mirabelli (Venice, 1507), s.v. *clementia*. Cf. *The Merchant of Venice*, IV, i, 184–5: 'it [mercy] becomes / The throned monarch better than his crown'.

32. Arden edition. Henry not only makes the antithesis between tyrant and king with which this paper is concerned. He also speaks here of the subordination of the passions (cf. Seneca's '*in voluptatem*' and Caesar's 'affections' which have not 'sway'd / More than his reason'). Moreover, he is 'Senecan' in dealing with the conspiracy of Scroop, Grey, and Cambridge in II, ii; he shows clemency to the drunkard who had railed against him but is harsh *ex causa ac necessitate* with these three hired assassins:

> Touching our person seek we no revenge;
> But we our kingdom's safety must so tender,
> Whose ruin you have sought, that to her laws
> We do deliver you. (II, ii, 174–7)

Shakespeare devotes nearly 200 lines to this episode.

33. The tradition of Caesar's self-justification goes back at least as far as John Lydgate's *The Serpent of Division*, where Caesar addresses Romulus, Remus, and the gods of ancient Troy at the Rubicon in legal language: 'I as hūble subiect vnto your deiti ful lowli besech & requir you of equiti & right to be wel willing & fauourable to promote my true quarel & cause, & beningly of your boūteous goodnes to fauour & fortune ỹ high enterprise which of iust tytle I purpose for lyfe or deth through your fauor to execut & not as enemy or rebell to Rome / but as a true citizen and a proued knight...' (Printed London, 1559, sig. B 8–B 8ᵛ).

34. See Maria Wickert, 'Antikes Gedankengut in Shakespeares *Julius Cäsar*', *Shakespeare-Jahrbuch*, LXXXII/LXXXIII (1948), 11–33 (esp. 25–33).

35. Ernest Schanzer, *The Problem Plays of Shakespeare* (1963), pp. 10–70; Mildred Hartsock, 'The Complexity of *Julius Caesar*', *Publications of the Modern Language Association*, LXXXI (1966), 56–62. Schanzer finds the characters morally ambivalent (Caesar, Antony, Cassius) or self-divided (Brutus), and reasons that the audience's response is accordingly a divided one. Miss Hartsock reads the play as 'a dramatic statement about the relative nature of truth'—Shakespeare's first tentative move toward the moral complexity of the great tragedies.

36. Cf. I, i, 48–50: 'And do you now...And do you now...And do you now...'; I, ii, 142–4: 'Write them...Sound them...Weigh them...'; I, iii, 91–2: 'Therein, ye gods...Therein, ye gods...' Kajal Basu has called attention to this feature of the play, which he calls 'repetitive jingle' and considers to be a vestige of Shakespeare's early, euphuistic style; see '*Julius Caesar* and *Henry V*', *Shakespeare Commemoration Volume*, ed. Taraknath Sen (Calcutta, 1966), pp. 89–124.

37. See also II, ii, 72; III, i, 141; IV, ii, 10.

38. *Ben Jonson's 'Timber' or 'Discoveries'*, ed. Ralph S. Walker (Syracuse University Press, 1952), pp. 78–9. In his 'List of the Principal Sources' (pp. 103–5), Walker gives *De Clementia* as one of Jonson's sources for this essay, 'On Statecraft'.

IA Plan of Elsinore from Braun and Hogenberg, *Civitatis Orbis Terrarum* (Cologne, 1588)

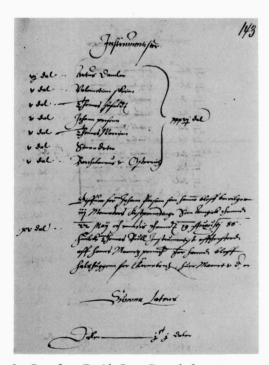

IB Page from Danish Court Records for 1586

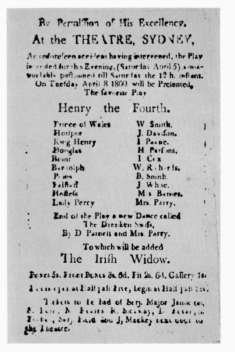

IC Playbill for a production of *Henry IV* at the Theatre, Sydney, 8 April 1800

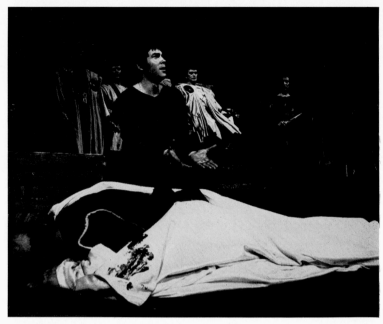

IIA *Julius Caesar*, Royal Shakespeare Theatre, 1968: directed by John Barton, settings by John Gunter. In the foreground, Charles Thomas as Mark Antony

IIB Ian Richardson (left) as Cassius and Derek Smith as Casca

III *The Merry Wives of Windsor*, Royal Shakespeare Theatre, 1968: directed by Terry Hands, settings by Timothy O'Brien. Brewster Mason as Falstaff

IV *As You Like It*, Royal Shakespeare Theatre, 1968: directed by David Jones, settings by Timothy O'Brien. Janet Suzman as Rosalind

VA *As You Like It:* Janet Suzman (Rosalind) and Michael Williams as Orlando

VB *King Lear,* Royal Shakespeare Theatre, 1968: directed by Trevor Nunn, settings by Christopher Morley. Left to right: Patrick Stewart as Cornwall, Susan Fleetwood as Regan, Sheila Allen as Goneril, Eric Porter as Lear, Diane Fletcher as Cordelia and Terrence Hardiman as Albany

VI *Troilus and Cressida*, Royal Shakespeare Theatre, 1968: directed by John Barton, settings by Timothy O'Brien. Helen Mirren as Cressida and David Waller as Pandarus

VIIA *Troilus and Cressida:* Helen Mirren (Cressida), David Waller (Pandarus) and Michael Williams as Troilus

VIIB Alan Howard (centre) as Achilles, with the Myrmidons

VIIIA *Doctor Faustus*, Royal Shakespeare
Theatre, 1968: directed by Clifford
Williams, settings by Abd'elkader
Farrah. Terrence Hardiman (left)
as Mephistophilis and Eric Porter
as Faustus

VIIIB Hugh Keays Byrne as Sloth, Sara Kestelman as Lechery and Eric Porter (Faustus)

THOMAS BULL AND OTHER 'ENGLISH INSTRUMENTALISTS' IN DENMARK IN THE 1580s

BY

GUNNAR SJÖGREN

E. K. Chambers[1] gives a list of Elizabethan actors which includes the following:

> BULL, THOMAS, Denmark, 1579–80
> KIRCK (KIRCKMANN), JOHN, Denmark, 1579–80
> KRAFFT, JOHN, Denmark, 1579–80
> PERSONN, JOHANN, Denmark, 1579–80

E. Nungezer[2] adds that these actors were members of a troupe of English players at the Danish court and gives as source an article by Johannes Bolte.[3]

These players were first recognized by V. C. Ravn,[4] who pieced together information in the *Rentemester Regnskaber* (R.R.)—account books of the receiver of the Revenue—and in the associated *Maaneds og Kostpenge Registeret* (Kp.R.)—the register of monthly wages and board-wages. These are now in Rigsarkivet in Copenhagen.

This paper is based on a new study of these documents and of other available sources which yield some supplementary information concerning these and other supposedly English artists at the court of Frederick II. A full account is also given of the fate of one of them, Thomas Bull, which is not without human interest.

The musical establishment at the court in 1577 and 1578 consisted of some ten trumpeters, twelve singers and six instrumentalists, four of them fiddlers. At the beginning of 1579 three instrumentalists were dismissed and replaced on 18 January by four new ones: Artus Damler, Johann Krafft, Johann Persen and Johann Kirckmann. At some later date, not specified, a dancer, Mathias Zoega, was attached to the court and on St. John's day another name, that of Thomas Bull, was added to the list.

These six are grouped together in the monthly accounts of the *Kp.R.* until December 1579, when Artus Damler was transferred to the other group which was made up of the remaining three instrumentalists—a bassoon-player and two fiddlers.

In the *Kp.R.* for the first month of 1580 the names are arranged under the heading 'Instrumentalists and fiddlers' in this way:

Mathias Zoega Dantzer
Johann Krafft ⎤
Johann Personn ⎬ *Engelsche Instrumentister*
Johann Kirck[5] ⎟
Thomas Bull ⎦

Artus Damler
Valentinn Skein
Andreas Tide
Thomas Sefeldt

This entry does not seem to have been noticed before.

In the following months the two groups are always treated as separate units, and are arranged in the same manner. In the *Kp.R.* for the fifth month the groups change place and the designation 'English instrumentalists' is repeated, but this time Zoega is bracketed with them.[6]

The bracketing suggests that this designation referred not so much to their nationality—Mathias Zoega was in all probability an exiled Italian nobleman—as to the kind of entertainment they were supposed to provide. Their talents would be employed not only in making music but also in dancing, tumbling and the acting of interludes. It is significant that during the whole of their period at court they were paid more than the ordinary musicians. Zoega received eighty daler a year, the other four in this group thirty daler, while the remaining three instrumentalists were paid only twenty daler. Although transferred to this latter group, Damler retained a fee of fifty daler a year. They also received board-wages, except in periods when they boarded with the court—six daler for Zoega, five and a half for Damler, and five for the rest.

Krafft, Personn, Kirck and Bull were undoubtedly Englishmen. It is possible that Artus Damler, who was engaged at the same time as Krafft, Personn and Kirck, was also English. Names were germanized and spelling is somewhat haphazard in this register. Artus is the German form for Arthur and his surname may have been something like Daymar or Damer (Daimer).[7] He may have proved more useful as a musician and thus transferred to the other group.

In January 1581 Zoega was discharged and deprived of employment by the king himself, on what grounds we do not know. In 1583 Kirck dropped out and was replaced by Thomas Warrin—an English-sounding name. Warrin received fifteen daler a year, a sum which would seem to indicate that he was a boy. If this is indeed so, it would support the supposition that the group acted, for they would need a boy for the female parts. Towards the end of 1584 Krafft left the group and was replaced, some months later, by a man called Simon Detre. He may also have been English, with a name something like Deuters (Dutere).[8] But by now all the instrumentalists are grouped together in the *Kp.R.* so that the 'English instrumentalists' cannot be separated out.

In 1585 the city of Elsinore had to pay four skilling for the repair of a wooden paling which 'people rode down when the Englishmen acted in the town-hall courtyard'.[9] As no other English players are known to have been in Denmark at that time, the king's 'English instrumentalists' may be the performers referred to.

On the other hand companies of foreign players may have paid short visits to the Danish court without leaving any trace. Normally they would have been paid out of the king's own pocket and taken their meals at court. Unfortunately the relevant accounts are lost and we only get glimpses of the king's private expenses when he momentarily ran dry and had to borrow from the receiver of the revenue. Such entries do not give any details, thus in 1592 sixteen daler are paid to 'some tumblers', and in 1593 thirty daler to 'those who acted before his Majesty'.

That acting, not only of interludes during meals, but on a rather grand scale, was at least meant to be a frequent form of entertainment when the Royal family lived at Kronborg Castle at Elsinore can be inferred from a contemporary description of the courtyard of the castle: *In qua, institutis theatris & scenis, comoediae exhiberi, ignes volatiles protici, spectacula, ludi, triumphi, decursiones equestres, solennia hastarum ludicra instituti possunt.*[10]

This description was probably supplied by an elder statesman, Henrik Ranzau, whose son, Gert Ranzau, was governor of Kronborg.

In April 1586 the Danish chancellor Henrik Ramel sailed for England on a very important mission—the proposal of Danish mediation between England and Spain.[11] His considerable retinue included nine trumpeters and eight instrumentalists, including Artus Damler, Johann Personn, Thomas Bull, Thomas Warrin and Simon Detre.[12] The embassy returned on 16 June. From the 17th board-wages were paid to two new groups of English instrumentalists, who had presumably come from England in one of the ambassador's three ships.[13]

These Englishmen are the two well-known groups, 'William Kempe, instrumentalist' and his boy, Daniel Jonns, who stayed two months and received an extra month's board-wages as a gift, and the five 'instrumentalists and tumblers', including Shakespeare's later colleagues George Bryan and Thomas Pope, who stayed for three months and three days.[14] Their wages are not recorded in *R.R* and it seems probable, therefore, that they were paid by the king. Eventually he passed them on to the Elector of Saxony.[15]

While they were still in Denmark, tragedy befell their colleague Thomas Bull. In a fit of jealousy he killed a compatriot called Thomas Boltum (Bolton?).

The murder took place at an inn in Elsinore owned by Gertrud Cletten, who was probably the widow of an English-born naval captain Raf Cletton or Klethen (Clayton?). This man was engaged in chasing pirates in the 1570s and is often mentioned in letters from the Royal chancellery.[16] In 1574 he was sent to England to buy a ship and enlist a crew and was obliged to advance the money for this project out of his own pocket. More than a year later he was still demanding payment of the seven hundred and fifty daler he had advanced and for which he had had to mortgage his house in England. In 1576 he went to England again, but in April 1577 he was chasing Polish pirates in the Baltic. Three months later by royal letters patent Gertrud, Raf Klethon's widow, was given permission to stay in Copenhagen and granted the right to earn her living like any other subject.

The widow apparently soon moved to Elsinore, where—due to the collection of the Sound Toll—the influx of foreigners would make it more profitable for her to keep an inn. Money could also be made from the trains of foreign ambassadors who often arrived by ship at the port. (The most important inn-keeper who catered for this clientele was an English or Scottish merchant, Richard Wedderborn.)

Thomas Bull was in the king's service and therefore under the jurisdiction of the Governor of Kronborg Castle, Gert Ranzau. But as the crime was committed in Elsinore the governor ordered the mayor to investigate the matter. The recording-clerk took the following notes, which I quote in full from the report of the proceedings:[17]

In the year of our Lord 1586, on the 25th of August, at the request of his Lordship Giertt Ranntzou, on behalf of his Majesty the King, the mayor, councillors and sheriff met at the town hall to find out what happened between Thomas Bull and Thomas Boltum when the latter was killed.

[In the margin] On a homicide between Thomas Bull and Thomas Boltum.

The said Thomas Bull, who did the deed, was first brought in and asked on his oath to confess how this calamity had happened and how their quarrel had started.

The said Thomas Bull, who is still alive, deposed that, some time ago, he had told the said Thomas Boltum in confidence that this woman Elsabe [Elizabeth] 'is now so much in love with you, but you shall know that she told me once that there was nobody in the world she loved more than me. This I tell you in confidence and entreat you not to pass on to her'. Shortly afterwards Thomas Bull went to Elsabe's house as he was wont to do, and then she said harshly 'because you, Thomas, shall know that I will have that man Thomas Boltum, I ask you to keep out of my house in the future'. And because the woman had given him such words he believed that Thomas Boltum had told the woman what he had said to him, as mentioned before. This she denied that he had done. And that, he asserted, was the beginning of their quarrel. And there were no witnesses to this. Thomas Bull was now asked on his holiest oath to confess if Elsabe at any time, secretly or openly, had promised to marry him, to which he answered no.

Then Thomas Bull deposed that yesterday when he had been walking about in Gertrud Cletten's tap-room, Thomas Boltum had entered and sat down on a stool, and Thomas Bull said to him, 'you did not right in revealing what I told you in secrecy'; to which Boltum, who is now dead, answered, 'thou liest like a knave, I have not done that'; and Thomas Bull, who is still alive, hit him with his hand on his head. And Boltum rose from the stool and hit him back on the mouth, and then Thomas Bull ran out through the door.

And as no men or other witnesses were there, two servant girls who had been in the room when this started, were brought in.

[In the margin] Deposition of witnesses.

Jehanne Thygis Daatter was first brought in and asked on her holy oath to tell everything that she knew in truth about this. Then she deposed that she sat in the room spinning and that Thomas Bull was walking about in the room when Thomas Boltum came in and sat down on the folding-stool. Then she heard that heated words were exchanged between Thomas Bull and the said Boltum, which she could not understand. Then Thomas Bull hit him with his hand on the head, and the other one, who is now dead, rose and hit him on the mouth, whereupon Thomas Bull ran out through the door.

The other girl, called Suenndtz Daatter, deposed that at the same time she was sitting spinning in the room and Thomas Bull was walking about on the floor when Thomas Boltum, who is now dead, came in and sat down on the stool and they exchanged a few heated words which she did not under-stand [presumably they were speaking English], and then Thomas Bull hit the said Boltum on his head with his hand and then Boltum rose and dealt him a blow or two on the mouth. Then Thomas Bull ran out of the room and up to the attic to get his rapier. Then the girl deposed that she barred the door so that he should not be able to get at the other one. And the other girl ran out to her mistress Gertruid and told her that they were trying to murder each other in the room. And when Gertruid ran out into the hall Thomas Bull was there with his rapier and Gertruid entreated him for God's sake to think of his salvation, and not to throw away his life and got him out of the front door. And the other, who is now dead, stayed in the room.

Further the said Gertruid deposed that she went to Elsabe her daughter immediately and told her what had happened, and the daughter returned with her to her house. Then Thomas Boltum came out and met them at the front door and started to accompany Elsabe back to her own house again.

And according to what Eliisabet deposed, Thomas Bull appeared round the corner of the alley and came against them with his rapier and Elsebe implored her betrothed Thomas Boltum to run. So he ran back and into the porch and, as he came to the door and turned round and looked back, Thomas Bull ran his rapier into his breast, right through. The said woman deposed on her holy oath that it had happened in this way, which he himself could not deny.

Lastly master Hanns Bardskier [Barber] was brought in and asked what he thought about the dead man's body and death, if he was stabbed from the front or from the back, to which he answered on his oath that, so far as he could judge, the said Thomas Boltum was pierced from the front and out at the back right through the body. As said before.[18]

Judging by this record the trial seems to have been fair. Bull did nothing to defend himself; he did not deny that he started the brawl, nor did he maintain that Elsabe had promised him marriage—which might have been the sole extenuating circumstance. Having examined the case the town-council left it to Gert Ranzau to pronounce sentence. Bull could hardly escape being sent to the block—the usual punishment for homicide. (Thieves were sent to the gallows.) Nevertheless the outcome would have been open to doubt if the name of Thomas Bull did not crop up in the *Kp.R.* three months later, in November 1586. Evidently board-wages had been due to him for the period 22 May to 19 August. This amount, fifteen daler, was now paid out to Johann Personn for his colleague, '*som bleff halshuggin for Kronnborg*'—who was beheaded at Kronborg.

The small band of English players must have been hard hit by this pathetic tragedy, which also may have exposed them to the displeasure of the king. Whatever the case, Damler, Personn, Warrin and Detre left his service in November 1586. Of the original instrumentalists who had been together since 1579 only Valentin Skein, the bassoon-player, and Andreas Tide, now promoted to organist, remained. A small Dutch orchestra, consisting of a conductor and six musicians, was engaged from January 1587.

Soon after the death of Frederick II in 1588 the names of Damler, Warrin and Detre reappear in the *R.R.* (The *Kp.R.* after 1586 is not extant.) Damler collected some money due to him since 1586, which suggests that he had left in a hurry. Thomas Warrin and Simon Detre re-entered the service of the court. Warrin stayed only nine months but Detre remained until August 1590. After this no instrumentalists who could also have been actors seem to have been employed at the Danish court.

© GUNNAR SJÖGREN 1969

NOTES

1. *The Elizabethan Stage* (Oxford, 1923), II, 272.

2. *A Dictionary of Actors* (New Haven, 1929), pp. 65, 226, 230, 279.

3. 'Englische Komödianten in Dänemark und Schweden', *Shakespeare-Jahrbuch*, XXIII (1888), 99 ff.

4. *For Idé og Virkelighed*, (Copenhagen, 1870). An English translation, 'English Instrumentalists at the Danish Court in the time of Shakespeare', was published in *Sammelbände der Internationalen Musik-Gesellschaft* (Leipzig, 1905–6), VII, pp. 550–63.

5. Called Kirckmann in the *R.R.*

6. This entry is quoted and commented on by Ravn, *op. cit.* p. 553.

7. P. H. Reaney, *A Dictionary of British Surnames* (1958), p. 91.

8. *Ibid.* p. 93.

9. Bolte, *op. cit.* p. 100.

10. Braun and Hogenberg, *Civitatis Orbis Terrarum*, Book IV, Plate 26 (Cologne, 1588).

11. Walter Kirchner, 'England and Denmark, 1558–1588', *The Journal of Modern History*, XVII (1945), 1–15.

12. *Kp.R.*, 22 April–23 May 1586.

13. *Kp.R.*, 20 August–18 September 1586.

14. Chambers, *op. cit.* p. 272.

15. The rather amusing correspondence on this subject is quoted in full by Bolte, *op. cit.* pp. 104–6.

16. *Kancelliets Brevbøger*, 1571, 1573–7.

17. *Helsingør Købstads tingbog*, A.A. No. 10, 1583–6, fol. 156ᵇ ff. (now in Landsarkivet for Sjaelland, Copenhagen).

18. A summary in Danish was published by Laurits Pedersen in *Kronborg Have* (Copenhagen, 1920), pp. 76–7.

SHAKESPEARE IN THE EARLY SYDNEY THEATRE

BY

ERIC IRVIN

A great many of Australia's first colonists were drawn from that section of eighteenth-century society described by moralists of the day as 'undesirables who frequent play-houses'. As well as a genuine love of the drama—sometimes as onlookers, sometimes as performers of the more menial theatrical characters and tasks—they had a love for the easy pickings and the good times to be had in theatre company. But while most of them gave up, or were forced to give up their evil ways on arrival at Port Jackson, none of them lost his or her love of the theatre. They had been brought up with it; it was almost the sole and certainly the most popular form of public amusement available to them.

In all the theatres left behind them by these men and women the fare had been basically the same. There was always the solid core of old favourites, including the many rewritten or other-wise arranged versions of Shakespeare's *Richard III, Hamlet, Othello, Macbeth*, and *Romeo and Juliet*, and the comedies such as the Garrick version of *The Taming of the Shrew*. No wonder that in their idle moments—and there were to be plenty of these, as well as hungry ones—the thoughts of Australia's unwilling first colonists should turn to the theatre. Only seventeen days away from their new country a group of men on at least one of the ships of the First Fleet 'made a play for the benefit of their masters and fellows', and 'sang many songs'.[1] What was done on this ship was no doubt also done on some of the others of the fleet on that tedious eight-month voyage from England.

The first theatre in Australia was a crude hut fitted by the convicts for a performance of George Farquhar's comedy, *The Recruiting Officer*, presented as part of the king's birthday celebrations on 4 June 1789. Not until 1796 was the first real theatre established, a theatre open to free and convicted alike, and here, among other plays, were presented two of Shakespeare's that we know of, though possibly there were more—*Henry the Fourth* and *Romeo and Juliet*.

This theatre was, according to a contemporary account, in all components 'a miniature resemblance of a country theatre at home. There was a stage, there were scenes fitted to it, there were footlights, there was a pit and a gallery, and there were side-boxes in which the Sydney "quality" might take their ease...the gallery was much larger than any other part of the theatre'.[2]

A far from complete record exists of the plays given at this theatre between 1796 and 1800, when it was closed by order of the Governor, Captain John Hunter. One copy only exists of the playbill for the performance of *Henry the Fourth* given on 8 April 1800. This was printed on the battered wooden hand-press brought out by the First Fleet. The copy is in the Mitchell Library, Sydney. But that this theatre also presented *Romeo and Juliet* at least once may be deduced from the following extract.

Botany Bay Theatricals. *Romeo and Juliet* was one of the earliest performances of the Thespian corps in the land of 'immigrant personages', and the governor having announced his intention of honouring it with his presence, the police magistrate took the very necessary precaution of surrounding the house with a double row of constables to secure the performance proceeding to a straightforward close, without that prolific garnishing of convulsive hiccupings, sentimental sighs, heigh-ho's, fainting fits, and other significant tokens of *spiritual overpowering* which had heretofore prolonged the performance to a very late hour. Things glided on most smoothly till the last scene, where the pensive Romeo was seen staggering towards the tomb of his dear Juliet, vociferating her name in a manner which too evidently showed *how* he was affected. To his repeated tender exclamations of *Juliet, Juliet!* not even a sigh was returned; the audience became impatient; but their murmurs of impatience were converted into one universal shudder of horror, on Romeo exclaiming, with a wild shriek, 'She is dead!' which was apparent to the whole auditory, on perceiving her heels sticking up out of the tomb. The fond Romeo passionately seized the protruding members, and dragged her feelingly forth from her place of rest, making, however, such a display of her charms in the chivalrous attempt, as forced the lady visitors to a hasty flight from this 'too theatric' sight. All eyes were now riveted to this tragic spectacle of youth and beauty, and 'dead, dead!' burst in one unbroken exclamation from every part of the house. 'Yes', sighed the sentimental Romeo—'*dead drunk!*'

On the surface, a certain air of mystery surrounds this extract. It is prefaced with the words 'Botany Bay Theatricals', which places it in the period roughly 1788 to 1820, when, as far as English newspapers were concerned, any report from the new colony of New South Wales was prefaced with the words 'Botany Bay', for that was the First Fleet's original destination. But the extract is known to us today only because it was reprinted in the issue of *The Sydney Gazette* of 25 June 1827. At this time Barnett Levey, the father of the Australian theatre, was making his initial and for a time unsuccessful attempts to establish the first permanent Sydney theatre. It is conceivable that the *Gazette*, siding as it did with the Governor against the establishment of a theatre, maliciously printed this extract (without either provenance or comment) as a warning of what might be expected with the advent of the drama. Certainly there had been no theatrical performances in Sydney since 1800, so it must have been anti-theatrical 'ammunition' supplied by the *Gazette* itself, or by one of its readers, from a conveniently remembered copy of a much earlier English or Scottish newspaper. For five years Barnett Levey had to fight a tight-lipped, dour and vindictive group of Sydney 'moralists' who believed, or professed to believe, that the introduction of the theatre in Sydney would be the moral undoing of the colony.

Levey, born in Whitechapel, arrived in Australia as an emigrant at the age of about twenty-two on 21 December 1821. He brought with him an absolute passion for the theatre, and once he had established himself commercially he set about building the theatre Sydney lacked. His every move was blocked by the Governor of his day, Lieutenant-General Ralph Darling, who even had a special Act passed by the Legislative Council to prevent him or anyone else using his theatre once it had been completed. Concerts were permitted, but not the drama. Levey had to wait for the arrival of his successor, Major-General Sir Richard Bourke, before he got his licence in 1832 to open the first permanent theatre in Sydney, and to conduct theatricals. This he did in the saloon of the Royal Hotel in George Street while his real theatre, at the rear of the hotel, was being enlarged and redecorated. By this time New South Wales had a population of 55,954. Of this, 43.1 per cent were convicts. In the Sydney area the population was about 16,000, with the proportion of free to convicted persons slightly higher than in the colony as a whole.

Barnett Levey's Theatre Royal players were no more or less ambitious than their counterparts at any period in the history of the English or Australian theatre. They played in the stock money-making melodramas, the comedies, farces, and semi-operas of the day; but in their hearts, it seems, many of them yearned for higher things. Though all were untrained and lacked previous theatrical experience of any real depth, there was a small but solid core of them who worked hard and long to be worthy of the better plays and the approval of their audiences. The highest peak they could achieve, they knew, was to perform successfully in one of Shakespeare's plays, but such fare would not be acceptable in the normal programme for each season, for 'the vulgar like not the sound of Shakespeare's name, when attached to a play-bill', as one Sydney critic was later to write. He said audiences regarded his work as 'dry stuff'.

But the players soon found a way of overcoming the major obstacle—by means of a benefit or other special performance. So Shakespeare, Sydney Theatre Royal version, made his bow to a Sydney audience after an absence of thirty-three years at the first anniversary of the Theatre Royal in December 1833, and thereafter at benefits given for or by some of the theatre's leading actors.

Taking the first ten years of the first permanent Sydney theatre, it is found that from December 1833 to February 1843 fourteen of Shakespeare's plays were given first performances. All had at least two performances, initially, and some, such as *Richard III*, *Hamlet*, *Othello*, *The Merchant of Venice*, and *Macbeth* were many times performed. The first performances in this ten-year period were: *Richard III* (26 December 1833), *The Taming of the Shrew* (22 February 1834), *Othello* (26 July 1834), *Hamlet* (18 August 1834), *Macbeth* (7 September 1835), *The Merchant of Venice* (17 September 1835), *Romeo and Juliet* (28 September 1835), *Henry IV, Part I* (14 April 1836), *King Lear* (23 January 1837), *Cymbeline* (13 August 1838), *Julius Caesar* (4 September 1838), *The Tempest* (15 July 1839), *The Comedy of Errors* (18 January 1841), *King John* (6 February 1843).

In this period, 1833–43, the Theatre Royal was replaced by the Victoria Theatre (in 1838) following the death of Levey in 1837, but as Levey's original company made up at least 80 per cent of the Victoria company for its first five years or more, the use of the term 'the first permanent Sydney theatre' still holds good.

A great many of these Shakespearian performances received little more from the Press than a mention that they would take place, or had taken place, because most of them were given as benefit performances; these the Press covered only if there was nothing else to do. Not until the 1838 performance of *Hamlet* were there at least five lengthy reports, for this was a dual occasion—the opening of a new season at the Victoria and the return of the stage favourite, Conrad Knowles, from his unsuccessful trip to England. Only one other production had an equally wide coverage, and that was the first Shakespearian performance at Barnett Levey's theatre, in which the riot which ensued rather than the performance got most of the publicity.

Of the actors who took part in these Shakespearian productions, the names of six occur again and again, all of them free emigrants (the use of convicts in the theatre was not permitted). The first, and most prominent because most ambitious, was the Royal's leading actor, Conrad

Knowles, followed by John Meredith and Joseph Simmons. Among the women the most consistent were Mrs Maria Taylor, Mrs Harriet Jones (also known as Mrs Knowles), Mrs Cameron, Miss Douglass, and Miss Eliza Winstanley (later known as both Mrs O'Flaherty and Mrs Eliza Winstanley, and the first Australian-trained actress to play in both London and New York).

There were no doubt many reasons why Levey's actors attempted Shakespeare, but not the least of them must have been because of a benefit performance given on 12 June 1833 for two of the lesser players of the company, Dyball and Palmer. Novelty and a rich diet were the snares set to catch benefit audiences, and this one had a house packed to the doors to witness Colman's comedy *The Review; or, The Wags of Windsor* (1800), the favourite melodrama *Black Ey'd Susan* (1829) by Douglas Jerrold, and, starring Mr Palmer, the Tent Scene from *Richard III*. Newspaper comment on this performance was limited, but it was said that both the comedy and the melodrama pleased the audience, whereas the Tent Scene from *Richard III* '...was not beyond mediocrity, the stage is not large enough for such an exhibition'. There, perhaps, the matter would have rested, had it not been for at least two things which disturbed the equilibrium of the theatre. One was that Palmer had apparently annoyed one or two of the Theatre Royal's would-be tragedians by stealing the Shakespearian limelight from his 'betters' (these being, in their opinion at least, John Meredith and Conrad Knowles). The other was the decision by Barnett Levey, announced on 20 December, to celebrate the first anniversary of his Theatre Royal on 26 December with a programme consisting of *Richard III* (Cibber version) and a pantomime. By now the Theatre Royal players were in the theatre proper.

It seems that while this decision delighted Meredith and Knowles (who had possibly helped engineer it, and had certainly appropriated the best parts for themselves), it infuriated Palmer because he—of them all the only one who had 'done' the Tent Scene—had been relegated to one of the least significant parts. He was not one to take such an insult without a murmur, and so he not only 'left' the theatre on the morning of 26 December, but also told his tale of woe during the day to all his tap-room cronies and whoever else would listen.

From newspaper reports of this performance it is known that Meredith played Richard, his wife played Queen Elizabeth, and Grove played Catesby. Knowles was also in the cast, but although he was said to have been the only adequate player of them all the part he played is not mentioned. The four Sydney newspapers damned the Royal's performance of *Richard III*, but it seems they damned something which they were largely unable to hear, and at times could not even see. For this gala night the house was packed to the doors, and long before the rising of the green baize curtain people eager to gain admittance had to be turned away. When the curtain did rise, however, there was not the expected or customary hush for the opening of the play. No sooner did Meredith appear on the stage as Richard than the theatre was filled with cries for Mr Palmer. For some time there was so much noise it was impossible for Meredith to be heard, but when a lull did come he stepped forward and announced that Mr Palmer had left the theatre of his own accord and would not be appearing. 'From that time forward', one newspaper reported, 'there was an incessant roar in the house so that the speeches of the actors... could but be imperfectly heard. The pit and galleries hissed incessantly and the boxes laughed incessantly, joining ever and anon in the hissing'. Women had to be rescued from the turmoil in the pit, the most unruly area in the house, and take momentary refuge on the stage, from where they were conveyed out of the theatre. The musicians were forced out of the orchestra pit, and members of the audience started to climb on to the stage, despite the spikes fronting it and designed to prevent such a happening. Then followed an even wilder scene during which the thwarted and infuriated Richard threw two or three men down into the pit as fast as they climbed up from it. The inglorious night finished, at the end of the pantomime, with an actor trying to announce from the stage the bill for the next night, while a number of boys who had clambered on to the stage mimicked him 'to the infinite amusement of the *gods*'.

Palmer, it must be admitted, was at least a determined Shakespearian. Almost twelve months later he staged *Richard III* for his benefit, with himself in the name part. On 8 October 1834 the curtain rose on what one newspaper called his 'lofty and daring flight'. The writer said he did not know whether to commend Palmer's courage or condemn his presumption. But a writer in another paper found that he 'sustained the character throughout very respectable' [*sic*].

In February 1834 the players again gave their audience Shakespeare, eighteenth-century version. This was David Garrick's arrangement of *The Taming of the Shrew*, called *Catherine and Petruchio* (1756). By this time Joseph Simmons, 'lately from London' and said to have had previous theatrical experience on the English stage, was a partner with Levey and had ousted Meredith as stage manager and therefore as principal player. The *Monitor* found that under his control all the 'irregularities under former managements' had disappeared, although because of those irregularities the better class of people had ceased to attend the theatre. It regretted they were not present to see his Petruchio, 'the best hit he has yet made', though it found Mrs Meredith as Catherine 'quite out of the line of acting she is qualified to assume'. This lady excepted, the newspaper pronounced the performance to be 'infinitely superior to any that have yet been attempted'.

Nearly five months later the 'gentleman' of the Sydney stage, Conrad Knowles, was seen in the first Australian production of *Othello*, with Joseph Simmons as Iago. This was the first Shakespearian production at the Theatre Royal to be worthy of, and to receive, detailed treatment from the Press. Its many faults were not overlooked, but neither were its virtues. The *Gazette* reported, somewhat incoherently, that 'the attempt (we cannot call it by any other name) at representing one of Shakespeare's greatest efforts of genius, is far too gigantic to be compassed by the present theatrical company'. It drew a large and respectable crowd, said this newspaper, but was a miserable failure, '. . . the only even tolerable piece of acting in it being Mr Simmons's Iago, and the representation of that fell very far short of the intentions of the author'. It found the dresses were 'in the very extreme of the ridiculous', and the scene in the Senate house something 'only equalled by one of the lowest tap-rooms in Kent Street' (a street which at that time catered for the flotsam and jetsam of the Sydney waterfront).

The *Australian* was not nearly so harsh in its judgement, feeling that 'upon the whole, the company may be congratulated on their success'. The audience, it said, manifested throughout the highest satisfaction and pleasure. Knowles misconstrued the character, with a forced attempt at theatrical stateliness; Mrs Meredith as Desdemona did not show enough tenderness and simplicity; Mrs Taylor's Emilia was not sufficiently energetic, while Simmons's Iago was marred by melodramatic gesticulations. But, despite all this, 'no one who witnessed it on Saturday night can call it a failure'.

The *Monitor* reported that Knowles as Othello would not have disgraced a provincial theatre in England, '...he was greeted throughout with continual applause'. It said Simmons was tolerable as Iago, Mrs Meredith was dull and monotonous as Desdemona, while only Mrs Taylor's last scene was notable. A little more attention was needed to the scenery and properties to make the play a great favourite, it concluded.

The *Herald*, sure that a great many in the large audience thought the performance of *Othello* would share the same fate as *Richard III*, and had attended merely to indulge their curiosity, was just as sure they were agreeably disappointed. Knowles' Othello was on the whole a respectable personification of the character; the Iago was creditable, but wanted more of the villain in it; Desdemona was 'respectable', and Emilia was played with deep feeling and repeatedly applauded.

That all four writers were reporting on one and the same performance seems hard to believe, but this marked variation in opinion was to be exhibited again and again during the performance of some of the remaining Shakespeare plays in the ten-year period under review.

About three weeks after the performance of *Othello* already noted, it was produced again with a change of cast, Simmons playing Othello, Knowles Iago, Mrs Taylor Desdemona, and Mrs. Meredith Emilia. Not one of them was 'up in the part', and it was said of the performance that 'Shakespeare never could have been so maltreated (before), and it is hoped never will again'. The audience, one critic said, was convulsed with laughter when it was not hissing.

The critics were next able to give their attention to the first Australian performance of *Hamlet*, on 18 August 1834, with Knowles in the name part. Two of the five newspapers of this time 'noticed' the performance, the others ignoring it. The first found that it was a creditable attempt; that all the performers 'exerted themselves', and that Knowles's Hamlet, Mrs Taylor's Queen, and Mrs Jones's Ophelia were the best sustained characters of the evening.

The second newspaper thought Knowles looked the part of Hamlet very well, but lacked 'that quiet solemnity of manner which ought to distinguish it'. It said the most barbarous butchery was frequently perpetrated upon the text. It liked Simmons as Horatio, but thought Ophelia quite out of Mrs Jones's line. Her mad scenes were said to have been highly ludicrous, and her singing of snatches of songs to some nondescript tunes 'most farcical'. (At this time Ophelia seems to have been looked upon as principally a *singing* role, if the remarks made on various Sydney performances of *Hamlet* up to at least 1840 are to be believed.) This paper then criticized Meredith for appearing first as the Ghost and then as the First Gravedigger. 'It altogether destroys the illusion of the scene, for we defy anyone then present to forget that the facetious Gravedigger had just before been masquerading in a suit of armour, as a ghost'.

After this Knowles announced, on 9 October 1834, that a performance of *Romeo and Juliet* would be given on 31 October for the benefit of Mr Winstanley, the theatre's scene-painter. The Juliet was to be Mr Winstanley's elder daughter, Eliza, who would make her first stage appearance, but for reasons not hard to guess this performance did not take place.

And then came the turn of *Macbeth*. Unfortunately, only one newspaper reported on this performance, although it was given three times in the one week. For the first time a complete list of the players and their parts was included in the theatre advertisement, and from it we learn that Mrs Jones played Donalbin; Mr Mackay, Banquo; Mr Knowles, Macduff; Mr Simmons, Macbeth; Mrs Taylor, Ross; and a newcomer, Miss Douglass, played Lady Macbeth. The play was billed as *Macbeth; or, The Three Weird Sisters* (Davenant version). The three witches were played by Messrs Grove, Buckingham, and Dyball, recalling Fanny Kemble's note in her Journal under the date 18 February 1833: 'It has always been customary—heaven only knows why—to make low comedians act the witches, and to dress them like old fish-women... with as due a proportion of petticoats as any woman, letting alone a witch, might desire, jocose red faces, peaked hats, and broomsticks'.[3]

The *Gazette* notice of the Sydney Theatre Royal's first *Macbeth* was favourable. It said it was 'far superior to that which we anticipated it would have been', and 'altogether much better than might have been expected'. The playing of Simmons, Knowles, and Mackay was praised, particularly that of Mackay as Banquo. Mrs Taylor as Ross, 'in the affecting interview with Macduff and Malcolm...acquitted herself in a manner highly creditable to herself and with satisfaction to the audience'. Lady Macbeth, it said, was not well done, because it is a very difficult character, and because Miss Douglass was indisposed. The scene where the spirits pass before Macbeth was well managed, also the banquet scene, but the witches failed to please entirely—'...the garment of one of them was rather too short for the legs; or the legs too long for the garment'. The dresses and scenery were also praised.

Some ten days later Knowles announced a performance of *The Merchant of Venice* for his benefit. In this Knowles played Shylock to Miss Douglass's Portia, with Simmons as Lorenzo and Mrs Taylor as Jessica. In the course of the play there were interpolated a number of solos and duets sung by Mrs Taylor and Simmons. For this performance the house was again crowded in all parts.

Shylock by Knowles was said by the *Herald* to be his most successful effort during the season— 'It is paying him no compliment to say he has no competition on the Sydney boards'. The *Gazette* believed exactly the opposite on this occasion, finding the outstanding performances to have been those of Mackay as Gratiano, Mrs Taylor as Jessica, and Simmons as Lorenzo. The songs, it said, were introduced with good effect, 'although not in strict accord with the plan intended by Shakespeare'.

In a matter of another eleven days yet another of Shakespeare's plays was presented for the first time—*Romeo and Juliet*, for Miss Douglass's benefit. Knowles played Romeo, Simmons Mercutio, Miss Douglass Juliet, and Mrs Larra the Nurse. The *Gazette*, the only newspaper to comment on this performance, said it was 'on the whole pretty well got through'.

For his benefit on 12 April 1836 Knowles chose *Henry the Fourth; or, The Battle of Shrewsbury*, which was, of course, the current version of *1 Henry IV*. The newspapers ignored this, but it is known from an advertisement that the versatile Knowles played Falstaff; Miss Jones played Prince John; Simmons, Hotspur; and Mackay played the Prince of Wales. Mrs Larra was Mistress Quickly.

King Lear was the next play attempted, the most ambitious yet undertaken. In the Nahum Tate version, it had Knowles as Lear, and as the three daughters Miss Douglass, Mrs Taylor, and Mrs Cameron. The play was too much for the Sydney audience of the time, too incomprehensible, and it was restless and talkative throughout. The *Monitor* said it would have been very respectably performed to a well-behaved house, half-filled, 'but, whenever our Sydney theatre is *full*, the vulgarity of the people breaks forth, turns all the pathetic scenes into ridicule, and the tragic into burlesque'. This newspaper said Knowles played the first act well, but after that he knew nothing of his part. The three daughters, it said, all dressed and acted well, and the scenery and dresses were generally good. The *Herald* said Knowles *could* play Lear, if he did not come on stage so imperfect in his part. On the other hand, it was admitted that he was called on to do what was well nigh impossible—to study many new parts each week, and week after week.

After this, seventeen months passed before another first performance was essayed. This time it was *Cymbeline*, presented at the newly opened Victoria Theatre. The newly arrived *Commercial Journal* was the only newspaper to comment on this production. 'It would be a task far beyond our simple talents to attempt a description of the play or players', it said. 'The only way we can mercifully dispose of them is to say nothing about them.' It added the pious hope that Mr Wyatt, proprietor of the Victoria Theatre, would not again drag Shakespeare before an audience until he had found 'performers to *read* him'. By way of reply, perhaps, next month this theatre presented the first Australian performance of *Julius Caesar*. It was ignored by every newspaper.

Again there was a break, this time of ten months, before the next 'first'—*The Tempest; or, The Enchanted Island*, the Dryden version of the original. This was given the year after William Macready in London restored the original play to the stage. Knowles, of course, played Prospero, and his performance again had a mixed reception. Surprisingly, both the *Commercial Journal* and the *Herald* criticized the management for producing this non-Shakespearian version of *The Tempest*, indicating a growing awareness not only of the importance of the theatre but also of the contemporary theatre in London. 'Why is not the *real* play produced?' asked the *Commercial Journal*. 'It would draw a better house than did the *calm Tempest*.'

Knowles was again imperfect in his part, and according to the *Sydney Standard* appeared to play the last act *ad lib.*, 'anxiously watching the prompter's word'. The *Herald* said that as Prospero he appeared to want *repose*, thus giving support to the *Standard*'s complaint about his 'melodramatic and unnatural positions'. The women were the worst in the cast, said the *Herald*, adding that Mrs Taylor as Miranda knew as much of the character 'as the man (or the woman) in the moon'. But it did conclude its report with the fair statement that 'it is due to the manager to say that he has introduced some admirable scenery in *The Tempest*'.

Of the 1841 performance of *The Comedy of Errors* nothing is known excepting the advertisement announcing that it would be performed.[4] Perhaps the newspapers thought it another *Cymbeline*. There were six newspapers in Sydney at this time, and all of them ignored it. But they also seem to have ignored the theatre's other performances during this month.

From this time until 6 February 1843, although many performances of Shakespeare's plays were given none was a first performance. There were repeats of Cibber's popular version of *Richard III*, of *The Merchant of Venice*, *Hamlet*, and even *King Lear* (in which, this time, Knowles earned the highest possible praise) but no first performance until that of *King John* on 6 February. This was again a Knowles benefit, with Frank Nesbitt (a newcomer from England who had ousted Knowles in popularity) in the title role and Knowles playing Faulconbridge. Mrs Jones (Mrs Knowles) played Prince John. One newspaper reported that only those parts played by Nesbitt and Knowles were well sustained. As it was a benefit performance no other mention of it was made.

From this time onwards Sydney's original 'theatricals' began to fade into the background. It was in the early 1840s that the first of the English provincial players emigrated to Sydney.

Some of these the Sydney critics found to be better than the local players; some merely equal to them. In the 1850s, following the discovery of gold in California and Australia, there came a flood of actors from both England and America, but chiefly America, including Mr and Mrs James Stark who appeared in *Hamlet*, *Othello*, *King Lear*, *Macbeth*, *Richard III*, *The Merchant of Venice*, and *Catherine and Petruchio*. Next came Mr and Mrs D. Waller (Emma Waller), who appeared in *Romeo and Juliet*, and *Othello*; followed by Laura Keene and Edmund Booth in *The Merchant of Venice*, *Hamlet*, *Much Ado About Nothing*, and *Richard III*. In a return visit the Wallers appeared in *Macbeth*, *The Merchant of Venice*, *Hamlet*, and *Richard III*, as well as the two plays presented during their earlier visit. The Starks followed them with their return visit, when they appeared again in all the Shakespearian plays of their first visit except *The Merchant of Venice* and *Catherine and Petruchio*.

By the 1860s the Australian 'circuit' was well known, and attracted may English actors, including Charles and Ellen Kean. And from the 1870s onward the theatre in all the colonies—Sydney, Melbourne, and Adelaide particularly—continued to attract 'stars' from England, America, France, Germany, and even Italy, all of whom gave their version of at least one well-known Shakespearian character.

© ERIC IRVIN 1969

NOTES

1. *Memorandum of the Transactions of a Voyage From England to Botany Bay 1787–1793*, by John Easty, Private Marine, in the *Scarborough* Transport. Mitchell Library, Sydney.

2. Morgan McMahon, 'Australia's First Players', *The Lone Hand*, Sydney, 1 December 1910.

3. A. C. Sprague, *Shakespeare and the Actors* (Harvard, 1944), p. 224.

4. *The Sydney Herald*, 18 January 1841.

THE REASON WHY: THE ROYAL SHAKESPEARE SEASON 1968 REVIEWED

BY

GARETH LLOYD EVANS

It is an enormous achievement that the Royal Shakespeare Company, since 1960, has been able to maintain such a large head of steam in so many parts of its machine. When the theatre history of the sixties comes to be written this company will occupy a dominant position. The National Theatre (a later starter) still shows but few signs of catching up with the devious, athletic and exciting pace of its rival. Indeed, so far as Shakespeare is concerned, it has shown more signs of fruitless emulation than studied competitiveness. A *Much Ado* which seemed a self-congratulatory refugee from comic opera and an *As You Like It* from the Danny La Rue stable represent the image that most people carry with them of the National's inventive and creative conception of our national dramatist.

Peripatetic academics return annually to this country with optimistic but strangely frequent apologias about the events on the boards at Stratford Ontario and Connecticut. They remain in Stratford, England, awhile; they often fulminate about what they see at the Royal Shakespeare Theatre, but it is possible to detect, in the eyes, as they give you the last handshake, a look already of nostalgia for what they are leaving. So many of them tacitly seem to accept that, for all its shortcomings, the Royal Shakespeare Theatre is the true and vital home of Shakespeare at mid-century.

With the approach of the seventies and the attention paid to that contemporary assumption that the unit of the decade is of pregnant significance in the assessment of human affairs, it is perhaps timely to consider, in an interim way, the position of the Royal Shakespeare Theatre, with this season's productions fresh in the mind.

It owes its position (and has done for some time), first, to luck—both ill and good, and, second, to its own efforts, both worthy and unworthy. Stratford is a magnet. It is the envy of less happy places and envious men who, desperate at its easy ability to be an international town, do not seek, rationally, to find an explanation, but resort to an endearing lunacy. They hurl abuse at Stratford's alleged iniquitous treatment of tourists (quite unproven) or aver that the dislodgement of a few hundredweights of earth (with ecclesiastical sanction) will uncover the dread lie that the town has lived with, and upon, for four centuries. The town attracts the curious and the envious, the theatregoer and the non-theatregoer, but so far as the Royal Shakespeare Theatre is concerned, the particular importance of its being in Stratford (apart from obvious reasons) is that the town annihilates the customary and sharp distinctions between the knowledgeable theatregoer, the occasional theatregoer, and the positively anti-theatregoer. It is both an irony and a phenomenon that the avid theatregoer often cannot obtain tickets for performances, while people who, in most other towns, would not care whether they obtained a ticket or not, often find themselves borne into the auditorium by an all-in coach tour package-deal. Many sit there watching a play they have never heard of by an author whose reputation may well have been sullied by their school education. The Royal Shakespeare Theatre is in the enviable position of having an assured audience, but also in the difficult position, on an overall view of a season, of having an audience of which a variable proportion is present by accident or idle curiosity.

Actors at the theatre claim that it is the most unpredictable audience in the world. 'You feel', one said, 'that there is a play going on there in the auditorium and that you, on stage, are the audience. It makes contact difficult'. Others express the same problem differently, and cover up under the phrase—'It's a challenge'.

The theatre is, therefore, in the ironic situation of quantitative assurance and qualitative dubiety about its audience. No theatre can afford to despise its audience, but the Royal Shakespeare Theatre must sometimes look at its own quizzically. Its fragmented nature is increased by its internal constituents. An example of the kind of problem this raises is indicated by the number of young foreign students who attend the theatre, often in groups, many of whom have little English and a mere passing comprehension of Shakespeare. Even when their knowledge, often theoretical, is good, there is no guarantee (why should there be?) about their reaction to a play. No play, of course, is ever guaranteed the responses desired by the author, the director or the actors, but in the case of the Royal Shakespeare Theatre the matter can be extreme in its implications. It is unnervingly interesting to sit next to a Japanese who finds difficulty in controlling his laughter at this year's *King Lear*—'Oh, no, no, not because it is bad, oh, no. The actors are highly excellent, most worthy performers, but you westerners have such a quaint view of tragedy'.

It is probably beyond the capabilities of an outsider to know to what extent the Royal Shakespeare Theatre is conscious of the influence of this extraordinary audience upon its policy, its productions and the interpretation of individual plays. If the remarks of the players are to be counted upon then it would seem that they find the experience of playing at Stratford a constant mixture of difficulty and invigoration. There is evidence that the administrative and artistic hierarchy are sensitive (and rightly so) to the box-office, and that they show it in what some would call their timorous frugality in presenting non-Shakespeare plays; yet whether any conscious knowledge they have deeply affects their policy it is not possible to know, and dangerous to guess.

There are, however, certain features of this nearly completed decade which tend to isolate it from the past history of this theatre. These features, it is inferred, represent, at the very least, a strong unconscious response to the kind of audience the Royal Shakespeare Theatre has increasingly had in the sixties. This season's productions, in fact, seem to sharpen the validity of the inferences that can be made.

The first, and most dominant, was discussed in *Shakespeare Survey 20* by the present writer. It is the avowed and demonstrated policy initiated by Peter Hall (and dutifully continued by his fellows) of making the plays speak to the twentieth century. The discussion concentrated upon thematic interpretation. It may be pertinent now to enquire into the other implications of this policy—in terms of the unique audience which the theatre attracts. The question is—'Does the Royal Shakespeare Theatre consciously or unconsciously direct its productions not just to a twentieth-century audience, but to an international one with extremes of receptivity?'

Some of the effects which are made in production, this season, are of the same nature as, but greater in quantity than, those that have been noted in the past eight years. An ungracious explanation would be that they are baffling examples of an intermittent but total dissociation of sensibility by directors. It is as if, at times, a self-destroying irresponsibility descends, and the result forces even temperate critics to the darkest conclusions. Yet those very directors, like John Barton, who are prone to these aberrations, have otherwise shown ample proof of intelligence and imaginative discipline.

A close examination of some of these effects might lead to a different conclusion. Is it because, one wonders, the audience is so diverse in taste, understanding and nationality, that there seems to be an increase, over the last three seasons, of dissociated action in productions? Is it for the same reason that there is such an amount of acting which, at best, is impersonation and, at worst, what I have called mere behaviourism? Is it the same reason which accounts for the growing examples, in comedies, of business unrelated either to character or plot?

These effects are both visual and aural, and it is not easy to award either predominance in their obtrusions into the productions. There is an increasing use of lengthy and entirely visual introductions and episodes to accompany what are, after all, verbal masterpieces. In some cases these are brilliantly justified, as in Clifford Williams' mime introduction to *The Comedy of Errors* (1965); on other occasions they give the impression of having originated as part of a unity of conception, as in the ritual semi-dances of *The Revenger's Tragedy* (1967) and the splendid parade of barbaric splendour which heralds this season's *King Lear*. Strangely, however, one finds, too often, that such episodes, as performed, seem to draw attention to themselves—the mind has to work hard to realize the unity which might involve them. *Troilus and Cressida*, this season, has one such episode of visual emphasis; its implications, thematically, are discussed later, but two aspects of it can be mentioned now. First, it was sensational in appearance, being no more and no less than a slightly ritualized performance of sodomy; second, witnesses testify to its having been conspicuously muted in performance subsequent to the first night. If this is true, it will not go unremarked by those who believe that its presence was dissociatively obtrusive—to say the least. If it is not true, its appearance can only be justified by its relationship to the play and the production.

The manner in which some of the visual underlinings draw attention to themselves gives an impression of a show-within-a-play, and it is astonishing how much of it is dumb-show. Television has given us the opportunity of seeing foreign circuses whose acts are obviously designed to be filmed and sold on the international market. They exhibit a firm, and under the circumstances of that art, a justifiable reliance on the international language of dumb-show. Yet a Shakespeare play is not a circus—his verbal world is underlined, replaced or decorated, at great peril.

Verse-speaking is one of the first victims of an undue concentration on the visual. Since 1960 it has had intermittent hours of glory at the Royal Shakespeare Theatre but, significantly, most often in the mouths of the already accomplished. This theatre has a distinguished record, in this period, which must be applauded, of bringing young actors to the fore, but few of its graduates have achieved distinction in speaking. What is more melancholy is that some young players who, in past productions, have shown some grasp of the necessities of Shakespeare's language, show no consistency—no more, indeed, than some of their directorial colleagues. A notable example is Michael Williams who (in the only slightly less demanding role of

Petruchio had tonal variety and an intelligent sense of pausing) has, as Troilus, declined into a verbal condition risible in its inefficiency. There is no question of singling out this actor (indeed, as Lear's Fool, his speaking shows intelligence) but he is a prominent example.

The general verse-speaking faults are as follows:

(1) Repeated examples of phrasing which suggest either that the voice is being wrongly produced—i.e. the breathing is faulty and so the phrase length cannot be achieved—or a total misunderstanding of the meaning of the line. This is noticeable in supernumerary work, but also appears in major characters. For example, Sebastian Shaw's speaking of Ulysses' degree speech shows none of the mellifluous precision which characterized his king in last year's *All's Well*. One is inclined, in a Barton production, to ascribe this fault to technical reasons rather than to lack of understanding. This may be evidenced by the persistent complaints (which the theatre would do well to heed) about the difficulty of actually hearing many speeches.

(2) Tonal ugliness. The mellifluous extrovertism of the past is easily decried and when, as often, it was unaccompanied by intellectual understanding, it was justifiably decried. The ear now, however, yearns for voices which intelligently attempt to correspond to the music of the Shakespearian line. The lack of music this season is the more surprising in view of the emphasis both Hall and Barton have placed on the musical structure of Shakespeare. The Royal Shakespeare Theatre seems to have forgotten, too often this season, that the truth of Shakespearian character lies in a double-focus. First, the 'truth' to human nature—to this extent most of his characters are 'naturalistic'; second, the poetic grandeur or subtlety of the means they are given to communicate themselves. A merely 'naturalistic' interpretation of character will inevitably bring with it non-poetic speaking. The need to speak to the twentieth century can well persuade a director, and hence an actor, that rhythm, pausing, the musical noise of words based on a sensitivity to the line, are to be avoided or played down. This runs the risk of speaking to the twentieth century at the expense of ignoring the totality of what Shakespeare's characters *are*, and how they express themselves. This season at Stratford, there seem to be two basic procedures which shy away from a total grasp of the line—and therefore of character. One is an a-tonal phrase-chopping, the other is a substitution of a mechanical tinkling as a substitute for rich musicality. Janet Suzman exhibits this surrogate music. She is an actress of great agility of mind and body. There is a sense of energy about everything that she does and speaks. At its best, as in Joan of Arc in the *Henry VI* trilogy, this quality is engaging. At its worst, what emerges is a kind of restlessness, as if the actress were seeking to find a still perch upon which to rest her interpretation. Her Rosalind, this season, demonstrates well the disadvantageous effects of her acting and speaking. The character is denuded of that quality of poise, of sweet gravity, beneath the devious and witty comic play of the actions in which she is involved. Miss Suzman, whose tone is attractive, tends, however, to thump upon the verse. It is as if, determined to be a gay Rosalind, she jumps up and down upon the iambic with trampoline regularity. No foreigner in the audience would have any doubts that this is a happy Rosalind, but equally no sensitive native Englishman would be satisfied that he had seen anything other than a happy Rosalind. What is also significant is Miss Suzman's speaking of the prose. She brings exactly the same thumping insouciance to it; the net result is to rob both verse and prose of its individuality and reduce both to mechanical, if joyful, tinkling. Miss Suzman has all of Rosalind's youthfulness, courage and witty purposefulness, but not her control over situations or her

sweet gravity. Her speaking has the unfortunate effect of reducing Rosalind to an elegant-looking, gay, superior, pantomime principal boy.

In a season where there is a general weakness in the speaking it is fair to consider whether there is a particular and overriding reason, external to the players themselves, which can account for it. In this respect it is noticeable that *King Lear*, the first part of *As You Like It*, and *Troilus and Cressida*, are staged with few props. In both *Lear* and *Troilus* the proscenium area of the stage seems vast and empty, inhabited occasionally by small props. One may speculate that some general agreement had been reached between the different directors on an overall style of presentation—particularly in the three examples quoted. Some might call it 'abstract', others might call it 'bare-staged'. There is more emphasis, particularly in *King Lear*, on action which takes place in a void than on any attempt to localize it. The dramatic results remain to be discussed; the practical effects may very well be the factor that has deracinated the speaking this season. Voices give the effect of disappearing into the flies when the actors stand directly beneath the proscenium arch (which is often). The impression is given that some actors, conscious of the vast empty spaces behind them, have resorted to a pushing and chopping technique in an attempt to reach the audience. If this explanation has any validity then it is to be regretted that the long-heralded major changes to Stratford's stage have again been postponed. This theatre has, since its erection, been hag-ridden by the inept original design of the stage and back-stage areas.

These considerations about the possible effect of its audience, the desire to speak to the twentieth century, the speaking, and the mechanics of the stage, play a dominant part in one's experience and assessment of the season. The repertory had great variety—*The Merry Wives of Windsor*, *Julius Caesar*, *King Lear*, *Doctor Faustus*, *Troilus and Cressida*, *As You Like It* (re-produced from last season) and *Much Ado About Nothing*.[1] Of these the most successful, by far, was *The Merry Wives*, and for a simple reason—its cast was composed of mature and experienced members of the company who had not been put under any obligation to make the play say more than it does. Elizabeth Spriggs, Ian Richardson, Brenda Bruce and Brewster Mason created a sharp sense of the uniquely class-conscious world of Windsor, and created its comedy with a joyous subtlety of pace and invention. The dominant impression was of a coordinated exploration of visual comedy, but this did not inhibit a shrewd appreciation of the possibilities (small though they are in the play) of characterization. The inherent snobbishness, the flashes of jealousy, anger and sentimentality which Richardson, Spriggs and Bruce invoked, made a world of reality inside which the comedy was firmly held. Brewster Mason's Falstaff was a remarkable justification for the return of the fat knight into the canon. He avoided the customary depiction of the character as a declined and farcical idiot; this Falstaff had dignity and a true if soiled knighthood. Something of Falstaff's former grandeur remained, but within a context of vulnerability; he became a victim of circumstances which made him look foolish but did not reduce him to total absurdity.

As You Like It, less satisfying than in its original production of last season, still shows evidences of thoughtful direction. It has been curiously underrated by the critics, yet, in some ways, it is the most interesting of this season's repertoire. David Jones, the director, had deliberately avoided the traditional conception of a 'golden glow' comedy, and equally deliberately emphasized the darker elements. In his production the forest is, itself, a *dramatis persona*—its beneficial influence is shown to be the element which transforms dalliance to love, irrascibility to patience and rancour to humility. Because this transforming process is so clearly maintained in the production, characters like Duke Frederick and Oliver are explicable in thematic terms—they become, so to speak, extreme examples of how the world of Arden can turn bad to good. Jaques, as played by an exciting young actor—Alan Howard—is an eccentric and youngish man. He has experienced all seasons and found them wanting; Mr Howard and the director have taken a cue from the Duke's speech in which he says:

> For thou thyself hast been a libertine,
> As sensual as the brutish sting itself;
> And all th'embossed sores and headed evils
> That thou with license of free foot hast caught
> Wouldst thou disgorge into the general world. (II, vii, 65–9)

This Jaques is psychologically affected by the physical results of libertinism. He clutches his cloak about his lower parts as if to hide 'embossed sores' from us. His melancholy is part guilt at his own excesses and, in David Jones's world of Arden, he is the one being who, though he tentatively and poignantly attempts to feel the blessings of the place, is untouched by it.

The overall interpretation of the play is mature but its execution suffers, this season, from the absence of Dorothy Tutin as Rosalind, and from the effects of the 'abstract' staging mentioned above. The interpretation depends upon the audience's total acceptance of the effects of location upon character, but it is turned awry because the first part is robbed of a sense of location in favour of a grey limbo.

Julius Caesar might well have been the most distinguished production of the season, but it fell far short of the expectations it intermittently aroused. Brewster Mason's Caesar—powerful in voice and with a patina of decay on his large frame—was the true husk of the colossus of the text; Ian Richardson's Cassius had within it the authentic tension of a character in whom cynical politics are at war with a nervous humanity; the set evoked sharply the rich severity of Rome's architecture—there was, blessedly no 'abstract' art here. Yet these virtues were, as it were, unconnected with anything. The majority of individual scenes contained some virtue—the Brutus/Cassius scene before Philippi, the Caesar/Calpurnia relationship—but each one gave the impression of having been conceived separately. On this occasion one felt that John Barton's academic knowledge of text and source had completely dominated his theatrical instincts. On the one hand it is possible to applaud the wise readings of the text, on the other to wonder why there was so much uncoordinated movement, why the crowd listening to Antony and Brutus was so ridiculously small and so artificial in its movements. One wondered why the assassination scene, produced with care as to speech and movement, put so much emphasis on the Caesar/Casca relationship and left the Caesar/Brutus relationship a kind of afterthought—perhaps Mr Barton had read his Plutarch too closely? The questions crowded upon one out of this production and, inevitably, what one suspects was conceived with thought and care, lost all hold upon the imagination.

Stratford made its most explicit committal to the era of permissiveness when it announced that Helen in *Doctor Faustus* was to appear naked. The result of this decision and of the attention it incited was a mere confirmation that she did, in fact, appear naked—and that is all. It is a respectable and traditional view that a sweet disorder in dress kindles wantonness, and that total exposure has an anaesthetic effect. Helen's appearance proved this. At one stroke the expectations of the lascivious were dampened and the wanton and desperate passion of Faustus's speech to Helen reduced to superfluous triviality. The best answer to any theory the director may have had that a naked Helen was essential to his interpretation is the fact that the understudy appeared fully clothed and Eric Porter's speech gained immensely in evocative power.

This production is, indeed, noteworthy for other qualities. Visually it was the most inventive of the whole season, and often successfully. The claustrophobic and dark recesses of Faustus's study were exactly and economically achieved—the designer had resisted the usual temptation of depicting 'Elizabethanism' by a vast clutter of dusty books, skulls, astrolabes and olde mappes. Hell enclosed about Faustus in a sensational explosion of colour, noise and shape—a medieval conception boosted by twentieth-century technical aids. The Seven Deadly Sins, out of Bosch by Gerald Scarfe, cavorted and shrieked. They were startlingly ugly and malformed and had a great theatrical impact. At the same time they raised the question, 'Would Faustus or anyone be tempted by such grotesque ugliness?' In a way Faustus is a demonstration of Wilde's dictum that the only way to resist temptation is to yield to it. These Sins made a mockery of any urge to yield. Perhaps the director had concluded that their appearance is calculated less to allure Faustus than to convince him of Lucifer's theatrical inventiveness; if this is so, it begs many questions about the relationship of Faustus to the Devil and, more pertinently, of the meaning of the bond.

Eric Porter, in the name part, created, with thoughtful precision, the various stages of Faustus's spiritual and physical journey—the curiosity, the doubt, the urge for more and yet more sensation, the regret, the terror. Technically and intellectually, his reading of the text was excellent. What was lacking (and this where it was most needed—in the final monologue) was passion. At any point in this performance one could sense a strong intellectual engagement with the character, but missed the sense of a heart and soul moving in parallel with the mind's experience. The pathos of this play comes from our observation of a man wasting great gifts and entering into a trap. It was Terrence Hardiman's Mephistopheles, rather than Faustus, who induced the pity of it in a performance characterized by quiet grief, mordant humour, and resigned dignity. His performance was the more touching since the overall interpretation stressed wryness and grim humour—this was increased by the brilliantly controlled and realized comic scenes. These did not attempt comic relief (for which Marlowe's text is not conspicuously well equipped) but underlined the dangerous absurdity of playing with the devil's fire.

Eric Porter brought to King Lear exactly the same intellectual clarity that informed his Faustus. The great virtue of this actor is that an audience always knows where it stands with him. The 'meaning' of a line is rarely in doubt. It often seems as if he deliberately eschews any attempt to 'move' an audience, being more concerned to teach it to understand. His Lear was, therefore, distinguished by intellectual clarity and a corresponding lack of passion. The agony, grief, anger and madness all remained inside the words. Loss of mental and emotional control are, paradoxically, carefully constructed verbally by Porter, but are rarely completely embodied by the voice or the movements. Trevor Nunn seems to see the play as a kind of parable of the fall of man. Lear stands for Man who, compact of splendour and greatness, is stripped (and strips himself) of everything. The filial themes of the play become subservient to this over-riding conception—as if an abstract psychological reading had overborne the basically simple human actions of the story. Thus the divesting of clothes in the storm scene, although visually naturalistic, has the effect of psychological symbolism. Edgar, having lost all before Lear, is almost totally naked; Lear, still clinging to something (his sanity) strips to the point where his trousers hang about his ankles—the final divesting not yet achieved. Kent, brilliantly played by David Waller, as a bluff, accented man of oak, is part of the sacrificial movement of Lear's descent to nothing. His last speech is more than a declaration of his utter love and duty to Lear—it is a logical committal of himself to the same final nothing. Gloucester (a distinguished per-formance by Sebastian Shaw) is less the chief character in a related sub-plot about filial ingrati-tude, than part of the declension from human riches to rags.

The interpretation is consistent, but the execution, with certain exceptions, leaves much to be desired. Goneril, Regan and Cordelia were simply deficient in speaking and movement, the storm scene was an uneasy mixture of naturalism and impressionism in its effects, and the vast empty stage, while it increased the symbolic overtones, swallowed speech. The production, fascinating for its reading of the play, could not, with certain exceptions, justify, in execution, the subtle acting and direction which the reading demands.

It was John Barton's production of *Troilus and Cressida* which intensified speculation about the kind of considerations which are discussed in the early part of this article. The production has been much discussed in print and reactions have been mixed. The testimony of spoken criticism is held, by many theatre people, to be less valid even than written criticism, so it is certain that the unusual amount of adverse audience reaction expressed in conversation would not be considered as reasonable evidence. Yet one cannot avoid reporting that many members of the audience found it offensive. It is only right, however, to reflect that British theatre audiences are naturally thin-skinned about what they deem proper and improper in stage production; as to the foreigners they are less available for comment. Perhaps they do not display the crabbed puritanism which is a dominant critical response for the majority of British theatre-goers. One reports an unusual amount of spoken verbal comment for what it is worth. Only when the realities of the play, the nature of the production, and the main burden of public disapproval are put together, can some conclusion be reached.

This play is one of, and about, contrasts. It allows of a variety of detailed emphases by actor and director, because of the richness of its characterization. Yet whatever way is sought, in detail, to 'depict' Cressida or Pandarus or the various Greeks and Trojans, it must minister to the play's demonstration of the bitter irony of contrasts. Love is one thing, but love in practice becomes another; Honour is one thing, but its theoretical status is shattered by the sickening perfidy of Hector's death; a grand enunciation of the value of Degree and Order is one thing, but it is demolished by the actual facts of disorder in the wars; the courage and glory that War engenders are rhetorically magnificent, but the reality is the blustering of Ajax and the puny grounds upon which it is, in fact, fought. Shakespeare's tragedies preserve, in the end, the idea of human dignity and perfectibility, but this play puts the abstractions, by which humanity preserves its dignity and attests its perfectibility, against the usages of human behaviour, and leaves us nothing to believe in—unless it be that reality is vicious and illusions ludicrous. John Barton's rehearsal notes imply that he began with the idea of contrast in mind:

We use abstract words like Honour, Fame, Beauty and Truth to sanction what we do and give our-selves a sense of order and meaning. We need these to smooth over the confusion of life, and to avoid acknowledging the chaos within ourselves'.[2]

A play generated by the idea of ironic contrast requires a pivot for successful communication—this is Thersites. He is the most privileged voyeur in history and, like the most accomplished voyeur, knows that he can be guaranteed (such is man) that the worst of reality will always overcome the best of illusion.

Mr Barton has sat upon one end of the see-saw himself, and allowed Thersites to slide amok into a perfidious commitment to the lower earth of his production. His rehearsal notes say one thing but his production demonstrates quite another, in fact a set of other things:

(1) Thersites, far from being observer and commentator, in fact a Fool described by Achilles himself as one who 'is a privileg'd man', becomes a deformed boil-covered (on what authority?) grotesque. He is, as it were, the conductor of a perverted orchestration of homosexual behaviour in which the first player is Achilles, accompanied by virtually naked myrmidons whose actions are only too obviously representational.

(2) Achilles is no warrior (at one point he coyly bares his chest to back-stage as if to apologize for the discrepancy between his reputation as warrior and the pale weak reality). He is given to female impersonation—visually, at one point, he appears in 'drag'. Mr Barton has not only homosexualized (to an extreme) on the basis of slender textual evidence, but has been unfaithful even to his own grotesque conception, since Patroclus behaves in anything but a homosexual manner.

(3) The Greek commanders' behaviour is made to range from the irresponsibly doddery (Nestor) to the ludicrous—Agamemnon sports a straw hat which he tilts bucolically when Aeneas visits the Greek camp and does not recognize him.

These three elements are the dominant impressions of a production which only marginally conveys any sense of the contrast between abstraction and reality. Critical comment finds itself hamstrung between deprecating the perversity of the conception and the ineptitude of a great deal of the execution. Troilus is small and seems afraid of his lyrical speeches; Cressida is bouncy and jumps upon her lines like a teenage pop singer; Sebastian Shaw unbelievably turns the Degree speech into tedious, ill-spoken irrelevancy. The mind, having tried to cope with the vulgarity of such treatment, is jolted back to the conception when Thersites releases, from behind a grinning codpiece, a tail/penis which he swings with monotonous exultation. Try as one will to reconcile Mr Barton's theory of the play with what is seen in this production, it cannot be done.

This production most clearly shows the perils of the various deliberately expressed policies and the, perhaps unconscious, responses which seem to inform the work of the Royal Shake-speare Theatre. There is something forced about John Barton's reference to Vietnam in his programme notes:

the war (is) an image of a Vietnam situation, where both sides are inexorably committed...

—not because it is improbable that we should relate this play to Vietnam, but because what we see on the stage is grotesquely remote not only from Vietnam but from anything that Shakespeare's own chorus announces—in any case why cannot we be content, for once, not to have an image of Vietnam, or any other modern equivalent, but one of the wars of the Greeks and Trojans, which is what the play is about. There comes a point when speaking to the twentieth century ends in a special pleading which is both meaningless and irritating.

There is something vulgar about the reduction of Ajax to 'A Jakes' in pronunciation, perhaps to give a knowing wink to the British members of the audience that they have not been forgotten. The international audience is presumably catered for by the spectacle of a Greek running from the stage giving one of those high-fisted jumps so beloved of modern footballers when they have scored a goal.

There is something self-indulgent about the sensational visual episodes which make their meaning only too clear. Another result of this was pointed out by W. A. Darlington in *The Daily Telegraph*[3]—'Mr Barton's decorations made it a three-and-three-quarter-hour job'. This elongation of the play is achieved, it may be noted, with only one interval.

There is something timorous, to say the least, about speaking which rarely seems to try to come to grips with Shakespeare's language. It is as if directors have begun to feel that they will bore their audiences if they give them too much 'poetry', and that the message for the twentieth century will be lost unless speaking approaches the naturalism of conversational vernacular.

Regret that Mr Barton, of all people, should provide the strongest occasion for these conclusions, is made melancholy by the fact that *Troilus and Cressida* is only an extreme example of what seems a general condition. Perhaps the efforts of the last eight years have exhausted the Royal Shakespeare Theatre. Perhaps...perhaps. Whether there is one basic reason, or a combination of several, one cannot help feeling unease about the present situation. Shakespeare seems to be moving inexorably into the background, to be replaced by image-making which at its best is merely vivid and, at its worst, separated from the reality of the plays.

© GARETH LLOYD EVANS 1969

NOTES

1. *Much Ado About Nothing* appeared too late in the season to be included in this review.

2. John Barton's rehearsal notes published in the Royal Shakespeare Theatre programme for *Troilus and Cressida*.

3. W. A. Darlington, 'A Queer Twist to Shakespeare', in *The Daily Telegraph*, 19 August 1968.

THE YEAR'S CONTRIBUTIONS TO
SHAKESPEARIAN STUDY

1. CRITICAL STUDIES

reviewed by G. R. HIBBARD

Faced with a body of material as heterogeneous and sometimes as strange as that dramatized in *Pericles, Prince of Tyre*, and with a scene that is, to quote Malone, set 'dispersedly in various countries', the present reviewer, seeking to make a 'true Relation' not of 'the whole Historie' but of as much of it as has come his way, cannot but be grateful for having been provided with an 'ancient Gower' to serve as Prologue and even on occasions as Chorus. Walter Whiter died in 1832, yet there are two good reasons why his *A Specimen of a Commentary on Shakespeare*, admirably edited by the late Alan Over and Mary Bell,[1] should appear in this context. First, there is much here that has never been published before, since the editors have wisely chosen to include the additions and revisions Whiter made for a projected second edition of his original publication (1794) that was never called for. Secondly, however, Whiter is, in a sense, a modern critic, because it is only during the last thirty years or so that the significance of his approach and findings has come to be recognized. His main aim, at least when he began his work, was to establish the validity of his theory, based on the ideas of Locke, about the role of association in creative writing. He says: 'I define therefore the power of this *association* over the genius of the poet, to consist in supplying him with words and with ideas, which have been suggested to the mind by a principle of union unperceived by himself, and independent of the subject to which they are applied' (pp. 62–3). And he goes on to insist that the writer is 'totally unconscious of the effect and principle of their union' (p. 64). But interest in the theory as such rapidly gave way to a fascination with Shakespeare's image clusters for their own sake; and, in his efforts to elucidate the unifying factors within the clusters, Whiter came to see, as no one had seen before him, just how much the imagery in Shakespeare owed to the life of Elizabethan England and, in particular, to the theatre itself and to the masques and pageants of the time. At least one of the articles noticed later acknowledges a specific debt to him on this score, and it seems likely that his fertilizing influence will grow, now that his seminal work has at last been made generally accessible.

Freud may fairly be regarded as the counterpart in our age to Locke in Whiter's. Norman N. Holland's *Psychoanalysis and Shakespeare*[2] is a work of considerable importance, especially in its conclusions which point towards new lines of enquiry. It falls into three clearly defined parts. The first is a succinct account of Freud's theory of literature, correcting some misconceptions that are still common. The second, beginning with a survey of Freud's comments on Shakespeare, then proceeds to a lucid and entertaining summary of the observations, including the

1 Methuen; Barnes and Noble, New York, 1967.
2 McGraw-Hill, New York, Toronto, London, 1964, 1966.

engagingly dotty ones, that have been made by psychoanalytical critics about the individual plays, about specific characters, and about the *œuvre* in general. From this it emerges that the basic split among the psychoanalytical critics is the same as that among literary critics: between the 'realistic' attitude to the plays and the 'anti-realistic'. In the final and most valuable section of his book Holland sets two groups of findings in opposition to each other. The first set, which he labels 'Logical', are the bases of most modern criticism: the idea that a play must be seen as an artifact, and that the tendency of psychoanalytical criticism to treat the characters as though they were historical figures with an independent life of their own is therefore a mistaken one. The second set, labelled 'Not so Logical', give Holland's own position and provide the *raison d'être* for his work. Here he takes the line that the psychoanalytical critic is, or ought to be, engaged in a different kind of activity from that of the literary critic proper. The latter tries to establish what a work means, the former to understand how it succeeds in moving us. And, as soon as we begin to consider the responses of an audience to a play, we have to admit that it does see the characters as 'real people'. Indeed, since those characters are represented on the stage by living actors, it has no alternative to doing so. It is in this field of audience response, Holland suggests, that the psychoanalytical criticism of Shakespeare has its true role and future.

This thesis receives indirect support from Sitansu Maitra who, because he is concerned primarily with meaning, rejects Freud's theory of art as being too exclusively devoted to problems that belong to the individual, and prefers to find help in the ideas of Jung. The centre of his *Psychological Realism and Archetypes: The Trickster in Shakespeare*[1] is an attempt 'to show that Shakespeare was right in causing Falstaff's rejection and also right in causing us pain at his rejection and yet again right in violating psychological realism for the sake of achieving greater truth to life'. Maitra aligns himself with the romantic critics, attacking Stoll and the whole school of 'historical' criticism on the grounds that there is a kind of poetry which belongs to the 'visionary' mode, as distinct from the 'psychological', and which draws its power from the 'collective unconscious' and from our instinctive response to archetypes. Falstaff is identified as Hal's 'shadow', 'the trickster', the dark unconscious side of his being. Hal, whose conscious public role is that of the order figure, must, in the end, throw off this other side of himself, but the process is necessarily a painful one. The book is not, however, restricted to the case of Hal and Falstaff. Using his knowledge of Indian myth to good purpose, the author offers fresh insights into the significance of complementary characters in dramatic literature.

There is a connexion between this sort of thinking and that of Norman Rabkin, who invokes the Buddha's readiness to admit the existence of absolute yet necessary contradictions as part of the very nature of things in support of his main thesis. His wide-ranging book, *Shakespeare and the Common Understanding*,[2] plunges straight into the problem of *Hamlet*, arguing that the confusions in which it involves us are, in fact, under the author's control, because the entire drama is built on a dialectic between conflicting ethical systems which are mutually exclusive yet equally demanding, thus leading to a series of unanswerable questions. This way of seeing things is, Rabkin contends, the authentic Shakespearian vision of life—it bears an obvious relationship, though he does not mention it, to the Keatsian idea of 'negative capability'—but it is not something confined to Shakespeare; it can also be seen in the work of others as diverse

[1] Bookland Private Limited, Calcutta, 1967. [2] The Free Press, New York, 1967.

as Homer, Vergil, Dante, Chaucer, and Tolstoy. It is, indeed, a mirror of life as we know it: something that cannot be reduced to any kind of logical consistency, but which has, nevertheless, its own harmonies. Moreover, this sort of vision finds a parallel in the ideas of some modern physicists, such as Nils Bohr and J. Robert Oppenheimer, whose book, *Science and the Common Understanding* (1954), Rabkin alludes to in his own title, for in it Oppenheimer sets out the notion of 'complementarity', an application to difficult problems in physics of the double vision we all have of the world we live in, seeing it simultaneously as that which exists outside and independent of us and also as that which is filtered through the individual subjective consciousness. From this original and impressive opening Rabkin goes on to develop an analysis of a number of the plays, designed to show not merely that Shakespeare had this sense of 'complementarity' and that his art was built on it, but also the manner in which the art and the vision modified each other by reciprocal action. There are, of course, interpretations about which one is disposed to quibble, but the overall theory commands a high degree of assent not only by virtue of its cogency but also because of the unassuming and reasonable tone in which it is advanced.

Wilbur Sanders, on the other hand, in his *The Dramatist and the Received Idea*[1] adopts a quite unnecessarily aggressive manner that is bound to antagonize many, is far too prone to scold those of whom he disapproves, and is not above practising a critical sleight of hand that does much to undercut the moral seriousness that he parades. It is simply not fair to draw a disparaging contrast between a soliloquy from *Edward II* and Hamlet's first soliloquy without mentioning that Shakespeare himself had written nothing at all comparable with Hamlet's lines at the time when Marlowe died. In fact, Sanders deliberately uses Marlowe as a whipping-boy and admits to having done so. Contrasting Shakespeare's poised response to the rich life of his time with that of the lesser men who could only react to the age with 'more or less unsatisfactory adjustments, ranging from ruinous dependence on a debased social code to an independence which is in danger of toppling over into mere assertiveness or a random impulse to *épater-les-bourgeois*', he adds: 'I have cast Marlowe to play this second and unenviable role' (p. 18). Furthermore, while much of the book is concerned with Elizabethan ideas about history, there is no mention in it of the work of such vitally important historians as Camden and Ralegh or of the modern historiographers, such as Fussner, who have done so much to make us see precisely what was happening to the writing of history at the time.

It has been necessary to clear the ground in this way because Sanders's book is, despite its asperities, a valuable one. It belongs to a critical tradition that has long been established at Cambridge, and that received its best-known formulation in recent years at the hands of L. C. Knights in his essay 'Historical Scholarship and the Interpretation of Shakespeare', first published in 1955 and since re-issued in *Further Explorations*. These *Studies in the Plays of Marlowe and Shakespeare*, to use Sanders's sub-title, are designed with two ends in view: first, to demonstrate that 'background studies' only assist in the appreciation of literature when they stem from, and are ancillary to, the critical response to that literature as a felt experience; and, secondly, to break what their author regards as the constricting stranglehold that historicism has now taken on our whole attitude to the Elizabethan–Jacobean period. The main targets of the attack are

[1] Cambridge University Press, 1968.

critics, such as E. M. W. Tillyard and Lily B. Campbell, who have concerned themselves with the 'Elizabethan World Picture' and with 'Mirrors of Policy' as valid lines of approach to the history plays, and others, such as W. C. Curry and Virgil K. Whitaker, who have seen the body of scholastic thinking, transmitted from the Middle Ages, as a decisive influence on Shakespeare's outlook, especially as it manifests itself in the tragedies. The plays considered in detail have been carefully chosen to serve the purposes of the argument. Convinced that Marlowe's reputation is 'distended', Sanders begins the process of deflation by examining *The Massacre at Paris*, which he sees as a betrayal of art, a jingoistic pandering to the worst tastes of the audience. Then follows a good discussion of *The Jew of Malta*, though there is no mention of the possibility that the play may be a demonstration of the ultimate emptiness of 'policy'; and this, in turn, leads on to a consideration of the political ideas of Machiavelli, which are found to be inadequate when weighed against the political insights of Shakespeare. Moving on at this point to *Richard III*, Sanders ditches the ending as unworthy of the rest of the play, saying nothing about its suitability as the ending of the first tetralogy, in order to concentrate—and very acutely he does it—on what he sees as the real heart of this drama: its subtle treatment of political problems when they cease to be abstract and become concrete, as they do, for example, in the scene of Clarence's murder. Unfortunately, the great abstract conception of providential history broods over the play in a manner that cannot be ignored; it is, therefore, regretted as a dramatic ineptitude, and then submitted to a hostile analysis for its inadequacy as a theory of history. *Edward II* is used to introduce a discussion of the relationship between the history play and morality, being compared, much to its disadvantage, with *Richard II*, which is regarded, following the lead given by E. W. Talbert, as a far more complex affair than it appears to those who see it as concerned essentially with 'the Divine Right of Kings'. For Sanders—and he writes very well about it—it is rather the product of what he describes as Shakespeare's political agnosticism, brought into play by the wide range of attitudes that existed at the time to such matters as the deposition of kings and the duties of subjects living in insecure states. An account of changing views on the subject of demonism preludes a useful analysis of *Doctor Faustus*, which raises the question of Marlowe's concern with the Calvinist doctrine of reprobation. The chapter devoted to this topic is really a protest against the horror of predestination as a theological idea, and a chiding of Marlowe for not realizing that it was a horror. There follows a chapter on *Macbeth*, which is to a considerable extent a return to the position of Bradley and Lascelles Abercrombie, and which is quite the best thing in the book. For Sanders, *Macbeth* is a play about the evil that exists both outside man and within him, something he can give himself to but also something that can take him over. Thomist notions of good and evil are dismissed as shallow and facile by comparison with the actual experience of evil that Shakespeare conveys. Here, as throughout the book, Sanders is at his best when writing sympathetically about something that matters deeply to him; his polemics never carry the same conviction.

Terence Eagleton's *Shakespeare and Society*[1] is a clumsy and unsuccessful attempt to enlist Shakespeare under the banner of Raymond Williams in the struggle for 'The Long Revolution'. His thesis is that after portraying conflicts between the individual and society in the tragedies and the dark comedies Shakespeare embodies his vision of how the two can work together in

---

[1] Chatto and Windus, 1967.

a harmonious and reciprocal fashion in the romances. Not surprisingly, Eagleton, knowing what he was looking for in Shakespeare, has found it, but only at the cost of doing considerable violence to the text. Like Humpty Dumpty, he makes words mean what he wants them to mean. Glaring examples appear at page 113, where a statement that Aufidius makes about himself is interpreted as a statement about Coriolanus, and again at page 128, where Cleopatra's rhapsodic praise of the absent Antony is described as biting satire. Factual errors abound; the author's English is slipshod; and the central argument is repeated time and again in the same limited vocabulary. The reader soon grows weary of 'spontaneity', 'authentic', 'reciprocal', 'gratuitous', and 'circular'. Eagleton admits in his introduction that he overworks the first three of these words, but excuses himself on the grounds 'that the terms will justify themselves, if the book is read as a whole'. The answer must be that they don't.

Repetitiveness is also the keynote, as the author himself says in the Preface, of G. Wilson Knight's *Shakespeare and Religion*,[1] a miscellaneous collection of essays, broadcast talks, reviews, and so forth, brought together partly as the result of a public demand, and partly because the appearance of R. M. Frye's *Shakespeare and Christian Doctrine* led Knight to the conclusion that much of what he had been saying had been misunderstood. The most interesting piece in it, from one point of view at least, is an essay entitled 'The Poet and Immortality' which first came out in 1928, for this brief work anticipates, especially in its treatment of Shakespeare's romances, a great deal in Knight's subsequent and better-known writing. In addition there is an introduction in which he tells us how he was first led into Shakespearian interpretation by a remark of his brother's, a long study of the Inca drama *Apu Ollantay* relating it to the romances, and a reprint of the article that came out in *Essays in Criticism*, xv (1965), rebutting the charges made against him by R. M. Frye and explaining precisely what the connexions between Shakespeare's work and the story of the New Testament, as he sees them, are. On the whole, however, it is not easy to discover any adequate justification for the publication of what are, in the main, occasional and ephemeral pieces that add little or nothing to the major works of their author.

Starting from the acknowledged fact that there has hitherto been too little study of Shakespeare's style and its development—probably because the whole subject is so extremely complex and difficult—Brian Vickers has written a long (over 450 pages) and ambitious book on the prose of the plays.[2] Convinced that the plays are poetic dramas, as distinct from dramatic poems, and that action and character are more basic than themes, he employs three main lines of approach in order to establish the nature and function of the prose passages in the plays where they occur. These are: first, through the imagery; secondly, through the linguistic structure of individual speeches; and, thirdly, through their rhetorical structure. Equipped with these tools, he then moves forward, in a roughly chronological fashion, treating the plays in groups. The heaviest stress falls naturally on the plays in which the prose is either dominant, as in *Much Ado About Nothing* and *As You Like It*, or at least as important as the verse, as in the two parts of *Henry IV*; but the advantages of handling the prose as an entity are particularly evident in the chapter dealing with Brutus and Hamlet as prose-speakers, and in that given over to the dark comedies, for in both these cases it serves to bring out aspects of the plays involved that are frequently overlooked—the relevance of the clown Lavache to *All's Well That Ends Well*, for

[1] Routledge and Kegan Paul, 1967.   [2] *The Artistry of Shakespeare's Prose* (Methuen, 1968).

example, and of the underworld of Vienna to *Measure for Measure*. Believing, with every justification, that Shakespeare mastered the art of prose before he mastered that of verse, Vickers thinks that the prose reached its maturity with the writing of *The Merchant of Venice*, and that thereafter the development that takes place is in the dramatic application of it rather than in any change within the structure of the prose as such; and he points to the fact that from the time of *Twelfth Night* onwards the witty solo speeches in prose, which are such a marked feature of *As You Like It* and of the plays in which Falstaff figures, give way to a prose of wit that is 'subordinated to character and situation more naturalistically conceived'. The observation seems just, but it does have the rather unfortunate consequence that the book loses some of its forward movement. This is further inhibited by the ruthless and unremitting fashion in which the author continues to apply his critical apparatus. One grows tired of seeing speech after speech set out on the page in such a way as to emphasize the isocolon, the parison, the antimetabole, and so forth that characterize it. The typographical devices are extremely useful for a time, but before the end they become wearisome. Furthermore, because passages with a strong rhetorical structure readily admit of analysis along these lines, they tend to receive an undue amount of attention at the expense not only of Shakespeare's development of a prose style that finds a place for speech rhythms, but also of the capacity he showed, especially evident in the speeches of Falstaff, for allowing poetic figures to work like leaven in the prose. Nevertheless, a great deal of new ground has been broken here, and both critics and editors will be grateful for the help they will find in these pages.

It would be hazardous to make the same prediction about Dorothy L. Sipe's *Shakespeare's Metrics*,[1] for this is not the general survey of Shakespeare's prosody that the title seems to promise, but rather an attempt to show that, contrary to the views of most critics, Shakespeare did not move towards a form of accentual verse but wrote 'carefully constructed *iambic* verse into which he introduced only those few minor variations considered permissible in his time. This means that his normative line consists of a succession of iambic feet, each containing two, and only two, syllables: the first unstressed, the second stressed...Shakespearian blank verse is overwhelmingly decasyllabic' (p. vii). The evidence for this statement is provided by a detailed examination of all the lines in which the choice of one word in preference to a syllabically different synonym (*bide* rather than *abide*, *'gainst* rather than *against*, etc.) was dictated, the author thinks, by purely metrical considerations. The lines involved run to about 13,000, yet only 63 of them 'show use of a variant that creates a trisyllabic or monosyllabic foot which could have been avoided had a synonym been chosen'. The method is ingenious, and the detailed discussion of synonyms that are syllabically different contains some useful ideas about how *OED* definitions might be improved; but it is hard not to conclude that the method followed has, at least in part, controlled the result. It does not follow that the five-sixths of Shakespeare's lines that have not been investigated fall into the same pattern. How for example, does Sipe scan Lear's 'Never, never, never, never, never'? One would like to see a full demonstration of the extent to which some of the speeches in the later plays conform to the decasyllabic iambic norm.

To revert to less technical matters, four lectures raise problems of a general interest. Taking

---

[1] Yale University Press, 1968.

up arms against a sea of Ph.D.s, G. K. Hunter[1] argues with wit and conciseness that there was no simple Senecan influence on Elizabethan tragedy. Ovid was at least as important, and so was the native tradition. In the first of a series of lectures given at the Folger Shakespeare Library in 1964,[2] which have now been published under the title *Shakespeare Celebrated*, C. V. Wedgwood deals with Shakespeare's depiction of the relations between rulers and ruled, connecting it with the historical situation. In the same volume Madeleine Doran[3] transfers Coleridge's description of the style of *Antony and Cleopatra, feliciter audax*, to Shakespeare's work in general, emphasizing that his natural gifts were for story-telling and for language, coupled with a constant urge to experiment. Wolfgang Clemen's Shakespeare Lecture to the British Academy[4] is of a more abstract nature. Taking up an idea first adumbrated in his *A Commentary on Shakespeare's 'Richard III'*, he examines the way in which the dramatist connects the past with the future in his plays.

A convenient transition to Shakespeare's first period is provided by A. C. Hamilton's *The Early Shakespeare*[5] which is based on the sound idea that the achievement of the first six or seven years can be far better appreciated if it is detached from the *œuvre* as a whole and treated as a separate entity. The book falls into five divisions: 'The Early History Plays' (*1, 2, and 3 Henry VI*) 'The Early Tragedy' (*Titus Andronicus*), 'The Early Comedies' (*The Comedy of Errors, The Two Gentlemen of Verona*, and *Love's Labour's Lost*), 'The Poems' (*Venus and Adonis* and *Lucrece*), and 'The Resolution of the Early Period' (*Richard III, Romeo and Juliet*, and *A Midsummer-Night's Dream*). The arrangement of the material is, perhaps, somewhat over-schematized, suggesting that the growth of Shakespeare's art was incredibly neat and sure; and, since *The Taming of the Shrew* is omitted with no explanation of why it has been left out, one has an uneasy suspicion that its inclusion might have disturbed the pattern. Nevertheless, the shift in perspective, together with Hamilton's readiness to look at these early works for what they are in themselves, asking to be judged by the standards of the time rather than in the light of Shakespeare's subsequent achievement, amply justify the experiment. He is especially illuminating on the subject of *Henry VI*, because he will have nothing to do with the idea that its primary purpose is didactic, and, consequently, is able to consider the three plays as pieces of dramatic writing. He is also extremely interesting on the vexed problem of *Titus Andronicus*, which he regards as an attempt to write the tragedy of terror, and which he relates very effectively to Book I of the *Metamorphoses*; and he has some good things to say about the connexions between the two narrative poems. About plays that have had their fair share of critical comment he has, naturally, less that is new to say; but the book as a whole is full of lively insights into the way in which Shakespeare's art was developing during the writing of these works.

Romeo and Juliet has certainly not been neglected by critics, yet there can be few who will not profit from Inge Leimberg's book-length study of it.[6] This thorough and well-organized

1 'Seneca and the Elizabethans: A Case-study in "Influence" ', *Shakespeare Survey 20* (Cambridge, 1967), 17–26.

2 'Shakespeare between Two Civil Wars', *Shakespeare Celebrated*, ed. Louis B. Wright (Cornell University Press, 1966), pp. 1–30.

3 'Shakespeare as an Experimental Dramatist', *ibid.* pp. 61–88.

4 'Past and Future in Shakespeare's Drama', *Proceedings of the British Academy*, LII (1966), 231–52.

5 The Huntington Library, San Marino, California, 1967.

6 *Shakespeare's 'Romeo und Julia'* (Wilhelm Fink Verlag, München, 1968).

monograph starts out from Kenneth Muir's view that generalizations about Shakespearian tragedy are useless, since there is no such thing: 'there are only Shakespearian tragedies'. Resisting strongly any tendency to moralize the play and to view the hero and heroine as slaves of passion, Leimberg takes much further than it has ever been taken before the idea tentatively set out by Molly Mahood in *Shakespeare's Wordplay* that *Romeo and Juliet* is, in fact, based on the *Liebestod* motive. This motive, it is suggested, came to Shakespeare and his age through the writings of the Neoplatonists, and especially from statements such as this by Ficino: 'love is a voluntary death...He who loves dies; for his consciousness, oblivious of himself, is devoted exclusively to the loved one...Therefore everyone who loves is dead in himself. But at least he lives in the other person'. This reading of the play is introduced and well supported by a brief examination of two earlier love tragedies: *Tancred and Gismund*, where there is already an attempt to create sympathy for the tragic figures as well as to teach; and *Soliman and Perseda*, in which Love, Fortune, and Death play such a large part. In these plays, however, the playwrights have no adequate means to hand for making feeling vocal. It was in the work of the sonneteers, Leimberg contends, and, above all, in that of Samuel Daniel, who is treated with great understanding and appreciation, that the Senecan tendency towards moralizing was finally overcome and replaced by an attitude that could regard myths, like those of Actaeon and Icarus, as something more potent and moving than mere warnings. As the sub-title of the book, *Von der Sonnetdichtung zur Liebestragödie*, indicates, the basis of Leimberg's interpretation of the play is that there was an intimate connexion between it and the Elizabethan sonnet sequence. A similar reading of the central significance of the play is offered by Warren D. Smith,[1] though he reaches his conclusion by another route, finding the reunion of the lovers on the other side of death as something that is implicit in Romeo's account, at the beginning of v, i, of his dream; and also by Joseph S. M. J. Chang,[2] who thinks that there are marks of uncertainty in Shakespeare's control of language throughout the play, but that the use of oxymorons is thematic, since the drama is about the intertwining of love and hate, body and soul, life and death.

The gaiety that might be expected in a shift from tragedy to comedy is certainly not evident in *Shakespeare's Early Comedies*, by Blaze Odell Bonazza.[3] Sub-titled *A Structural Analysis*, it makes the basic assumption—with which there is likely to be little quarrel—that *A Midsummer-Night's Dream* is a better play, and a more complex play from the structural point of view, than any of the previous comedies. The 'proof' offered is a detailed account of what happens in *The Comedy of Errors*, *Love's Labour's Lost*, and *The Two Gentlemen of Verona*, making the obvious point that in these plays there are only two or three interlocking plots, whereas *A Midsummer-Night's Dream* makes use of four. It does not, apparently, occur to the author that *The Comedy of Errors* and *Love's Labour's Lost* have a different plot structure from that of *A Midsummer-Night's Dream* because they are radically different plays from it, just as they are radically different from each other, the one depending largely on plot for its effect, and the other on near-absence of plot for its. Like Hamilton, Bonazza does not seem to consider the recalcitrant *Shrew* an early comedy. A modification of the approach to Shakespearian comedy set out in Northrop

1 'Romeo's Final Dream', *Modern Language Review*, LXII (1967), 579–83.
2 'The Language of Paradox in *Romeo and Juliet*', *Shakespeare Studies*, III (1967), 22–42.
3 Mouton and Co., The Hague, 1966.

Frye's *A Natural Perspective* is suggested by Sherman Hawkins,[1] who observes that the idea of 'the green world' is strictly applicable only to those comedies in which there are two sharply contrasted locales and does not really fit the others, like *Much Ado* and *Twelfth Night*, which are confined to one place, and where the action is precipitated by intrusion from without. He therefore proposes two patterns: that of the journey, as in *As You Like It*; and that of the siege, as in *Twelfth Night*. Taking a wider view, Analendu Bose in 'A Preface to Shakespearean Comedy'[2] sees Shakespeare's comic art as something derived from the Middle Ages, but informed by a spirit of freedom, and affirming a faith in life and in man.

Writing on *The Two Gentlemen of Verona*, Anselm Schlösser[3] distinguishes the concern with aristocratic and courtly values in the play from the middle-class *mores* of *The Comedy of Errors* and *The Taming of the Shrew*, and then goes on to argue that the difficult ending poses a real problem to which the idea of forgiveness is no satisfactory answer.

Taking the line that wit is only one aspect of a larger preoccupation in *Love's Labour's Lost* with the relationship between fancy and reality, Joseph Westlund[4] claims that this comedy is a prelude to the more extended discussion of the role of the imagination in *A Midsummer-Night's Dream*. The songs at the end of the play are the subject of an article by Catherine M. McLay,[5] arguing that they are strictly functional and provide the key to the unity of the work.

David P. Young's *Something of Great Constancy: The Art of 'A Midsummer-Night's Dream'*[6] is a good, unpretentious piece of critical writing, which, without making any claim to originality, in fact achieves it because the aim of understanding just what Shakespeare is doing is kept constantly in mind throughout. The conviction out of which it comes is the author's agreement with Frank Kermode that *A Midsummer-Night's Dream* is no apprentice work but, in many ways, 'Shakespeare's best comedy'. In order to substantiate this claim, Young seeks to synthesize the best that has been written about the play with his own personal response to it. The book falls into three sections: first, an examination of the dramatic and the non-dramatic background, with a strong emphasis on Shakespeare's manipulation of audience response; secondly, an analysis of the stylistic and structural virtuosity that has gone into its making; and, thirdly, an exploration of the themes, showing that they have a close connexion both with Shakespeare's art in general and with his attitude to that art. Each section is full and competent, though it is rather surprising that in a work which takes account of so much there is no mention of the stimulus Shakespeare must have found in the 'stuffed owl' quality of Golding's version of the story of Pyramus and Thisbe; that Muriel Bradbrook's stress on the unifying power of the idea of metamorphosis is ignored; and that no reference is made to Ernest Schanzer's essay on the Fairies. These omissions are, however, largely compensated for by the fullness and freshness of the last section, where Young uses Hippolyta's speech, from which he derives his title, as the

1 'The Two Worlds of Shakespearean Comedy', *Shakespeare Studies*, III (1967), 62–80.
2 *Essays on Shakespeare* (University of Burdwan Shakespeare Memorial Volume), ed. Bhabatosh Chatterjee (Calcutta, 1965), pp. 55–75.
3 'Betrachtungen über *Die Beide Veroneser*', *Shakespeare-Jahrbuch*, CIII (1967), 145–61.
4 'Fancy and Achievement in *Love's Labour's Lost*', *Shakespeare Quarterly*, XVIII (1967), 37–46.
5 'The Dialogue of Spring and Winter: A Key to the Unity of *Love's Labour's Lost*', *Shakespeare Quarterly*, XVIII (1967), 119–27.
6 Yale University Press, 1966.

lead-in to a valuable discussion of Elizabethan ideas about the imagination and its function, about the relation between art and nature, and about the nature of change which he regards as basic to the whole play. A similar interpretation, in a briefer compass, is given by John A. Allen,[1] who finds in the meeting of Bottom (the man become ass) and Titania (goddess of both fertility and chastity) the perfect expression of that 'concord of this discord' which lies at the heart of the comedy.

John W. Draper[2] seeks to relate *The Merchant of Venice* to Elizabethan history. Pointing out that Shakespeare transforms the shadowy figure of Ansaldo in *Il Pecorone* into 'the ideal man of commerce and affairs, as the Elizabethans conceived of that ideal', he draws an interesting parallel between Antonio and the great Elizabethan financier Sir Horatio Pallavicino who was in some difficulties about the time when the play was written.

A radical re-appraisal is proposed by Paul and Miriam Mueschke in their close-packed and well-argued article 'Illusion and Metamorphosis in *Much Ado About Nothing*'.[3] Far from being the gayest of the joyous comedies, it is, they contend, essentially reflective with marked tragic undertones. They see in it pronounced similarities to *Othello*, especially evident in its concern with honour, which they regard as the basic issue in it, and with the harm caused by a malicious villain. Parallels are also drawn with *Troilus and Cressida*. The writers do not, perhaps, allow sufficiently for the modifying effect that Dogberry and Verges have on the tone and tension of the play; but this is certainly an essay of fundamental importance. William G. McCollom,[4] on the other hand, thinks the comedy is about 'the struggle of true wit (or wise folly) in alliance with harmless folly against false wisdom'; while Denzell S. Smith[5] holds that its main concern is with confusion which reaches its climax in Beatrice's command 'Kill Claudio'. J. C. Maxwell has a useful note,[6] demonstrating that Antonio cannot be present at the Church scene.

'*Twelfth Night*' and *Shakespeare's Comic Art*[7] is a brief monograph on the play by Peter Bryant who argues that Orsino's initial folly is 'romanticised rather than satirised', and raises objections to the notion that the function of the action is to bring the characters to self-knowledge. He receives some support from Elias Schwarz, whose essay '*Twelfth Night* and the Meaning of Shakespearean Comedy'[8] is deeply indebted to the ideas of C. L. Barber.

Interest in the history plays appears to be on the decline, but Arthur R. Humphreys provides a concise and informative survey of the growth of historical writing in the sixteenth century, stressing Shakespeare's debt to it, as well as the capacity for historical thinking that he had, in his lecture 'Shakespeare and the Tudor Reception of History'.[9] Published posthumously and privately, Beryl Pogson's *Royalty of Nature* (1968) is not for sale to the public. The interpretation of the histories that it provides is a mixture of the narrative and the esoteric, but there are flashes of insight such as the comment that Richard III offers 'the ironical spectacle of a brilliant

1 'Bottom and Titania', *Shakespeare Quarterly*, XVIII (1967), 107–17.
2 'Shakespeare's Antonio and the Queen's Finance', *Neophilologus*, LI (1967), 178–85.
3 *Shakespeare Quarterly*, XVIII (1967), 53–65.
4 'The Role of Wit in *Much Ado About Nothing*', *Shakespeare Quarterly*, XIX (1968), 165–74.
5 'The Command "Kill Claudio" in *Much Ado About Nothing*', *English Language Notes*, IV (1966–7), 181–3.
6 'The Church Scene in *Much Ado*: the Absence of Antonio', *Notes and Queries*, n.s., XIV (1967), 135.
7 University of Port Elizabeth, 1967.
8 *College English*, XXVIII (1966–7), 508–19.   9 *Shakespeare Celebrated*, pp. 89–112.

intellect brought to ruin through *ignorance* of his relation to the universe'. Kenneth Muir crams a lot of matter into his article 'Image and Symbol in Shakespeare's Histories'.[1] He finds that the incidence of imagery in *1 Henry VI*, sometimes frequent, sometimes totally absent, supports the case for dual authorship; and that the quality of it in Young Clifford's speech over his father's body in *2 Henry VI* indicates that this passage must have been written at a later date than the rest of the play. He draws attention to the use of theatrical imagery in *Richard III*; and he concludes that the imagery of *Henry VIII* does not support the theory of dual author- ship. James L. Calderwood[2] has also examined the imagery of *2 Henry VI*, and thinks it was already beginning to fall into significant patterns. In 'Sidney, Shakespeare, and the "Slain-not- slain" '[3] Alan D. Isler makes comparisons and draws a contrast between Sidney's handling of the commons' revolt in Book II of his *Arcadia* and Shakespeare's treatment of the mob in *2 Henry VI* and *Julius Caesar*.

W. H. Clemen's monumental *Kommentar zu Shakespeare's 'Richard III'*, first published at Göttingen in 1957, has now been translated by Jean Bonheim under the title *A Commentary on Shakespeare's 'Richard III'*.[4] Moving forward slowly and methodically, scene by scene, it contains much acute observation of detail and some good comments on the relationship between Shake- speare's dramaturgy and that of his predecessors, but, even though the sections of the original work dealing with Shakespeare's treatment of his sources have been omitted from this English version, it still remains a long book. Ronald Berman in his 'Anarchy and Order in *Richard III* and *King John*'[5] sees the two plays as being set off from the other histories by the tough, cynical, and realistic wit of Richard and the Bastard. Both are 'new men', materialists and pragmatists, but, unlike Richard, the Bastard does ultimately become assimilated into the mystery of love for his country.

One aspect of the second tetralogy is the theme of a good article by Robert Hapgood that covers much ground. 'Shakespeare's Thematic Modes of Speech: *Richard II* to *Henry V*'[6] starts from the observation that *Hamlet* is governed by the interrogative mood. In *Richard II*, how- ever, denunciation is dominant; in *1 Henry IV*, retrospection; in *2 Henry IV*, report; and in *Henry V*, dispute. But, throughout the plays in which he appears, Hal represents the anti-mode, speaking directly, looking to the future, and calling for concord in a world of dissension.

Asking 'Who Deposed Richard the Second?'[7] A. L. French concludes that Richard deposed himself. He is wrong, however, in his belief that critics of the play have all thought the answer should be 'Bolingbroke'. Walter Pater knew better. More recently both Irving Ribner and E. W. Talbert have drawn attention to the inadequacy of Tillyard's interpretation, making precisely the points against it that French does. More important still, Talbert shows pretty con- clusively that the ambiguities concerning Richard's deposition, as they arise within the play, are not evidence, as French thinks, of a failure on Shakespeare's part, but of his extraordinarily percipient grasp both of the difficulties inherent in the matter he was handling and of the double- edged nature of the problem as it presented itself to Elizabethan eyes. Takako Uchigama[8] finds

1 *Bulletin of the John Rylands Library*, L (1967), 103–23.
2 'Shakespeare's Evolving Imagery: *2 Henry VI*', *English Studies*, XLVIII (1967), 481–93.
3 *University of Toronto Quarterly*, XXVII (1967–8), 175–85.   4 Methuen, 1968.
5 *Shakespeare Survey 20* (1967), 51–9.   6 *Ibid.* 41–8.   7 *Essays in Criticism*, XVII (1967), 411–33.
8 'The Three Themes in One Harmonious Chord', *Shakespeare Studies (Japan)*, V (1966–7), 88–118.

three themes in the play: the fall of England, the Tudor myth, and the personal tragedy of the king. There is a cogent note by J. C. Maxwell[1] on the significance of kings' long arms.

The old question of whether 'the education of the Prince' is, or is not, the theme of *Henry IV* continues to raise its head. David Berkeley and Donald Eidson[2] join voices to say no, because, as they see it, Hal does not change; instead, he practises dissimulation until he can show his true worth at Shrewsbury. Charles Mitchell, however, in 'The Education of the True Prince',[3] comes down on the other side, since he thinks that Part I corresponds to Hal's state as man, and Part II to his state as king. One cannot but welcome Alan Gerald Gross's attempt to cut the knot by arguing in 'The Text of Hal's First Soliloquy'[4] that the compositor is the real cause of the trouble. His view is that after Shakespeare wrote Hal's first soliloquy he changed his mind about the design of the play. Lines 1–9 and 14–23 represent the original version, and lines 10–13 ('If all the yeere...rare accidents') the revision. Unfortunately, the compositor printed both. Two independent articles, one by J. D. Schuchter[5] and the other by S. P. Zitner,[6] reach approximately the same conclusion about the puzzling scene between Hal and Francis in *1 Henry IV*, II, iv, namely, that Hal is making Francis feel the same pull of conflicting obligations that he is subject to himself: that of doing his duty, and that of rebelling against it. 'The Melancholy of Moor-Ditch: A Gloss of *1 Henry IV*, I, ii, 87–8', by Bridget Gilbert,[7] brings forward some new evidence to show that Moorfields was commonly associated with melancholy; and Richard L. McGuire emphasizes the importance of the play-acting in II, iv, both as marking the real end of the Hal–Falstaff relationship, and as a pre-view of III, ii.[8]

Northrop Frye's Alexander Lectures for 1966 are the obvious point of departure for any consideration of criticism of the tragedies. *Fools of Time*[9] begins well with the assertion that being in time, which is the essence of the ironic vision, is only part of the tragic vision where there is 'a counter-movement of being that we call the heroic'. It also ends well with the statement that when the tragedy is over 'it is not what the characters have learned from their tragic experience, but what we have learned from participating in it, that directly confronts us'. But the matter in between is disappointing. Frye tries to divide the tragedies up into three categories: tragedies of order (*Julius Caesar*, *Hamlet*, and *Macbeth*); tragedies of passion (*Romeo and Juliet*, *Troilus and Cressida*, *Coriolanus*, and *Antony and Cleopatra*); and tragedies of isolation (*Othello*, *King Lear*, and *Timon of Athens*). The scheme is much too arbitrary—*Macbeth* could equally well be a tragedy of isolation, *Lear* a tragedy of order, and *Hamlet* a tragedy of passion—and, in the event, Frye himself cannot keep his categories separate; the three chapters overlap with each other, and the outline becomes blurred. In fact, no clear-cut or precise line of argument emerges. There is much about *de jure* and *de facto* kingship, about the Apollonian and the Dionysian, about the White Goddess and Adonais (Frye even sees poor Ophelia's 'a-down-a' as a reference to him!), and about time and nemesis. But the mixture of political ideas, Nietzsche,

---

1 '*Richard II*, IV, i, 11–12', *Notes and Queries*, n.s., XIV (1967), 135.

2 'The Theme of *Henry IV, Part I*', *Shakespeare Quarterly*, XIX (1968), 25–31.

3 *Tennessee Studies in Literature*, XII (1967), 13–21.   4 *English Miscellany*, XVIII (1967), 49–54.

5 'Prince Hal and Francis: The Imitation of an Action', *Shakespeare Studies*, III (1967), 128–37.

6 'Anon, Anon: or, a Mirror for a Magistrate', *Shakespeare Quarterly*, XIX (1968), 63–70.

7 *Shakespeare Quarterly*, XVIII (1967), 70–1.   8 'The Play-within-the-play in *1 Henry IV*', *ibid.* 47–52.

9 Toronto University Press; Oxford University Press, 1967.

mythology, and so forth, never jells. Frye attempts to pull too many different approaches together, with the result that there is confusion of the kind typified by his remark that at the end of *Antony and Cleopatra* 'the two ends of the wheel confront each other' (p. 73).

Marco Mincoff, in his lecture 'Shakespeare, Fletcher and Baroque Tragedy',[1] is equally learned but far more precise. For him, the essence of Shakespearian tragedy lies in its concern with a state of war within the hero, a vision of the human predicament that was only possible when the pulls of religious ties on the one hand and social ties on the other were roughly equal, thus allowing independence of choice to the individual. In the early seventeenth century, however, especially among the upper class, morality became increasingly a social rather than a religious obligation, and it is this, he holds, that lies behind the tragedies of Fletcher, for here there is no sense of mystery. As a result, where Shakespearian tragedy finds its centre in a specific personality, Fletcherian finds its in a concept or theme. The analysis is borne out by a consideration of structure. Mincoff asserts that Shakespeare's tragedies have a firm pyramidal shape, whereas Baroque tragedy is far more hectic and unstable in its resort to one climax after another. Combining width of scholarship with critical penetration, this lecture is essentially a plea for a return to Bradley.

Three other essays on the tragedies may be grouped together. Marvin Spevack's 'Hero and Villain in Shakespeare: On Dualism and Tragedy'[2] argues that tragic drama is not a dualistic conflict. In Shakespearian tragedy villains are comparatively rare; it is the state of the hero, destined to defeat, that really matters. Nirmal Mustaph[3] is of the opinion that Shakespeare accepted the Thomist view of evil as the negation of good; and A. D. Mukherji,[4] after reviewing the final speeches in the tragedies, decides that the ending always represents a return to normality but excludes moralizing.

Ernest Schanzer's view that the Antony of *Julius Caesar* is different from the hero of *Antony and Cleopatra* is attacked by Lois Spencer in 'The Antony Perspective'.[5] She thinks that the Antony of Plutarch's narrative has a 'consistent inconsistency' which Shakespeare exploits in both plays. Jay L. Halio puts forward the thesis in '*Hamartia*, Brutus and the Failure of Personal Confrontation'[6] that Brutus, since he loved Caesar, should have sought to cure him not kill him.

Eleanor Prosser's *Hamlet and Revenge*[7] is exciting and provocative. It takes its rise out of her perception of a critical dilemma. Impressed by the exposition of orthodox Christian ideas on the subject of repentance that pervades Claudius's prayer, and, at the same time, appalled by the vindictive reasons Hamlet gives for his decision not to kill the king, she found it impossible to believe that Shakespeare either expected or desired his audience to approve of the hero at this point. She was thus led on to question, first the assumption that the desire to damn one's victim was an accepted convention of the revenge play, and then, more basically, the notion that the Ghost is 'an honest ghost'. The answer to her first question she has sought in a thorough examination of the ethics underlying the revenge plays shown between 1562 and 1607. Her conclusion is that with a few exceptions—the most notable being *Antonio's Revenge*—the man who takes

---

1 *Shakespeare Survey 20* (Cambridge,1967), 1–15.   2 *Tennessee Studies in Literature*, XII (1967), 1–11.
3 'Evil and the Shakespearian Prism', *Essays on Shakespeare*, pp. 85–108.
4 'Last Words in Shakespearean Tragedy', *ibid.* pp. 21–30.
5 *The London Review*, II (Autumn, 1967), 20–9.   6 *The Personalist*, XLVIII (1967–8), 42–55.
7 Stanford University Press, Stanford, California; Oxford University Press, 1967.

blood revenge is subject to moral condemnation, though he may well have engaged the sympathies of the audience on other grounds. There is, however, an element of plod about this part of the book. It really comes to life when Prosser turns to *Hamlet* itself, for her main thesis is that the Ghost is an instrument of darkness. To the present reviewer it seems that more is expected in the way of pneumatology on the part of the Elizabethan audience, and of their capacity to apply it during the course of an exciting action, than is reasonable; but there is no getting away from the fact that the Ghost, when it makes its revelation to Hamlet, is intensely vindictive, and that it lays an impossible burden on him when it tells him 'Taint not thy mind', since every word it utters is designed to have this effect. With the Ghost established as the agent of evil, the play becomes much tidier. Hamlet rightly weighs private revenge against the teaching of the Church, the Renaissance belief in action against the medieval virtue of patience—this, it is argued, is the essential matter of 'To be or not to be'—but his passions are deeply engaged, so that the Play Scene is conclusive. He commits himself to action, kills Polonius, sends Rosencrantz and Guildenstern to it without a qualm, and is, in fact, hell-bent up to the opening of Act v. Here a change takes place. Abandoning all ideas of private revenge—a view that hardly squares with the evidence of v, ii, 63–70—he entrusts things to Providence, which then produces an appropriate outcome, enabling him to carry out his task free from the stigma of contrived murder. Prosser's reading of the play has its attractions, especially as she remains aware throughout that Hamlet's situation must engage the sympathies of an audience on his side, but it has been reached by a process of simplification. Rabkin surely comes nearer to the heart of the matter.

So, too, does Nigel Alexander in a concise, witty essay, entitled 'Critical Disagreement about Œdipus and Hamlet',[1] that deals persuasively with difficult problems. The basic argument is that neither Sophocles in the *Oedipus Tyrannus*, nor Shakespeare in *Hamlet*, provide sufficient information at crucial points in their plays to enable us to give positive answers to the dilemmas they present. Being dramatists, both offer, not intellectual solutions, but dramatic resolutions. P. R. Grover,[2] though his main interest is in the attitudes towards *Hamlet* adopted by L. C. Knights and D. A. Traversi, does make the point that if the state is to be purged Hamlet has no alternative but to act. Jay L. Halio,[3] on the other hand, thinks that there are two other courses open to the hero, apart from that of killing the king: the exercise of Christian forbearance, and an effort to bring Claudius to repentance. Wendy Coppedge, in her prize essay 'Theater as Metaphor in *Hamlet*'[4] points out that many of the characters contrive scenes in order to manipulate others. Jagarnath Chakravorty[5] agrees substantially with Dr Johnson about the meaning of 'To be or not to be', while Toshikazu Oyama[6] attempts to relate it to the questions Hamlet puts to the Ghost in I, iv. Two critics write about Hamlet and Ophelia. Jasodhara Bagchi[7] thinks the bitterness with which Hamlet talks to her is a distillation of that crisis in humanism

1 *Shakespeare Survey 20* (Cambridge, 1967), 33–40.
2 'The Ghost of Dr. Johnson', *Essays in Criticism*, XVII (1967), 143–57.
3 'Hamlet's Alternatives', *Texas Studies in Literature and Language*, VIII (1966), 169–88.
4 Harvard University Press, 1967.
5 ' "To be or not to be": An Interpretation', *Essays on Shakespeare*, pp. 122–7.
6 'Hamlet's Dichotomy and the Elizabethan Demonology', *The English Review* (*Japan*), V (July 1967), 1–15.
7 'Hamlet and the Problem of Love', *Essays on Shakespeare*, pp. 145–59.

that came about around 1600; and Carol J. Carlisle[1] considers the comments that actors have made about the Nunnery Scene. 'Hamlet and Orestes',[2] by Jan Kott (translated by Boleslaw Taborski), is a confused and confusing attempt to relate the two figures. A more successful piece of comparison is '*The Spanish Tragedy* and Hamlet', the first and most recent essay in a volume of collected essays by Rudolph Stamm, entitled *The Shaping Powers at Work*.[3] Acknowledging Kyd as the first master of significant gesture in English drama, Stamm goes on to demonstrate how much more rapid, allusive, and organic gesture is in *Hamlet*. Challenging the generally accepted idea that 'blank' in such passages as *Hamlet* IV, i, 42 means 'the white spot in the centre of a target', J. R. Hale[4] brings forward a formidable amount of evidence to show that its real significance is 'point-blank range'.

The plays dealt with by William B. Toole in *Shakespeare's Problem Plays*[5] are the same four that E. M. W. Tillyard treated in his book of the same title. There the resemblance between the two works ends. Tillyard's criticism was always characterized by good sense; Toole's lucubrations are notably deficient in that quality. The assumption on which the book rests is that some of Shakespeare's plays are similar in pattern to *The Divine Comedy*, not because he knew Dante's work, but because he was aware of the native tradition of mystery cycles and moralities. A run-of-the-mill gallop through the history of medieval drama, intended to support this idea, generates unease. This is transformed into distinct distrust by Toole's readiness to assume that he knows what an Elizabethan audience would have felt and thought on any given occasion, and it hardens into active dissent when he says that they would have seen Malvolio's desire to marry Viola (*sic*) as evidence of his failure 'to accept God's construction of the universe' (p. 26). But there is worse to come. In his relentless pursuit of analogies, Toole commits himself to the statement that 'Helena's act in interposing her body to save Bertram from sin takes its significance from its correspondence to the act of Christ which afforded salvation to mankind' (p. 184), and he makes the same 'interpretation' of Mariana's taking Isabella's place in Angelo's bed. Now, quite apart from the question of whether Bertram has been saved from sin—he has certainly committed adultery in his heart—the obvious fact is that Helena has not sought to save him from doing so, but to conceive a child by him; and we are left in no doubt about Mariana's motives: she wants Angelo to make love to her because her passion for him has become 'violent and unruly' (III, i, 236), and in order to confirm her 'title to him' (IV, i, 72). These motives, surely, have nothing to do with the Atonement. That there are morality elements in both plays can be accepted, but the argument for them loses much from this kind of forcing. Moreover, Toole is altogether too sure about what God's purpose is in *Hamlet*—his notion that the killing of Claudius at prayer is part of it does little credit to God, nor does the view that Ophelia is the victim of his 'iron justice'.

Troilus and Cressida is too much for even Toole's analogical gymnastics to cope with, and has to be abandoned as 'something of an anomaly', though he does place it among the tragedies. So does J. Oates Smith[6] who defines its peculiar nature rather well by calling it 'the "tragedy"

---

1 'Hamlet's "Cruelty" in the Nunnery Scene: The Actors' View', *Shakespeare Quarterly*, XVIII (1967), 131–40.
2 *PMLA*, LXXXII (1967), 303–13. 3 Heidelberg, 1967.
4 'The True Shakespearian Blank', *Shakespeare Quarterly*, XIX (1968), 33–40.
5 Mouton and Co., The Hague, 1966.
6 'Essence and Existence in Shakespeare's *Troilus and Cressida*', *Philological Quarterly*, XLVI (1967), 167–85.

whose basis is the impossibility of conventional tragedy'. Its great theme is infidelity, and it leads to no affirmation of values, because it is concerned with the 'philosophic split between the realm of the eternal and that of the existential'. P. K. Guha, however, in his 'The Plot Structure of *Troilus and Cressida*',[1] thinks it is a comedy in which the love story and the story of the Trojan War are integrated with each other because in both the central theme is 'the un-manning influence of woman on man'. 'Cressida, Achilles, and the Finite Deed', by Charles Lyons,[2] is a good article, drawing attention to the parallel between Ulysses' attempt to make Achilles act as if he were the Achilles of his past exploits and Troilus' effort to maintain a con-stant Cressida. The play, he thinks, portrays the self-consuming nature of experience and the disintegration of the individual identity. Karl F. Thompson[3] seeks to reconcile the two conflict-ing views of Ulysses: that he is a model statesman; and that he is a manipulator of others who delights in exposing their follies. His solution is to suggest that Ulysses is a Stoic, who, while appreciating the nobility of statecraft, is also ready to laugh at the hazards involved in its practice. Taking up the difficult problem of Hector's *volte-face* in II, ii, Jean Gager[4] relates it to Renaissance ideas about humour, and especially to the belief that 'the imputation of coward-ice is a wrong too grievous for a mortal man to bear'.

As a follow-up to her recent book on *Measure for Measure*, Josephine Waters Bennett has now written a substantial article, entitled 'New Techniques of Comedy in *All's Well That Ends Well*',[5] adopting a similar line of approach. Contrary to the views of most critics, she is of the opinion that *All's Well* followed *Measure for Measure* and represents a 'marked advance in technique' over it. Her main reason for believing it to be the later of the two is that she con-siders that Shakespeare developed the character of Helena out of that of Mariana who also won her man by resorting to the bed-trick. The new technique that Shakespeare perfected in this play was, she contends, that of distancing the action in which Bertram and Helena are involved by forcing the audience to see it through the eyes of the old, thus preventing any undue engage-ment with it, and so preserving the over-all tone and atmosphere of comedy. The argument is pushed forward in a breezy, confident fashion, but it is hard not to feel that there is a certain insensitivity here to the reverberation of some of the poetry. G. Lambin[6] has two good notes on the play. He defends the reading 'gentle Astringer' (v, i, 7 S. D.) on the grounds that such a court official, appearing at Marseilles, adds a touch of local colour, since the marshes of the Rhone delta would be the perfect place for him to fly the royal hawks. He also relates 'young Charbon the puritan, and old Poysam the papist' (I, iii, 55) to an equivocal French proverb, 'Jeune chair et vieux Poisson'.

Moving away from current preconceptions about *Measure for Measure*, Roger Sale[7] holds that Shakespeare's primary concern in it is not with the well-being of his characters, still less with any kind of Christian allegory, but with doing the best that can be done, which involves the use of some shady devices, within a corrupt society. R. J. Kaufmann,[8] too, thinks that the

[1] *Essays on Shakespeare*, pp. 1–20. [2] *Études Anglaises*, XX (1967), 233–42.

[3] 'The Unknown Ulysses', *Shakespeare Quarterly*, XIX (1968), 125–8.

[4] 'Hector's Honor', ibid. 129–37. [5] *Shakespeare Quarterly*, XVIII (1967), 337–62.

[6] 'De Longues Notes sur de Brefs Passages Shakespeariens', *Études Anglaises*, XX (1967), 58–68.

[7] 'The Comic Mode of *Measure for Measure*', *Shakespeare Quarterly*, XIX (1968), 55–61.

[8] 'Bond Slaves and Counterfeits: Shakespeare's *Measure for Measure*', *Shakespeare Studies*, III (1967), 85–97.

play is about people, but for him these people are in bondage to their own limited notions about chastity, justice, and so on. Ronald Berman, in 'Shakespeare and the Law',[1] argues that such 'doctrine' as there is in the play is derived from Paul's Epistle to the Romans, the central authority for Reformation moral psychology.

Striving to restore Othello to the central position in the tragedy by making him primarily responsible for the disaster in which he is involved, R. N. Hallstead[2] offers an explicitly Christian reading of it that comes very close to Iago's. Indeed, the Ancient is quoted with approval on more than one occasion. The basic idea is that Othello elevates Desdemona to the position of God, but, at the same time, discovers his and her sexuality, thus opening the way for the disillusion that will lead him to murder her. For Hallstead, the pearl that Othello speaks of just before he stabs himself is his Christian faith; but John E. Seaman,[3] following up the possible reference to Matthew xiii, 45–6, concludes that it is Desdemona. 'Good Name in *Othello*', by Madeleine Doran,[4] is really helpful. It resorts to medieval law to establish that a man's good name is a property he was born with; that it can be lost or taken away; and that the restoration of it is possible, though difficult. The enemy of good fame is slander; and slander is Iago's weapon. Othello's final speech is meant, not to cheer himself up, but to clear himself of ill fame. Wayne Dodd's ' "But I'll Set down the Pegs that Make This Music" '[5] is important, since it argues that Iago does not mean that he will slacken the strings, but that he will call the tune. Rodney Poisson has two useful notes. In ' "Which heaven has forbid the Ottomites" ',[6] he suggests that these words are a reference to the much admired discipline of the Turkish forces; and in '*Othello* v, ii, 347: "The Base Indian" Yet Again'[7] he directs attention to two passages in Thomas Milles's *The Treasurie of Ancient and Moderne Times* which seems to have a bearing on the crux.

Paul A. Jorgensen's book, *Lear's Self-Discovery*,[8] is really an essay that has got out of hand; and the title is somewhat misleading. 'Self-discovery' suggests a process deliberately willed, which the experience Lear undergoes is not. Jorgensen is led to the use of this title by his awareness that 'self-knowledge' meant, for the Renaissance in general, a recognition of one's errors of judgment, and by his realization that a word of such a limited significance is quite inadequate to describe what Lear comes to understand, both about himself and about mankind, as a consequence of the suffering he is forced into, first by his own actions and then by those of others. What the author essentially says—and it is worth saying—is that Shakespeare in this play radically extended the whole meaning of 'self-knowledge'. But, in order to make a book of it, he tries to relate what is said and done in the play to a number of works on the subject of *nosce teipsum* that Shakespeare might, or might not, have read. Soji Iwasari's 'Time and Truth in *King Lear*'[9] is an interesting iconographical reading of the play which gains from not claiming too much for itself. The main idea in it is that Cordelia (*Veritas*) is *temporis filia*, and that after

1 *Shakespeare Quarterly*, XVIII (1967), 141–50.
2 'Idolatrous Love: A New Approach to *Othello*', *Shakespeare Quarterly*, XIX (1968), 107–24.
3 'Othello's Pearl', *ibid*. 81–5.   4 *Studies in English Literature*, VII (1967), 195–217.
5 *Neuphilologische Mitteilungen*, LXVIII (1967), 321–6.   6 *Shakespeare Quarterly*, XVIII (1967), 67–70.
7 *Modern Language Review*, LXII (1967), 209–11.
8 University of California Press, Berkeley and Los Angeles, 1967.
9 *Shakespeare Studies (Japan)*, V (1966–7), 1–42.

her banishment time is needed before she can reappear. Edmund, Goneril, and Regan are all compounds of Envy, Slander and Strife, while Lear is Innocence, but also Time. Betty Kantor Stuart[1] thinks that *King Lear* is not a Christian play, and that it makes no affirmation. What it offers is a true picture of life on this earth. H. A. Mason, in a discursive essay of considerable length,[2] contends that Lear learns nothing but 'dies an obstinately unreconstructed rebel', and that it is really Gloucester who is at the centre of Act III, since he stands for decency and suffers as a consequence. Russell A. Peck,[3] makes out a good case for the view that Edgar is the most important figure in the sub-plot, perhaps the second figure to Lear in the play, because his search for identity parallels the King's.

There are two articles about *Macbeth* to be noted. Harry Morris, writing on '*Macbeth*, Dante, and the Greatest Evil'[4] considers that Macbeth is guilty of all the sins for which Judas, Brutus, and Cassius are punished in the *Inferno*, and, without going so far as to state that Shakespeare had actually read the *Inferno*, thinks that he was, in some way, familiar with it. Herbert R. Couson, Jr. over-elaborates the case he makes out in his essay 'In Deepest Consequence: *Macbeth*'.[5] Relating the play to the Fall of the Angels, he advances three parallels: first, that Macbeth, like Adam, takes a conscious moral decision; secondly, that he is persuaded by a woman; and, thirdly, that all nature is involved in, and reacts against, the crime.

'*Timon of Athens* and the Growth of Discrimination', by R. Swigg,[6] is really a gloss on Apemantus' words about Timon: 'The middle of humanity thou never knew'st'. His view is that at the play's beginning neither Timon nor Athens has any capacity for discrimination, but, while Timon never alters, Athens is brought to see the importance of making valid judgements. Leonard Goldstein[7] finds the end of the play unusual in that revolt is apparently approved of, and tries to claim the tragedy for Marxism by describing it as a popular revolt. Dieter Hoffmeier[8] writes interestingly about two German adaptations of the play, both of which reduced its social content.

A. P. Riemer's book, *A Reading of Shakespeare's 'Antony and Cleopatra'*,[9] opens in a manner that inspires little confidence. Reviewing post-Bradleyan attitudes to Shakespeare, he cites L. C. Knights's 'How Many Children Had Lady Macbeth?', published in 1933, as the manifesto for a new approach to Shakespeare as practised by Wilson Knight among others, not realizing apparently, that *The Wheel of Fire* came out in 1930 and that Knights himself pays tribute to it in his essay. He also seems to be astray about the date of Caroline Spurgeon's *Shakespeare's Imagery*, and says nothing whatever about T. S. Eliot's brief, but extremely influential, comments on *Antony and Cleopatra* and *Coriolanus* in his essay on *Hamlet* (1919). The problem to which he eventually addresses himself, after a rather inadequate account of the play, is that posed by the fact that *Antony and Cleopatra* 'can be read as the fall of a great general, betrayed in his

1 'Truth and Tragedy in *King Lear*', *Shakespeare Quarterly*, XVIII (1967), 167–80.

2 '*King Lear*: The Central Stream', *Cambridge Quarterly*, II (1966–7), 23–48, 148–66, and 212–35.

3 'Edgar's Pilgrimage: High Comedy in *King Lear*', *Studies in English Literature*, VII (1967), 219–37.

4 *Tennessee Studies in Literature*, XII (1967), 23–38.   5 *Shakespeare Quarterly*, XVIII (1967), 375–88.

6 *Modern Language Review*, LXII (1967), 387–94.

7 'Alcibiades' Revolt in *Timon of Athens*', *Zeitschrift für Anglistik und Amerikanistik*, XV (1967), 256–78.

8 'Über die *Timon*-Bearbeitungen von Dalberg (1789) und Hans Rothe', *Shakespeare-Jahrbuch*, CIII (1967), 156–61.   9 Sydney University Press, 1968.

dotage by a treacherous strumpet, or else it can be viewed as a celebration of transcendental love'. Ignoring the possibility that this may be no problem at all, but rather the kind of paradox that tragedy so often portrays, he comes to the conclusion that the work is not really a tragedy, because it has no metaphysical content. More interesting is William Blissett's 'Dramatic Irony in *Antony and Cleopatra*'.[1] This sets out the idea that the play is permeated by an irony that reaches its culmination in the half-veiled references to the birth of Christ, which set the whole story in a context of which the characters know nothing but which was the central event in history for Shakespeare's audience. Ruth Nevo[2] also works out a good idea. She suggests that Act v dramatizes the working of Cleopatra's imagination as the thought of a triumph over Caesar takes possession of her mind, and that the form her dream takes owes much to that English tradition of pageants and masques, which, as Whiter noted, so appealed to Shakespeare. Robert E. Fitch,[3] however, is not moved by Act v. He sees it, and the play, as a magnificent spectacle that does not touch the heart.

In his longish essay '*Coriolanus*'[4] J. C. F. Littlewood moves back to the position taken by Bradley in his British Academy Lecture (1912), holding that the hero's creed, though narrow, is also noble. He wants his fellow patricians to be true to the essential Rome where *Virtus* is supreme. It is this identification of himself with the ideal of Rome, so cogently expressed in Act III, that disappears from the play in Acts IV and V, because Shakespeare's imagination is no longer absorbed by the hero. Writing on the fascinating similarities between Coriolanus and the mob, Michael McCanles[5] argues that the hero cannot do without those he despises because their hatred of him defines his superiority to them. 'The End of Coriolanus',[6] by E. A. M. Colman, seeks to justify the final scene as the right ending for the play, because in it the complex emotions of Coriolanus' tragic predicament are realized, appropriately, in action rather than words.

The idea that the final works of some of the world's major dramatists may have common characteristics is not a new one. Kenneth Muir, for example, made use of it in his *Last Periods of Shakespeare, Racine, and Ibsen* (1961). But, though David Grene is familiar with Muir's book, and though he also writes about Shakespeare and Ibsen in his *Reality and the Heroic Pattern*,[7] he links them with Sophocles, and his findings are his own. Arising out of the experience of giving courses of lectures on the plays concerned, the book bears the marks of its origins. The most interesting matter is contained in the Preface, where Grene sets out his general conclusions, and then in the introductory essays to each author. The most striking resemblance he discovers between these groups of last plays—*Pericles* is deliberately omitted from the section on Shakespeare—is that each playwright appears to be looking back on life in an effort to find some kind of significance in it. There is, therefore, in all the plays a constant preoccupation with the fact of time, because the passage of time can alter the meaning of events; and there is also, of course, a concern with death. Here, however, differences become evident. In Ibsen the death

1 *Shakespeare Quarterly*, XVIII (1967), 151–66.
2 'The Masque of Greatness', *Shakespeare Studies*, III (1967), 111–28.
3 'No Greater Crack', *Shakespeare Quarterly*, XIX (1968), 3–17.
4 *Cambridge Quarterly*, II (1966–7), 339–57 and III (1967–8), 28–50.
5 'The Dialectic of Transcendence in Shakespeare's *Coriolanus*', *PMLA*, LXXXII (1967), 44–53.
6 *ELH*, XXXIV (1967), 1–20.   7 University of Chicago Press, 1967.

of the hero is the dramatist's notion of a suitable death, asserting the character's private vision of himself. In Shakespeare there is little concern with personal death, and it is hard to say precisely what is affirmed as distinct from being presented. Sophocles sets the ways of men against the ways of the gods, and leaves it at that. The range of this book is attractive.

Starting from the assumption that the archaisms of speech and construction in *Pericles* are deliberate, Howard Felperin[1] argues that the play is an allegory, with Pericles as Everyman. Thelma N. Greenfield[2] prefers to see the protagonist as a kind of Ulysses, a solver of riddles, a born ruler of men. The puzzling geography of the play is the subject of an informative note by G. Lambin,[3] who also establishes the identity of the French ambassador who witnessed a performance of the play at Whitehall in May 1619. In an article that does not overstate its case, Arthur C. Kirsch[4] relates the manner of *Cymbeline* to that of the plays of Marston, as well as of Beaumont and Fletcher.

Norman Nathan takes up the problem of whether Leontes' jealousy is sudden or whether it has adequate motivation in his article 'Leontes' Provocation',[5] and reaches the comforting solution that it is both. Working from productions of *The Winter's Tale* and *The Tempest* at Weimar in 1964–5, Dieter Görne[6] argues that the personal experience of the characters in both plays reflects the political and social preoccupations of the age in which these dramas were written.

A. D. Nuttall's difficult and important book, *Two Concepts of Allegory*,[7] is not primarily about *The Tempest*, though it contains some excellent criticism of it. Shakespeare's play serves as a point of departure and a point of return. Beginning by outlining the extent to which *The Tempest* was allegorized by critics in the nineteenth century, he then poses his central questions: 'What sort of thing are people doing when they talk of allegorical significations; what sort of reasons prompt them to do so in connexion with *The Tempest*?' His search for the answers takes him far afield, but his basic conclusion is that there is a place for images in some kinds of conceptual thinking, because it is virtually impossible to think of 'the beyond' without resorting to them. His last two chapters bring him back to Shakespeare. Taking *Troilus and Cressida* as a relevant case, he stresses the inseparable connexion of love and value in the Elizabethan world, and then, turning to the Sonnets, he argues that in them the poet resorts increasingly to remedies, against the forces of time and change, that are of a metaphysical nature: the eternizing power of poetry, and love, the experience of which no disaster could deprive him. This conception of love achieves its final definition, Nuttall thinks, in Cleopatra's vision of Antony in v, ii, and it has much in common with Keats's idea of the Imagination as Adam's dream. Coming back to *The Tempest* in his final chapter, he brings out beautifully the extraordinary manner in which the play marries the material of romance with travellers' tales, creating a work of art that comes close to the world of dream and nightmare; that speaks, especially through the verse of Caliban

1 'Shakespeare's Miracle Play', *Shakespeare Quarterly*, XVIII (1967), 363–74.

2 'A Re-examination of the "Patient" Pericles', *Shakespeare Studies*, III (1967), 51–61.

3 'De Longues Notes sur de Brefs Passages Shakespeariens', *Études Anglaises*, XX (1967), 58–68.

4 'Cymbeline and Coterie Dramaturgy', *ELH*, XXXIV (1967), 285–306.

5 *Shakespeare Quarterly*, XIX (1968), 19–24.

6 'Bemerkungen zur Konzeption de Aufführungen des *Wintermärchens* und des *Sturms* an Deutschen National-Theater Weimar 1964–5', *Shakespeare-Jahrbuch*, CIII (1967), 162–76.   7 Routledge and Kegan Paul, 1967.

to primitive levels of consciousness; and that ultimately questions, through Prospero's great speech in IV, i, the reality of life itself. Because it has these qualities, *The Tempest*, he holds, both demands allegorical interpretation and evades it.

D. G. James has long been fascinated by the Last Plays. The final chapter of his *Scepticism and Poetry* (1937) was devoted to an exploration of them as myths. Now, in *The Dream of Prospero*,[1] he has come back to his first love, but by way of *The Dream of Learning* (1951), some of the essential matters of which he repeats at the opening of the present work, in order to give himself a starting-point from which he can move on to a consideration of *The Tempest* in relation to *Hamlet* and *King Lear*, and, more importantly, in relation to what was happening to European civilization at the time. James insists throughout on the centrality of Prospero and on the fact that he returns to Milan in order to rule it properly. Relating this to the dreamlike quality of the play, he suggests that, while the action is not presented as a dream, it is nevertheless as a dream of Prospero himself that the imagination receives it. The effect of this dream on Prospero is to make him choose 'between himself affirming the spiritual sources of society...and a society which rejects supernatural sanctions and in the event rejects morality itself'. James further hazards the theory that there is a connexion between the ending of the play, where Prospero drowns his book, and the supersession of that confused syncretism which is so characteristic of the Renaissance. It is suggestions of this kind that give the book a certain distinction, despite a repetitiveness that stems from the lecture form in which it was composed.

The main content of R. Berman's '*King Henry the Eighth*: History and Romance'[2] is implicit in the title. So is that of John P. Cutts's 'Shakespeare's Song and Masque Hand in *The Two Noble Kinsmen*',[3] a careful and detailed piece of work.

In a lecture on the Sonnets, Paul A. Bates[4] disposes of Mr. W. H., the rival poet, and the Dark Lady as 'creations of Shakespeare's imagination', and puts forward the thesis that in the sequence pastoral plots and characters are fused with Sonnet form, but there are no shepherds. Sergio Baldi, however, in his 'Shakespeare's Sonnets as Literature',[5] sees the Sonnets as representing the move from Elizabethan Platonism to Jacobean Mannerism, drawing attention to the way in which the nature imagery in them is interlaced with references of a commercial kind. Kalidas Bose[6] thinks the Sonnets are causing a clash between those critics who value lucidity and those who value complexity; while Hilton Landry[7] holds that the usual interpretations of Sonnet 116 are mistaken, since the 'impediments' lie in the speaker, not in the friend.

'Shakespeare's Unnecessary Characters',[8] an unassuming essay by Arthur Colby Sprague, puts forward some good reasons to justify the existence of figures such as Fabian, Cicero, and the like; Gary J. Scrimgeour studies 'The Messenger as a Dramatic Device in Shakespeare';[9] and Robert K. Presson uses the medieval distinction between 'somnium animale' and 'somnium naturale' as the basis for some observations on dreams in the work of Shakespeare and others in

1 Oxford University Press, 1967. 2 *English Studies*, XLVIII (1967), 112–21.

3 *English Miscellany*, XVIII (1967), 55–85.

4 'Shakespeare and Pastoral Poetry', *Shakespeare-Jahrbuch*, CIII (1967), 81–96.

5 *Shakespeare Celebrated*, pp. 133–54.

6 'The New Problem of Shakespeare's Sonnets', *Essays on Shakespeare*, pp. 128–44.

7 'The Marriage of True Minds: Truth and Error in Sonnet 116', *Shakespeare Studies*, III (1967), 98–110.

8 *Shakespeare Survey 20* (Cambridge, 1967), 75–82. 9 *Shakespeare Quarterly*, XIX (1968), 41–54.

his 'Two Types of Dreams in the Elizabethan Drama, and their Heritage: Somnium Animale and the Prick-of-Conscience'.[1] Halio[2] examines the use of the metaphor of conception to portray the workings of the imagination in *Troilus and Cressida* especially, and R. Holmes[3] shows that the years of Shakespeare's activity were a sort of trough between two waves of witchcraft mania.

The German interest in forms of speech and types of scene continues unabated. 'Rede-Konventionen des Vice von *Mankind* bis *Hamlet*'[4] is a long and careful study by Robert Weimann of the way in which the Vice's mixture of matter and impertinency was integrated into the dialogue of fifteenth- and sixteenth-century plays. Rudolph Böhm[5] stresses the frequency and variety of slander scenes in Elizabethan drama generally and especially in the work of Shakespeare; while N. Christoph de Nagy[6] examines a number of trial scenes with a view to establishing their connexion with medieval drama.

A series of lectures given at Weimar in 1966 relate Shakespeare's work to that of other writers and movements. Martin Lehnert spoke on 'Shakespeare und Chaucer';[7] Rolf Rohmer on 'Lessing und Shakespeare';[8] Wolfgang Stellmacher on 'Der Junge Herder und Shakespeare';[9] and Wilhelm Girnus on 'Deutsche Klassik und Shakespeare'.[10] Similar pieces are Walther Martin's 'Shakespeare und Cervantes'[11] and Zdeněk Stříbrný's 'Shakespeare in Czechoslovakia'.[12]

In his 'Keats on Shakespeare'[13] Bhabatosh Chatterjee traces the stages by which Keats became involved with Shakespeare's work; shows how phrases culled from it enrich the Letters; and concludes with a study of the importance that *King Lear* came to assume for him. 'A New Way to Pay Old Debts'[14] is a good description, by Mihir Kumar, of T. S. Eliot's use of Shakespeare in his poems; Sisirkumar Ghose gives a lively, if somewhat knock-about, account of the ways in which Shakespeare has been treated by his critics in his 'Which Shakespeare?';[15] and Alick West[16] argues that modern producers, in seeking to bring the plays into a significant relationship with the contemporary world, tend to empty them of their true meaning which depends on Shakespeare's perception of human greatness and dignity.

A number of works, whose value is so well established and recognized as to need no comment, have recently become available in paperback form: Elmer Edgar Stoll's *Poets and Playwrights* (1930);[17] W. B. C. Watkins's *Shakespeare and Spenser* (1950);[18] John Russell Brown's *Shakespeare and His Comedies* (1957);[19] M. M. Mahood's *Shakespeare's Wordplay* (1957);[20] H. S. Wilson's *On the Design of Shakespearian Tragedy* (1957);[21] Bertrand Evans's *Shakespeare's Comedies* (1960);[22] and Norman N. Holland's *The Shakespearian Imagination* (1964).[23]

© G. R. HIBBARD 1969

[1] *Studies in English Literature*, VII (1967), 239–56.
[2] 'The Metaphor of Conception and Elizabethan Theories of the Imagination', *Neophilologus*, L (1966), 454–61.
[3] 'Shakespeare and Witchcraft', *The Quarterly Review*, CCCV (1967), 179–88.
[4] *Zeitschrift für Anglistik und Amerikanistik*, XV (1967), 117–51.
[5] 'Die Verleumdungsszene bei Shakespeare', *Deutsche Shakespeare-Gesellschaft West Jahrbuch* (1967), pp. 221–36.
[6] 'Die Funktionen der Gerichtsszene bei Shakespeare und in der Tradition des älteren englischen Dramas', *ibid.* pp. 199–220. [7] *Shakespeare-Jahrbuch*, CIII (1967), 7–39. [8] *Ibid.* 40–53. [9] *Ibid.* 54–67. [10] *Ibid.* 68–80. [11] *Ibid.* 136–44. [12] *Shakespeare Celebrated*, pp. 113–32. [13] *Essays on Shakespeare*, pp. 169–230. [14] *Ibid.* pp. 109–21. [15] *Ibid.* pp. 76–84. [16] *Shakespeare-Jahrbuch*, CIII (1967), 97–107. [17] University of Minnesota Press, 1967. [18] Princeton University Press, 1966. [19] Methuen, 1968. [20] Methuen, 1968. [21] University of Toronto Press, 1968. [22] Oxford University Press, 1967. [23] Indiana University Press, 1968.

2. SHAKESPEARE'S LIFE, TIMES AND STAGE

reviewed by LEAH SCRAGG

The exuberant energy devoted in recent years to Shakespeare life studies seems at last to have ebbed away, and this year's contributions to the subject have been both meagre and restrained. With the exception of M. K. Naik, whose delightful, if not highly original, picture of a 'humanitarian' Shakespeare[1] is constructed by that process of judicious quotation from the text the dubious fruits of which we have long learned to suspect, scholars have eschewed the alluring paths of speculation and confined themselves to a rigorous re-appraisal of a number of items of evidence available to us. Thus the clothes in which the dramatist is depicted in the various contemporary representations of him,[2] the identity of the subjects of the 'Barnard' portraits,[3] the source of John Shakespeare's spiritual testament,[4] and fresh evidence that the 'upstart crow' reference may carry the implication of plagiarism[5] have all been carefully examined, while possible extensions to the Shakespearian canon in the shape of *The Double Falsehood*[6] or an early version of *Titus Andronicus* disguised as *Titus and Vespasian*[7] have both been discounted. Meanwhile Hallett Smith in *Shakespearean Research Opportunities*[8] urges the need for yet greater precision in the dating of the last plays and more certainty about the authorship of three of them.

Source scholarship continues to take two divergent paths, on the one hand suggesting material that may have influenced the dramatist and on the other making that material available to us. In the first category both Peter Milward, s.j.,[9] and Bettie Anne Doebler[10] have been concerned with Shakespeare's debt to the homiletic tradition, the former arguing that 'the thought of *Hamlet* and of its author was rooted in the sermon literature of his time', the latter discussing the final act of *Othello* in the light of the *ars moriendi* tradition. The influence exerted by continental drama has also been the subject of critical attention. Louise George Clubb has suggested[11] that the selection and organization of the dramatist's material in *The Comedy of Errors* indicates a knowledge of the *commedia grave*, Oscar M. Villarejo has maintained[12] (not entirely convincingly) that Shakespeare had an intimate acquaintance with Lope de Vega's *Castelvines y Monteses* when

1 'Humanitarianism in Shakespeare', *Shakespeare Quarterly*, XIX (1968), 139–47.

2 J. L. Nevinson, 'Shakespeare's Dress in His Portraits', *Shakespeare Quarterly*, XVIII (1967), 101–6.

3 F. Gordon Roe, 'Elizabeth Barnard: A Shakespearian Problem Restated', *Notes and Queries*, CCXIII (1968), 125–7.

4 James G. McManaway, 'John Shakespeare's "Spiritual Testament"', *Shakespeare Quarterly*, XVIII (1967), 197–205.

5 Arthur Freeman, 'Notes on the Text of "2 Henry VI", and the "Upstart Crow"', *Notes and Queries*, CCXIII (1968), 128–30.

6 Harriet C. Frazier, 'The Rifling of Beauty's Stores: Theobald and Shakespeare', *Neuphilologische Mitteilungen*, LXIX (1968), 232–56.

7 G. R. Proudfoot, 'A Note on "Titus and Vespasian"', *Notes and Queries*, CCXIII (1968), 131.

8 'Shakespeare's Last Plays: Facts and Problems', *Shakespearean Research Opportunities*, III (1967), 9–16.

9 'The Homiletic Tradition in Shakespeare's Plays', *Shakespeare Studies* (Japan), V (1966–7), 72–87.

10 'Othello's Angels: The *Ars Moriendi*', *ELH*, XXXIV (1967), 156–72.

11 'Italian Comedy and *The Comedy of Errors*', *Comparative Literature*, XIX (1967), 240–51.

12 'Shakespeare's "Romeo and Juliet": Its Spanish Source', *Shakespeare Survey 20* (Cambridge, 1967), 95–105.

he wrote *Romeo and Juliet*, and John Arthos has urged[1] that Elizabethan comic drama is better understood when seen against the background of such works as Baltazarini's *Ballet Comique de la Reine*. The current discussion of the *Ur-Shrew/A Shrew/The Shrew* complex has been joined by J. C. Maxwell with the heart-warming argument that to postulate the existence of an *Ur-Shrew* involves the multiplication of 'extraordinarily odd entities'.[2] Brian Vickers in a stimulating essay[3] has discussed paradox as a serious mode of philosophical debate in the Renaissance and cited some interesting parallels between Thomas Milles's *Treasurie of Ancient and Modern Times* and *King Lear*. And finally, in a more general study, Claus Uhlig[4] has examined Renaissance attitudes to a series of concepts (such as the lust/love dichotomy) and discussed Shakespeare's treatment of them.

Minor textual points have also been clarified by reference to sources. Bridget Gellert[5] has convinced one reader at least that Hamlet's remark (II, ii, 356–7) that he can distinguish between a hawk and a handsaw is derived from Bright's *A Treatise of Melancholie* and does not require emendation; Gunnar Sjögren has pointed out[6] that the interpretation of Polonius's 'Take this from this' as 'take my head from my body' is confirmed by the occurrence of a similar phrase in a scene between Ulysses and Thersites in *Iliad*, II (Shakespeare's source for *Troilus and Cressida*); while David R. Cheney[7] has contributed some fact and more speculation to the discussion about Hamlet's bird of dawning. Robert F. Fleissner has suggested[8] that Corderius's *Dialogues*, Colloquy no. LXVIII, may be a source for the play on the word 'nothing' in the love test scene of *Lear* and that a comparison with this work lends support to the Folio reading of the passage.

Straddling the borderline between those studies suggesting the range of Shakespeare's reading and those presenting the literature with which he was familiar to the modern reader is *Anglo–Polish Renaissance Texts*.[9] The volume contains facsimiles of seven popular late sixteenth- and early seventeenth-century works all concerned with the early phase of Anglo–Polish relations. Those of primary interest are Cromer's *A Notable Example of God's Vengeance upon a Murdering King* and Goslicius's *The Counsellor*, both of which the editor advances as possible sources of *Hamlet*.

Outstanding among the year's contributions to source studies is Judith M. Kennedy's edition of Yong's translation of George of Montemayor's *Diana* and Gil Polo's *Enamoured Diana*.[10] In the course of a long introduction, the editor analyses Shakespeare's debt to Yong's highly influential book, which, she claims, throws more light on the world of the 'romantic comedies' than any other single work. There is a full bibliography and the edition is beautifully produced. Less ambitiously, T. J. B. Spencer has edited[11] eight Elizabethan love stories for the Penguin

---

1 'The Forming of the Early Comedies', *Shakespearean Research Opportunities*, III (1967), 1–8.
2 ' "The Shrew" and "A Shrew"; The Suitors and the Sisters', *Notes and Queries*, CCXIII (1968), 130–1.
3 ' "King Lear" and Renaissance Paradoxes', *The Modern Language Review*, LXIII (1968), 305–14.
4 *Traditionelle Denkformen in Shakespeares tragischer Kunst* (Cram, de Gruyter and Co., Hamburg, 1967).
5 'Note on "Hamlet", II. ii. 356–7', *Notes and Queries*, CCXIII (1968), 139–40.
6 ' "Take This from This": Polonius and Ulysses', *ibid.* 139.
7 'The Cock Crowing at Christmas in "Hamlet" ', *ibid.* 136–7.
8 'King Lear's Love-Test: A Latin Derivation', *ibid.* 143–4.
9 Ed. Witold Chwalewik (Polish Scientific Publishers, Warsaw, 1968).
10 *A Critical Edition of Yong's Translation of George of Montemayor's* Diana *and Gil Polo's* Enamoured Diana (Clarendon Press, Oxford, 1968).   11 *Elizabethan Love Stories* (Harmondsworth, 1968).

Shakespeare Library and equipped them with an elementary introduction showing the relationship between each story and the relevant Shakespearian play. While providing undergraduates with a useful introduction to source studies, the book will do double duty as a selection of Elizabethan prose—thus allowing the reviewer to pass imperceptibly from Shakespeare's life to his times.

A welcome addition to the bibliographical material available to the Renaissance scholar is *Shakespearean Research Opportunities'* selective list of non-literary Renaissance studies, 1966–7.[1] Such topics as socio-economics, education, ethics, law, music, etc. are included and future lists, it is promised, will be more comprehensive. Of the wealth of material published on a variety of aspects of the Renaissance during the year, the widest ranging is Robert Ergang's *The Renaissance*,[2] a well-produced, richly documented work purporting to offer 'an interpretive account of the beginnings of our modern secular civilization, with special emphasis on culture'. It is hard, however, to see for what audience the work is intended. The section on 'English Literature of the Renaissance Period' is of such an elementary kind it casts doubt on the value of the 'cultural' aspect of the whole survey. Among other reservations, one wonders whether the assertion that the English Renaissance dates from Chaucer will find many supporters among either Renaissance scholars or medievalists. More specialized are two studies of the religious movements of the sixteenth century, Patrick Collinson's *The Elizabethan Puritan Movement*,[3] a detailed, scholarly account of what constituted one of the major forces in the history of the period, and Patrick McGrath's *Papists and Puritans Under Elizabeth I*,[4] which examines the two conflicting movements and discusses their differences and similarities. Phoebe Sheavyn's *The Literary Profession in the Elizabethan Age* (1909) has been brought up to date by J. W. Saunders,[5] but, though greater space is now devoted to dramatists and the necessity for patronage in other literary fields has been emphasized, errors continue to abound. John Morris, in an interesting article,[6] has traced the history of the struggle between the university and the Stationers' Company consequent upon the setting up of a printing press at Cambridge, while in the educational field, Lawrence V. Ryan's admirable modern spelling edition of Roger Ascham's *The Schoolmaster* (1570)[7] has made accessible one of the most influential books of the period. The law has been the subject of two works of particular interest to the Shakespearian scholar, W. J. Jones's *The Elizabethan Court of Chancery*[8] and George W. Keeton's *Shakespeare's Legal and Political Background*.[9] The former combines impressive scholarship with lucidity in a fascinating account of 'one of the largest organs of the Elizabethan state', but the latter, while

1 'Shakespeare and Renaissance Intellectual Contexts: A Selective, Annotated List, 1966–7', pp. 64–91.

2 D. van Nostrand Co. Inc., 1967. Here, perhaps, should be mentioned A. A. Mendilow and Alice Shalvi, *The World and Art of Shakespeare* (Israel Universities Press, Jerusalem, 1967), an elementary study designed to explain Shakespeare's world to the foreign student. The book covers Shakespeare's life, pre-Shakespearian drama, the Elizabethan theatre, changing theatrical taste, etc., with commendable clarity. Though directed to a non-Christian audience (e.g. references to Christ as Lamb are explained) the book could possibly form a useful addition to an English school library. 3 Jonathan Cape, 1967. 4 Blandford Press, 1967.

5 Manchester University Press, 1967.

6 'Restrictive Practices in the Elizabethan Book Trade: The Stationers' Company *v* Thomas Thomas 1583–8', *Transactions of the Cambridge Bibliographical Society*, IV (1964–7), 276–90.

7 The Folger Shakespeare Library (Cornell University Press, Ithaca, New York, 1967).
9 Pitman, 1967.

8 Clarendon Press, Oxford, 1967.

promising to supply a long-felt need, is an unequal book, disappointing in its failure to tackle the subject systematically. Though some chapters discuss specific topics, e.g. 'The Law of Debt in Shakespeare', others confine themselves to problems within single plays and fail to notice related issues in others. (For example, the chapter devoted to 'The Bastardy of Falconbridge' would have been more useful as a study of bastardy in the plays as a whole, with comment on such points as the bastardizing of the Princes in *Richard III*.) Omissions too are evident. It is surprising to find no mention of the marriage contract (cf. *Measure for Measure*, *Richard III*). And the chapters devoted to Shakespeare's political background do not advance any ideas with which we have not been long familiar.

A number of other studies have also been concerned with viewing the plays against their social and intellectual background. Sir Mungo MacCallum's monumental *Shakespeare's Roman Plays and their Background* has been re-issued,[1] and A. L. Soens has warned us[2] against interpreting Shakespeare's fencing terms in the light of the illustrations of the period without careful study of the accompanying text.

Conveniently bridging the gap between studies of Shakespeare in his time and works devoted to his contemporaries is Eric Laguardia's *Nature Redeemed*,[3] a critical analysis of Spenser's *Faerie Queen III* and *IV*, Milton's *Comus*, and *All's Well That Ends Well* as poetic evocations of a world poised between its tendency towards corruption and potentiality for redemption. The application of the thesis to *All's Well* is far from satisfactory. Minor incidents (e.g. the conversation between Helena and Parolles in I, i) are given undue prominence, the interpretation of some passages (e.g. the Countess's speech I, iii, 134–9) is forced, and the view of the play's theme as the 'initiation' of Helena into womanhood and the 'purification' of Bertram (and Parolles!) does not convince. Of the general argument, little more need be said beyond the author's own admission that it is advanced in spite of 'insufficient evidence and the fact that...[it]... violates chronology'.

Elizabethan poets and poetry have been the subject of a number of volumes during the year. Nigel Alexander has edited a useful selection[4] of Elizabethan narrative verse 1560–1610, including (among others) poems by Daniel and Drayton, each of whom has been the subject of a book from Twayne publishers.[5] Two complementary works on Sir Philip Sidney have appeared, one concerned with his public, the other with his literary, career. Roger Howell's biography[6] sets out to place 'the shepherd knight' firmly in historical perspective and to emphasize his importance in non-literary spheres, while Neil L. Rudenstine's critical study[7] concentrates upon style and technique in order to demonstrate a 'pattern of unbroken continuity' in his

[1] Macmillan, 1967.

[2] 'Two Rapier Points: Analysing Elizabethan Fighting Methods', *Notes and Queries*, CCXIII (1968), 127–8.

[3] Mouton and Co., The Hague, 1966.

[4] *Elizabethan Narrative Verse*, Stratford-on-Avon Library 3 (Edward Arnold, 1967).

[5] Cecil Seronsy, *Samuel Daniel* (New York, 1967), includes discussion of cross-fertilization with Shakespeare. Joseph A. Berthelot, *Michael Drayton* (New York, 1967), presents Drayton as 'the complete Renaissance poet, one who wrote effectively in almost all of the poetical forms of his day'. Also on Drayton see Richard F. Hardin, 'Convention and Design in Drayton's *Heroicall Epistles*', *PMLA*, LXXXIII (1968), 35–41.

[6] *Sir Philip Sidney. The Shepherd Knight* (Hutchinson, 1968).

[7] *Sidney's Poetic Development* (Harvard University Press, Cambridge, Mass., 1967).

poetic development. Alan D. Isler has produced two articles in defence of aspects of the *Arcadia*,[1] of particular interest here being his comparison between the knights' attack on the mob in *Arcadia*, Book II, and the mob's attack on Cinna the poet in *Julius Caesar*. In both he finds the victims to be of a cartoonistic 'slain–notslain' variety and argues that humour, not horror, predominates. As far as *Julius Caesar* is concerned, I find myself unable to agree with him.

Outstanding among the new books devoted to Shakespeare's fellow dramatists is Arthur Freeman's *Thomas Kyd: Facts and Problems*.[2] Aiming to provide 'a broad basis for the study of Kyd's works' in the absence of a full-length account in English, and avoiding the labyrinths of *Ur-Hamlet/Ur-Andronicus* speculation, the author has carefully assembled the available facts, discussed the problems inherent in an account of Kyd's life, work and influence with admirable clear-sightedness, and made some perceptive remarks on the plays. It is thus a most welcome addition to a relatively neglected field. It is regrettable that as much cannot be said for David L. Frost's *The School of Shakespeare*[3] which sets out to trace the influence of the dramatist on his contemporaries and successors. Though the subject of his book must be of immediate interest to every Shakespearian scholar, and many of Mr Frost's views (e.g. on the influence of Shakespeare on the Revenge play and the Romance) are stimulating, his book as a whole suffers from a belligerent manner, a readiness to make glib assumptions ('presumably Middleton planned and Rowley botched'), and a willingness to transform a hypothesis on p. 37 into a fact by p. 39. More importantly, it seems doubtful whether the title 'School of Shakespeare' is applicable to a collection of dramatists of whom it is claimed that one wrote a single 'Shakespearian' play, one was influenced by the word not the spirit, and two were 'anti-Shakespearian'. With reference to the individual dramatists discussed, it seems a pity that the chapter on Middleton should have placed such emphasis on the dubious *The Revenger's Tragedy*. In all a disappointing book. Another work breaking fresh ground to some extent is Brian Gibbons's *Jacobean City Comedy*[4] which traces the development of citizen comedy from Jonson's early comical satires through to *The Devil is an Ass*, while offering a fresh appraisal of the work of Jonson, Marston and Middleton. An interesting book, but it is hard to agree with many of the points made (e.g. the ridicule is described as 'urbane though taut' in the scene in *The Revenger's Tragedy* in which Vendice pretends to share Lussurioso's anticipated seduction of his sister). And, incidentally, the type face is not attractive.

Chapman has been the subject of a number of studies. Charlotte Spivack has analysed[5] the whole corpus of his work, defending his poetry from the charge of obscurity and rejecting the view that he was reluctant to write for the stage; G. R. Hibbard[6] has shown how Chapman's neoplatonism, together with his apprehension that it is right versus right that is often productive of tragedy, militate against the limitations imposed by his providential view of history; the same writer, in an extended essay,[7] has discussed his tragedies in relation to Jonson's; and Akihiro

1 'Heroic Poetry and Sidney's Two *Arcadias*', *PMLA*, LXXXIII (1968), 368–79, and 'Sidney, Shakespeare, and the "Slain–notslain" ', *University of Toronto Quarterly*, XXXVII (1968), 175–85.

2 Clarendon Press, Oxford, 1967.　　　　　　　　　　　3 Cambridge University Press, 1968.

4 Rupert Hart-Davis, 1968.　　　　　5 *George Chapman* (Twayne Publishers Inc., New York), 1967.

6 'George Chapman: Tragedy and the Providential View of History', *Shakespeare Survey 20* (1967), 27–31.

7 'Goodness And Greatness: An Essay On The Tragedies Of Ben Jonson And George Chapman', *Renaissance and Modern Studies*, XI (1967), 5–54.

Yamada[1] has examined the 1599 Quarto of *A Humorous Day's Mirth*. Other contributions to our knowledge of the contemporary stage include articles on *The Devil's Law Case*,[2] *The Changeling*,[3] the possibility that the Vices of the late morality play might have been dressed as the four knaves of a pack of cards,[4] and the nature of the connexions linking the various actions of Elizabethan multi-plot drama.[5] Notable among this year's crop of editions is *The Alchemist*, which has been added to the Revels plays.[6] In the more obscure regions of Elizabethan dramatic studies, the blurred figures of five of the eight collaborators in Hughes's *The Misfortunes of Arthur* have been sketched in for us a little more clearly.[7]

A book[8] and a collection of essays[9] on the related field of the masque, the former including some remarks on the influence of the genre on Shakespeare, the latter covering a wide variety of topics ranging from the evolution of 'disguising' to the evaluation of the work of individual writers, together with a selection of Dekker's prose[10] and a detailed study of Bacon's,[11] bring to a close the year's additions to our understanding of Shakespeare's contemporaries.

Medieval and pre-Shakespearian Renaissance dramaturgy continues to receive an increasing share of critical attention, though Murray Roston's *Biblical Drama in England*,[12] which traces the history of religious drama in this country from the Middle Ages to the present day, does scant justice to the medieval period which is dismissed in a bare 29 pages compared with 73 for, one would have imagined, the less fruitful 'Modern Era'. His neglect is amply compensated by R. Weimann's lengthy book on Shakespeare and the popular drama,[13] which discusses mime, folk shows, mysteries, moralities, interludes, etc. and considers their influence on the Elizabethan–Jacobean stage. Particularly worthy of note is J. M. R. Margeson's *The Origins of English Tragedy*,[14] which examines the range and variety of episodes capable of tragic development in medieval and early Renaissance drama and suggests that the richness of this background made

1 'Bibliographical Studies of George Chapman's *An Humorous Day's Mirth* (1599)', *Shakespeare Studies* (Japan), V (1966–7), 119–49.

2 D. C. Gunby, ' "The Devil's Law-Case": An Interpretation', *The Modern Language Review*, LXIII (1968), 545–58.

3 Dorothy M. Farr, 'The Changeling', *The Modern Language Review*, LXII (1967), 586–97.

4 Alan C. Dessen, 'Jonson's "Knaue of Clubs" and "The Play of the Cards" ', *ibid.* 584–5.

5 Richard Levin, 'The Unity of Elizabethan Multiple-Plot Drama', *ELH*, XXXIV (1967), 425–46.

6 Ed. F. H. Mares (Methuen, 1967).

7 Jacques Ramel, 'Biographical Notices on the Authors of "The Misfortunes of Arthur" (1588)', *Notes and Queries*, CCXII (1967), 461–7.

8 Marie-Thérèse Jones-Davies, *Inigo Jones, Ben Jonson et le Masque* (Librairie Marcel Didier, Paris, 1967).

9 *Renaissance Drama*, n.s. 1 (1968).

10 *Thomas Dekker: Selected Prose Writings*, ed. Eric Pendry, Stratford-on-Avon Library (Edward Arnold, 1967). Also for a possible borrowing by Dekker from Shakespeare see J. R. Weeks, 'A Masticke Patch and Masticke Jaws', *Notes and Queries*, CCXIII (1968), 140–1.

11 Brian Vickers, *Francis Bacon and Renaissance Prose* (Cambridge University Press, 1968).

12 Faber and Faber, 1968.

13 *Shakespeare und die Tradition des Volkstheaters* (Henschelverlag, Berlin, 1967). A number of articles on related topics have appeared by the same writer, cf. 'Realismus und Simultankonvention im Misteriendrama', *Shakespeare-Jahrbuch*, CIII (1967), 108–35; 'Die furchtbare komik des Herodes. Dramaturgie und Figurenaufbau des vorshake-speareschen Schurken', *Archiv für das Studium der neueren Sprachen und Literaturen*, CCIV (1967), 113–23; 'Antiker Mimus und Shakespeare-Theater', *Lebende Antike*, ed. Horst Meller and Hans-Joachim Zimmermann, ((West) Berlin, 1967), 181–96.   14 Clarendon Press, Oxford, 1967.

possible several quite distinct forms of tragedy in the later period. A similar position is taken by G. K. Hunter,[1] who argues against that 'diagram of development that sees Elizabethan tragedy beginning from the Senecan translations of the 1560s' and urges us to 'look more closely at the tradition of repertory drama' in order to see, 'inside a single acting tradition, a gradual but continuous adaptation of the discursive and moralizing drama of the late Middle Ages into the polydimensional story-drama of the mature theatre'. How respectable pre-Shakespearian drama has become of late years!

While on the subject of theatrical traditions, perhaps one should note here Robert Egan's article relating *Henry V* to *Tamburlaine* as a 'conqueror' play[2] (the reviewer, alas, was unconvinced) and possibly James E. Robinson's discussion of *A Midsummer-Night's Dream* in terms of ritual and rhetorical argument.[3]

The vexed question of the nature of the Elizabethan stage continues to be debated. C. Walter Hodges's lavishly produced book, *The Globe Restored*, has been revised[4] and now includes, among other fresh illustrations, a 'conjectural reconstruction' of the Globe. The existence of five aspects of the 'typical' Elizabethan playhouse, including the inner stage, shown, with reservations by the author, in Mr Hodges's drawing, is disputed by Richard Hosley,[5] who comes to the conclusion that the multiple stage is a figment of our imagination, possibly derived from our familiarity with Victorian production methods. Arthur Freeman has suggested[6] that the difference between Quarto and Folio versions of *2 Henry VI* suggest that the Folio was revised for a theatre lacking an inner stage, which implies that theatres both with and without this facility existed during the period. On aspects of production as opposed to staging, David Klein[7] has argued against the traffic of the stage being of two hours' duration, Irwin Smith[8] has examined the sixteen occasions when Shakespeare's characters appear to enter directly after making their exit and has shown that it is unlikely that any of them involve immediate re-entrance (a point for both editors and producers to note), and John Shaw[9] has postulated the way in which parallel scenes in *1 Henry IV* may have been produced in Shakespeare's time. The linguistic process by which the themes of a play (*Tamburlaine I* provides the exemplum) are communicated to the audience has also been analysed[10] though little is achieved beyond clothing the obvious in complex terminology.

Many of the aspects of Elizabethan dramaturgy mentioned above are discussed in J. L. Styan's *Shakespeare's Stagecraft*.[11] The author begins with a factual outline of those points of the Elizabethan stage of which we are reasonably confident, and then proceeds through careful analysis

1 'Seneca and the Elizabethans: A Case-study in "Influence" ', *Shakespeare Survey 20* (Cambridge, 1967), 17–26.

2 'A Muse of Fire: *Henry V* in the light of *Tamburlaine*', *Modern Language Quarterly*, XXIX (1968), 15–28.

3 'The Ritual and Rhetoric of *A Midsummer-Night's Dream*', *PMLA*, LXXXIII (1968), 380–91.

4 Oxford University Press, London, 1968.

5 'The Origins of the So-Called Elizabethan Multiple Stage', *The Drama Review*, XII (1968), 28–50.

6 'Notes on the Text of "2 Henry VI", and the "Upstart Crow" ', *Notes and Queries*, CCXIII (1968), 128–30.

7 'Time Allotted for an Elizabethan Performance', *Shakespeare Quarterly*, XVIII (1967), 434–38.

8 'Their Exits and Reentrances', *ibid.* 7–16.

9 'The Staging of Parody and Parallels in "1 Henry IV" ', *Shakespeare Survey 20* (Cambridge, 1967), 61–73.

10 Siegfried Wyler, 'Marlowe's Technique of Communicating with his Audience, as seen in his *Tamburlaine Part I*', *English Studies*, XLVIII (1967), 306–16.

11 Cambridge University Press, 1967.

of Shakespeare's text to deduce the way in which stage action, grouping of characters, movements, etc. were managed and speeches delivered. This is a study of Shakespeare as a man of the theatre acutely conscious of theatrical effects, as a writer whose work becomes more meaningful seen in the context for which it was created. As such, providing a balance to purely literary studies, it is useful to students and scholars alike. The effect of a particular theatrical context upon Shakespeare's work is also the subject of a study by Arthur C. Kirsch[1] who argues that the move to Blackfriars and thus to a milieu fostering a self-conscious dramaturgy accounts in some measure for the stylized techniques of the last plays. As the author himself admits, however, the theory, interesting in itself, fails to account for *Pericles*, which antedates the King's Men's acquisition of Blackfriars.

Probably the most enduring of the year's contributions to the study of Renaissance drama, and certainly the most important that have fallen to my share, are the two concluding volumes of *The Jacobean and Caroline Stage*.[2] It would be superfluous to praise Professor Bentley's scholarship and erudition at this juncture when the earlier volumes of his work have so long been one of the indispensable tools of seventeenth-century criticism. His two latest volumes are devoted to the private, public, court and projected theatre buildings (Vol. VI) and to appendices on Sunday and Lenten performances, a chronological list of dramatic and non-dramatic events, and an index to all seven volumes (Vol. VII). The appearance of the index and its inclusion of subjects not specifically discussed by Professor Bentley himself will increase the usefulness of a work already of incalculable value.

Two articles on the late Renaissance stage are worthy of note before turning to the vicissitudes of the Shakespearian corpus in its descent to modern times. Ann Haaker[3] has shown the implications of the plague to both dramatists and actors in tracing Brome's dispute with the Salisbury Court Theatre and Marco Mincoff[4] has suggested some interesting differences between Shakespearian and later seventeenth-century tragedy.

The stage history of Shakespeare's plays in successive centuries and a variety of languages has been unusually richly documented. A Restoration cast list of *Julius Caesar* has been discovered,[5] the actors mentioned giving some indication of the way the leading roles were interpreted. Esther K. Sheldon, in a fascinating account[6] of Thomas Sheridan's rise and fall as a theatre manager, devotes considerable space to his celebrated Shakespeare series, giving details of the plays staged, number of performances, cast lists, etc. It is gratifying to know that in eighteenth-century Dublin, at least, the production of a sequence of Shakespeare's plays resulted in packed theatres and soaring profits. The 'Romantic' approach to tragic character has been the subject of an article by Joseph W. Donohue, Jr,[7] who, in describing the Kemble–Mrs Siddons interpretation of *Macbeth*, attempts to show how 'the study of a major actor and actress in a play of unquestioned merit can lead to a knowledge of how theatrical performance faithfully

---

[1] '*Cymbeline* and Coterie Dramaturgy', *ELH*, XXXIV (1967), 285–306.　　　[2] Clarendon Press, Oxford, 1968.

[3] 'The Plague, the Theater, and the Poet', *Renaissance Drama*, n.s. 1 (1968), 283–306.

[4] 'Shakespeare, Fletcher and Baroque Tragedy', *Shakespeare Survey 20* (Cambridge, 1967), 1–15.

[5] John W. Velz, 'A Restoration Cast List for "Julius Caesar"', *Notes and Queries*, CCXIII (1968), 132–3.

[6] *Thomas Sheridan of Smock-Alley* (Princeton University Press, 1967).

[7] 'Kemble and Mrs Siddons in *Macbeth*: The Romantic Approach to Tragic Character', *Theatre Notebook*, XXII (1967–8), 65–86.

mirrors an age'. A discussion by Sybil Rosenfeld of the Grieves spectacular stage effects[1] and the London Museum's illustrated catalogue[2] of costumes and properties from the mid-eighteenth century to the present day also throw light on changing taste in theatrical presentation. Moving further afield, Shakespearian productions in Brazil,[3] Czechoslovakia,[4] and Romania[5] have been described and the history of the plays in Yiddish[6] has been traced. Reviews of contemporary productions in Britain, the United States, Canada, East and West Germany have appeared,[7] and the Berliner Ensemble's production of Brecht's adaptation of *Coriolanus* has been discussed by both actors[8] and critics.[9] A number of valuable articles have been devoted to the process of presenting a Shakespearian play to a modern audience. Stanley Wells has sketched the evolution of our attitude to the text and discussed the ethics of adaptation,[10] Weimann has argued that it is not possible to produce a Shakespearian play in solely twentieth-century terms,[11] and Gareth Lloyd Evans, in an extremely perceptive study of recent Royal Shakespeare Theatre performances,[12] has indicated the strengths, weaknesses and dangers inherent in an attempt to do so. Other items of note are a cross-section of opinions on *Hamlet* recorded at a public discussion of the play in Karl-Marx-Stadt,[13] and a collection of essays by critics on critics.[14]

Richly documented too is Shakespeare's influence on non-dramatic literature. Shakespeare and Defoe,[15] Diderot,[16] Keats,[17] pre-Raphaelite painting,[18] and nineteenth-century Russian literature,[19] together with the influence of *King Lear* on *Moby Dick*,[20] have all been the subject of essays. And finally, to demonstrate the continuing fertility of the products of the Elizabethan–Jacobean stage, one must note that the translation of tragedy of blood into modern novel has

1 'The Grieves Shakespearian Scene Designs', *Shakespeare Survey 20* (Cambridge, 1967), 107–12.

2 M. R. Holmes, *Stage Costume and Accessories in the London Museum* (H.M. Stationery Office, 1968).

3 Barbara Heliodora C. de M. F. de Almeida, 'Shakespeare in Brazil', *Shakespeare Survey 20* (1967), 121–4.

4 Ljuba Klosová, 'Shakespeare sur la scène tchèque pendant la deuxième moitié du 19ème siècle', *Theatre Research*, IX (1967–8), 72–87.

5 Alexandru Duțu, 'Recent Shakespeare Performances in Romania', *Shakespeare Survey 20* (1967), 125–31.

6 Leonard Prager, 'Shakespeare in Yiddish', *Shakespeare Quarterly*, XIX (1968), 149–63.

7 See *Shakespeare Quarterly*, XVIII (1967); *Shakespeare-Jahrbuch*, CIII (1967); *Deutsche Shakespeare-Gesellschaft West Jahrbuch* (1967).   8 *The Drama Review*, XII (1967–8), 112–17.

9 Dieter Hoffmeier, 'Notate zu Bertolt Brechts Bearbeitung von Shakespeares *Coriolan*, zur Bühnenfassung und zur Inszenierung des Berliner Ensembles', *Shakespeare-Jahrbuch*, CIII (1967), 177–95.

10 'Shakespeare's Text on the Modern Stage', *Deutsche Shakespeare-Gesellschaft West Jahrbuch* (1967), 175–93.

11 'Shakespeare on the Modern Stage: Past Significance and Present Meaning', *Shakespeare Survey 20* (1967), 113–20.   12 'Shakespeare, the Twentieth Century and "Behaviourism"', *ibid.* 133–42.

13 Ilse Jäger, 'Aus einer Publikumsdiskussion über die *Hamlet*-Inszenierung der Städtischen Theater Karl-Marx-Stadt', *Shakespeare-Jahrbuch*, CIII (1967), 226–9.

14 See *Deutsche Shakespeare-Gesellschaft West Jahrbuch* (1967).

15 John Robert Moore, 'Defoe and Shakespeare', *Shakespeare Quarterly*, XIX (1968), 71–80.

16 R. Desné, 'Diderot et Shakespeare', *Revue de Littérature Comparée*, XLI (1967), 532–71.

17 Bhabatosh Chatterjee, 'Keats on Shakespeare', *Essays on Shakespeare*, University of Burdwan Shakespeare Memorial Volume, ed. Bhabatosh Chatterjee (Orient Longmans, 1965).

18 S. N. Roy, 'Shakespeare in Pre-Raphaelite Painting', *ibid.*

19 Yu. D. Levin, *Shekspir v Russkoy Literature XIX Veka (ot Romantisma k Realizmu)* (Ministerstvo Prosveshcheniya RSFSR, Leningrad, 1968).

20 Julian Markels, '*King Lear* and *Moby Dick*: The Cultural Connection', *The Massachusetts Review*, IX (1968), 169–76.

been accomplished.[1] Clearly, in the words of Sisirkumar Ghose, whose humorous essay[2] on Shakespeare's life and reputation provides an ironic comment on the subject matter of this article, 'their revels are not ended'.

© LEAH SCRAGG 1969

3. TEXTUAL STUDIES

reviewed by RICHARD PROUDFOOT

Marvin Spevack[3] has used the resources of the German Computing Centre, Darmstadt, to compile a new and unprecedentedly complete concordance to the works of Shakespeare. The first two volumes contain separate concordances to the comedies and histories and to each of their characters, and the second ends with separate and consolidated concordances to the non-dramatic works. Volume three is to cover the tragedies, *Pericles*, *The Two Noble Kinsmen* and the Shakespearian portion of *Sir Thomas More*, while a further three volumes will be occupied by a consolidated concordance to the complete works. The present volumes supply exhaustive statistical information about the vocabulary of the texts they include, beginning with act, scene and line reference for every occurrence of every word, and extending to data about the incidence of verse and prose and about the vocabulary of every speaking part. The concordance is based on a modernized, American-spelling text which is to be published by the Houghton Mifflin Company. Wherever this text departs from the readings of the early text on which it is based, the concordance indicates the fact, but does not record the rejected reading. Homographs differently etymologized by the *O.E.D.* are separately listed and indicated with an asterisk. This concordance will clearly be an indispensable tool for future analysts of Shakespeare's language.

It is hardly surprising that one or two of the many difficult decisions of policy involved in such an undertaking seem to have been taken in a way that is open to question. The completeness of the concordance is slightly impaired by the omission of all stage directions and of the folio lists of *dramatis personae* for *The Tempest*, *Measure for Measure*, *The Winter's Tale* and *2 Henry IV*, as well as by that of the dedicatory epistles to *Venus and Adonis* and *Lucrece* and of the argument of *Lucrece*. *The Passionate Pilgrim*, however, is included in its entirety. The decision not to include either rejected readings from the basic early text or any variants from other early texts may have been unavoidable, but it has led to the exclusion of many readings, for instance from the first Quarto of *Richard III*, which are not certainly un-Shakespearian, and will presumably lead to the exclusion of many more from the early texts of *Troilus and Cressida*, *Hamlet*

[1] N. L. Goodrich, 'Le Moulin de Pologne, Modern Novel and Elizabethan Tragedy', *Revue de Littérature Comparée*, XLI (1967), 88–97.

[2] 'Which Shakespeare?', *Essays on Shakespeare*, University of Burdwan Shakespeare Memorial Volume, ed. Bhabatosh Chatterjee (Orient Longmans, 1965).

[3] *A Complete and Systematic Concordance to the Works of Shakespeare* (Hildesheim, 1968), Vol. I, *Drama and Character Concordances to the Folio Comedies*; Vol. II, *Drama and Character Concordances to the Folio Histories. Concordances to the Non-Dramatic Works*.

and *Othello*. The index lists of these volumes contain only the single words referred to, followed by statistical information and the full record of occurrences. This makes common words hard to trace, as the line numbering of the chosen text differs from other standard systems, especially in prose. 'Meaningful contexts' are promised in the three volumes of the consolidated concordance, and these should make the work easier to use, particularly for homographs of different grammatical function, which are not distinguished.

Peter J. Seng's *The Vocal Songs in the Plays of Shakespeare*[1] is a handsome work of reference which will be of use to future editors as well as to students of the songs. The texts of seventy songs are given in facsimile reprint, each followed by an exhaustive commentary on the principles of the New Variorum Shakespeare, as well as full references to early musical settings and brief critical notes on the dramatic function of the songs, in which alone the author voices his own opinions. Not the least valuable part of the book is its extensive bibliography. When so much is given, it may seem ungrateful to regret that the scheme did not allow for the printing of any of the early settings.

The scale of the undertaking makes it the more unfortunate that some of Seng's methods detract slightly from the comprehensiveness and reliability of the book. He defines 'vocal song' as 'any lyric passage which was originally intended to be sung on the stage by the actor to whom it is assigned, that intention being manifested either by a stage direction in the original source, or by a clear reference to the lyric as a song, or to the actor as a singer in the approximate context'. By this definition the dirge in *Cymbeline* is, most reasonably, admitted, although the dialogue directs that it is to be spoken, because it is called a song, whereas Touchstone's jingle 'O sweet Oliver' in *As You Like It*, III, iii, which echoes a ballad, is excluded, presumably for lack of clear reference to it as a song. Other criteria for exclusion are the lack of 'certain texts' and occurrence in 'plays or parts of plays outside the generally accepted Shakespeare canon', of which the first removes the Witches' songs at *Macbeth*, III, v, 33 and IV, i, 43, although their texts might be more accurately described as 'un-Shakespearian' than as uncertain, while the second covers the exclusion of 'Orpheus with his lute' from *Henry VIII* and the bridal song from *The Two Noble Kinsmen*, I, i, one of the scenes most generally accepted as Shakespeare's.

The texts reproduce exactly either the Folio or a substantive Quarto. Where two substantive texts exist, one is chosen and variants from the other are not always noted, so that Iago's drinking songs appear only in the text of the Quarto and the Folio's '*Oh, man's life's but a span*' at II, iii, 41, is nowhere mentioned. Conversely, six lines of commentary are devoted to discrediting Collier's spurious emendation 'wise as free' at *Two Gentlemen of Verona*, IV, ii, 41. That the choice of texts is a matter of methodology rather than of principle is suggested by Seng's readiness to discount the stage direction which precedes the song at *Merchant of Venice*, III, ii, 63, in the first Quarto, whose text he reprints. The direction reads '*A Song whilst Bassanio comments on the caskets to himselfe*'. J. R. Brown and others have used this direction as evidence against the view that Bassanio's choice is influenced by the song. Seng's defence of this view leads him to ignore his own text and to claim that 'Brown's argument is plausible only to the student who reads the play in the QI text; an audience witnessing this episode would be ignorant of the stage direction and would gather a wholly different impression'.

1 Harvard University Press, 1967.

The ample notes, quoted with corrections and additions from earlier editions, are not always correctly assigned: those on *Love's Labour's Lost*, v, ii, 905–6, which are attributed to the New Arden editor will be found in the Old Arden edition.

Nine new volumes of the New Penguin Shakespeare confirm the initial impression of the series as a valuable addition to the available paperback editions of separate plays. Their texts are soundly based on the good Quartos and the Folio and are cleared of much traditional editorial interference without any abdication of editorial responsibility where eclecticism or emendation is required. Musical settings are printed at the end of those plays which contain songs, with notes by F. W. Sternfeld. Some details of editorial policy vary from volume to volume, mainly in the scope and arrangement of the lists of collations, in which, for instance, the acknowledge-ment of emendations accepted from recent editions is not invariable. Modernization, as always, raises problems: the consistent adoption of 'an' for 'and', *if*, is a reasonable courtesy to modern readers, but instances need not, perhaps, be collated, any more than other spelling variants, such as 'thee' for 'the', or 'he's' for 'ha's'. It is unlikely that 'drovier', *Much Ado*, II, i, 178, and 'Beu', *As You Like It*, I, ii, 87, are more than obsolete spellings of 'drover' and 'Beau' and they are therefore out of place in a modernized text. A more serious doubt is raised by occasional modernization of verbal forms or of syntax: 'helped' for 'holp', *1 Henry IV*, I, iii, 13, or 'stand' for 'stands' and 'make' for 'makes', *Othello*, I, i, 152 and III, iii, 347, stand on the borderline between modernization and improvement of Shakespeare.

Three of the new editions are of plays for which the Folio is the only authority. Anne Righter's stress on the excellence of the text of *The Tempest* supports her conservative editing. She attributes this excellence to the careful scribal work of Ralph Crane in preparing the copy, but her unsupported suggestion that he was 'attached to Shakespeare's company as a scrivener' rather than being casually employed by them, leads her to lay too great an emphasis on the possibility that the fullness of the stage directions may be attributable to him. H. J. Oliver's *As You Like It* is also conservative, even, at times, where familiar emendations remove real difficulties of interpretation, as at III, ii, 101, where *O.E.D.* does not record the meaning *used in winter* which is necessary if the folio's 'Wintered' is to be retained, or where the folio reading makes for clumsiness of phrasing or emphasis, as at III, iv, 27 or IV, iii, 156, and where the error involved is so easy as the omission of 'a' or the misprinting of 'this' for 'his'. Such faith in the minutiae of the folio text is not wholly justified by his account of the transmission of the text, which draws attention to the problem of accurate 'casting-off' of copy and to the sporadic nature of the proof-correcting. M. M. Mahood recognizes that 'what is sense in the study is not always sense on the modern stage' and offers her collation of rejected emendations of *Twelfth Night* to any producer who may find her 'very conservative text' lacking in lucidity. She thinks that the folio was printed either from the prompt-book, which was not in Shake-speare's hand, or from a transcript of it, and admits no more than two dozen emendations into her text. She departs from the habit, normal since the late eighteenth century, of arranging half-lines by different speakers to make whole verse lines unless 'one character is responding fully to another'.

Two more plays for which the folio is the only basic text are *The Taming of the Shrew* and *Henry V*, although in each case editors have to take account of a Quarto as well. G. R. Hibbard gives a clear account of the dispute about *The Taming of a Shrew*, 1594, which he is inclined to regard as a bad quarto of Shakespeare's play. He believes that *The Shrew* was set up for the folio from a transcript of authorial papers and that it is the sole basis for the text. The later scenes involving Christopher Sly, which are found only in *A Shrew*, are reprinted in his edition at the end of *The Shrew*, but he argues that their absence from the folio was intended and reflects the need for doubling of parts in the later stages of the action. He attributes to the scribe of the copy for the folio many minor irregularities in the verse and makes many small alterations to rectify them. The need for these alterations is generally clearer when they entail adding words to make up defective lines than when they remove hypermetrical words present in the folio. It is questionable whether the second folio's 'Christophero' is really preferable to 'Christopher' at Induction, ii, 72, on metrical grounds. Other departures from the folio are well defended in the commentary, and include the happy assignment of the Messenger's speeches in Induction, ii, to the Lord, and a convincing rearrangement of v, ii, 75–6. A. R. Humphreys bases his text of *Henry V* on the Folio, agreeing with other recent editors that it was set up from Shakespeare's manuscript. While he accepts some twenty readings from the bad quarto of 1600 and follows its verse lining of Pistol's speeches, he is doubtful of its oaths and excludes them from his text on the grounds that, although the folio shows some signs of expurgation, enough oaths remain in it to vindicate its authority against the quarto in this particular. He proposes a new emendation at III, v, 26, replacing the familiar one from the second Folio, 'Poor we may call them' by 'Lest poor we call them', which clarifies the line of thought in the Constable's speech. Elsewhere, Humphreys retains more of the best established eighteenth-century emendations than some other New Penguin editors, including widespread correction of the French of Pistol's page and, of course, Theobald's 'a babbled of green fields', both of which are sanctioned more by editorial tradition than by the readings of the folio.

A quarto provides the only substantive text of *Much Ado About Nothing*, edited by R. A. Foakes, and of *1 Henry IV*, edited by P. H. Davison. Foakes provides an excellent text of *Much Ado*, which reinstates several quarto readings, and a full and helpful commentary. His account of the text slightly overestimates the authority of the folio in its textual alterations, and attributes to it the recovery of a line, I, i, 288–9, which, in fact, it omitted. Davison describes the textual situation of *1 Henry IV* with an amplitude uncharacteristic of the series. His conclusion, that the fragmentary first quarto of 1598 together with the second edition of the same year, now known as Q1, provide a very reliable text, is unexceptionable, but his position is more conjectural when he maintains that the copy for the first quarto was a manuscript in Shakespeare's hand, slightly revised by him for publication. He abandons a sound conservatism to try his hand at emending the obscure 'Oneyers' of the quarto at II, i, 77, offering 'O-yeas' in its place, a suggestion more ingenious than convincing as the emendation is quite as obscure and unprecedented as the quarto reading.

The high quality of the editing in the New Penguins is apparent in the two most problematic plays among the recent volumes, *Richard III* and *Othello*. The complicated editorial problem in *Richard III* is briefly and clearly stated by E. A. J. Honigmann. Neither the first quarto, 1597, nor the folio is a wholly reliable text, the quarto because of its memorial transmission, the folio because of its derivation from one or more of the later quartos and the incompleteness of the correction which was carried out by collating the quarto text with Shakespeare's own papers in preparing the folio copy. He offers no new suggestion on the vexed question of which quarto or quartos served as copy for the folio. He feels 'less pessimistic than other editors about the memorial contamination of Q, and more uneasy about the reliability of F', with the result that he has accepted a few dozen quarto readings where the folio has been preferred in other recent editions. Honigmann follows the quarto in some forty places where Dover Wilson followed the folio in his New Shakespeare edition. Of the rejected folio readings, twenty-five are in passages set by compositor B, whose work he characterizes as most careless, and fifteen in passages set by the more reliable A. The grounds for rejecting the folio are sometimes less apparent in A's stint than in B's: it is hard to see why the quarto's 'afar', III, i, 170, 'let us', III, ii, 93, and 'See', III, iv, 68, are preferred to the folio's 'far', 'let's' and 'Look'. If these variants are truly as indifferent as they seem to be, the remotest possibility that the folio alteration could be a correction might seem to argue for acceptance of its readings. The collation of readings accepted from later editions should include Spedding's 'accuse' for 'curse' at I, ii, 80.

Kenneth Muir's account of the texts of *Othello* draws attention to the uncertainties still surrounding the relationship of the 1622 quarto and the folio. He accepts the view that the folio was printed from a copy of the quarto corrected by comparison with the prompt-book, but concedes the possibility that 'sometimes where Q and F differ Shakespeare may have been responsible for both readings'. The extensive passages which are found only in the folio may have been omitted from the quarto or 'may result from later expansions after the first performance of the play'. Muir accepts the full editorial responsibility imposed by these uncertainties and supports his text with very full collations of rejected folio readings and of the more interesting and important rejected quarto readings. He accepts more readings from the quarto than the New Cambridge editors but less than M. R. Ridley in the New Arden edition and in so doing avoids the partizanship for one text or the other which is too apparent in those editions. Although he accepts the possibility of common error in the quarto and the folio, Muir follows the New Cambridge text in less than half of the passages where it initiated a departure from the common reading of quarto and folio. Agreement about every reading is hardly to be expected, the choice of the quarto's 'the lord of all my duty' at I, iii, 182, may serve as an instance, but overall this *Othello* is sensibly and sensitively edited.

The year has seen a number of welcome reprints. A. W. Pollard's pioneering work on the publication of Shakespeare, *Shakespeare's Fight with the Pirates*, 1920, and the collection of distinguished essays which he edited in 1923 as *Shakespeare's Hand in the Play of Sir Thomas More* are now published in a single volume.[1] *The Shakespeare Apocrypha*, edited by C. F. Tucker Brooke,[2] was last reprinted in 1929. It is slightly unfortunate that the present photolithographic reprint was made from the sheets of the 1908 edition, rather than from the 1918 reprint, which incorporated some ninety corrections, several of them prompted by Greg's Malone Society edition of *Sir Thomas More*, 1911. Six more volumes of the New Arden Shakespeare are now reprinted in paperback[3] as well as the first twenty-four volumes of the New Cambridge Shakespeare, in a slightly enlarged photolithographic form.

Photo-facsimiles of the Shakespeare quartos and folios are described by F. B. Williams, Jr,

---

[1] Cambridge, 1967. [2] Oxford, 1967.

[3] *King John*, ed. E. A. J. Honigmann; *King Henry IV*, Part 2, ed. A. R. Humphreys; *All's Well that Ends Well*, ed. G. K. Hunter; *Measure for Measure*, ed. J. W. Lever, 1967; *The Comedy of Errors* and *King Henry VIII*, ed. R. A. Foakes, 1968.

in 'Photo-facsimiles of *STC* Books: A Cautionary Check List'.[1] Three facsimiles of Shakespeare's poems from the Scolar Press[2] were published too late for inclusion in his list. They reproduce Malone's copies of *Venus and Adonis*, 1593, *Lucrece*, 1594 and *Shakespeares Sonnets*, 1609, now in the Bodleian Library.[3] The Xerox process used, with its lack of shading, has the disadvantage of exaggerating the effect of stains in the paper and of over-inking, but in other respects these facsimiles are more reliable than the Griggs facsimiles of 1886, which were extensively touched up. The reproduction is not good enough for editorial purposes and a cleaner copy of *Lucrece* could have been found. The description of the chosen copy of *Lucrece* as 'the earliest surviving impression of the first printing' is misleading when what is meant is that it has the inner forme of B and the outer forme of I in their uncorrected states.

E. A. J. Honigmann, in an important article 'On the Indifferent and One-Way Variants in Shakespeare',[4] urges the need for closer scrutiny by editors of indifferent variants in those plays which are extant in two or more substantive versions. He presents a detailed account of fifteen groups of frequent indifferent variants in order to demonstrate that a broad view of their incidence through several plays may reveal that they reflect the practice of a single agent in the transmission of the text, either the folio editor, or a compositor, or a scribe. The editorial implications of his argument can be seen most clearly in his first example. The folio texts of *1* and *2 Henry IV* and *Richard III* show a marked preference for 'yes' or 'I' over 'yea': editors of *Henry IV*, for which the basic texts are the quartos, would naturally restore 'yea', but the folio *Richard III* is the 'better text', so that editors of that play, unaware of the one-way traffic from 'yea' to 'yes' throughout several plays in the folio, have accepted its 'indifferent' variants in preference to the 'yea's' of the first quarto. Honigmann acknowledges the difficulty of interpreting some of his material—his own suggestion that the folio's 'yee' at *Richard III*, I, ii, 101, where the first quarto has 'yea', is a by-product of the 'folio editor's' dislike of 'yea' does not take full account of the fact that 'yee' is also the reading of the third and later quartos— but he makes a clear case that 'all supposedly indifferent variants should be rescrutinized, and the slightest hair's-breadth of a preference should justify a decision either way' and demonstrates some of the ways in which this scrutiny should be conducted.

In 'Compositor B, The Pavier Quartos, and Copy Spellings',[5] William S. Kable continues the study of William Jaggard's compositor B. He identifies him as the only compositor employed on the 1619 Shakespeare reprints for Thomas Pavier and presents the results of a comprehensive analysis of his spelling preferences, based on the collation of these texts with the earlier quartos used as copy. He qualifies the findings of earlier investigators of B's spelling preferences, discounting much that they found significant, and shows that B's spelling pattern in the Pavier quartos contains a high proportion of copy-spellings. He justifies his conclusion that B's departures from his consistent preferences are likely to reflect the influence of his copy by showing that of thirty-one such departures in B's six pages of folio *Love's Labour's Lost*, twenty-nine are in fact the spellings of the quarto used as copy. Kable's analysis will help editors to allow more precisely for B's effect on the folio texts which he set, but his claim that copy-

---

[1] *Studies in Bibliography*, XXI (1968), 109–30.   [2] Leeds, 1968.

[3] Shelf-marks: Malone 325; Malone 34(1); Malone 34(2).

[4] *The Library*, 5th series, XXII (1967), 189–204.   [5] *Studies in Bibliography*, XXI (1968), 131–61.

spellings can be identified in B's work when he was setting from manuscript copy is optimistic, as all the evidence is necessarily derived from B's habits when setting reprints from printed copy and there is no control situation comparable to that afforded by the Pavier quartos from which his treatment of copy-spellings when setting from manuscript can be determined.

Josephine Waters Bennett[1] challenges the received opinion that John Benson's publication of Shakespeare's sonnets in the *Poems* of 1640 was piratical. The copyright in the *Sonnets* had lapsed with the withdrawal of Thomas Thorpe from publishing about 1625 and William Jaggard's copyright in *The Passionate Pilgrim*, on which Benson also drew, had not been assigned to any other stationer. Thus, although Benson entered neither copy on the Stationers' Register, he may have established his right to both in the course of various transactions with the company from 1636 for the reprinting of copies 'which had come into the possession of the Stationers' Company'. Shakespeare's poems may have been granted to him in place of Davenant's *Albovine*, for which he paid forty shillings to the poor of the company in July 1639, but which he did not print. In any event, both Benson and his printer, Thomas Cotes, were in good standing with the company in 1640. His publication of Shakespeare's poems, however damaging to the text its alteration of the order and layout of the sonnets may have been, can be seen as an act of homage and an endeavour to rescue neglected works from oblivion.

R. H. A. Robbins[2] examines a version of Sonnet 128 on f. 34 of the Bodleian MS. Rawl. Poet. 152. It is derived from Thorpe's 1609 quarto and the fact that nearly fifty discrepancies exist between it and the quarto text 'with the verdicts of art and common-sense consistently on the side of the latter, testifies to the virtues of the Quarto'.

Standish Henning[3] confirms H. R. Hoppe's identification of Edward Allde as the printer of E–K in the first quarto of *Romeo and Juliet*, 1597, by tracing damaged types used in these sheets in three books printed by Allde in 1597 and 1599.

Patricia Ingham[4] takes a fresh look at those readings in the 1608 quarto of *King Lear* which have prompted the suggestion that recitation by an actor played a part in the transmission of the text, because they appear to result from phonetic transcription of words rightly heard but misunderstood. She finds seven, or at most eight, readings which are both clearly erroneous and representative of feasible contemporary pronunciations of the words misunderstood, and concludes that of the errors in the quarto text 'those unmistakably aural are fewer than generally supposed, and that whoever was responsible for them used an advanced or vulgar form of speech'.

The following notes relate to particular readings in several plays. Arthur Freeman[5] discusses the bad quarto and folio readings at *2 Henry VI*, II, iii, 71–91, and suggests that the reported text of the combat of Horner and Peter (reported by an actor who had played Horner) should be chosen as the basis of a modern text as standing closer to the source in Hall than the more sober and dignified folio version, which may be 'a theatrical alteration of Shakespeare's original'. At line 93 of the same scene, the words 'Sound Trumpets, Alarum to the Combattants', assigned

---

1 *Ibid.* 235–48.

2 'A Seventeenth-Century Manuscript of Shakespeare's Sonnet 128', *Notes and Queries*, XIV (1967), 137–8.

3 'The Printer of *Romeo and Juliet*, Q1', *Publications of the Bibliographical Society of America*, LX (1966), 363–4.

4 'A Note on the Aural Errors in the First Quarto of *King Lear*', *Shakespeare Studies*, III (1967), 81–4.

5 'Notes on the Text of *2 Henry VI*, and the "Upstart Crow"', *Notes and Queries*, XV (1968), 128–30.

to York in the folio, should perhaps have been printed as a stage direction equivalent to the quarto's 'Alarmes...'. R. Hosley[1] recommends Charles Knight's emendation at *Romeo and Juliet*, I, iii, 72, of the second quarto's 'your mother' to 'a mother' as the simplest resolution of the inconsistency of references to the age of Lady Capulet: if Juliet is not her first child, no need remains to suppose her so young as twenty-eight.

Thomas Clayton[2] proposes the emendation 'surety' at *Hamlet*, I, iii, 21, on the grounds that it suits the context better than Theobald's 'sanity' and is palaeographically as likely a source for the second quarto's 'safety'. He does not mention the quarto's reverse error of 'sanctity' for 'sanity' at II, ii, 210. Elis Fridner[3] defends the second quarto at *Hamlet*, I, iii, 73, taking 'chiefe' as a verb meaning 'lead', 'are most prominent', 'excel'. 'It is an affected even far-fetched way of speaking, and in the usual manner of Polonius'. He would read 'the chiefe ranck' in line 74, taking 'chiefe' from the first quarto in place of 'best', and so afford Polonius a quibble on 'chief'. Jane Crawford[4] challenges recent editors of *Hamlet* for accepting the reading 'miching mallecho' at III, ii, 146, and for 'explaining "miching" as a word obsolete except in dialect and "mallecho" as a borrowing of the Spanish *malhecho*'. Returning to the second quarto's 'Marry this munching *Mallico*, it means mischiefe', she proposes the reading 'Marry, this munching malice, it means mischief'. She notes Capell's support of 'munching' and finds the *O.E.D.*s definition, 'To eat with continuous and noticeable action of the jaws', suitable to the context. As she points out, the case for 'malice' is stronger than that for 'munching', unless the folio's 'Miching' results from contamination from the first quarto, which reads 'myching'.

Sheldon P. Zitner[5] upholds the authenticity of *King Lear*, III, ii, 76–80, because of 'its connection with both the plot sequence and the main themes of the play' and points out that 'there is no clear textual basis for labelling the Prophecy spurious'. He rejects all attempts to alter the folio sequence of lines, finding the essence of the speech in its anti-climax. James G. McManaway[6] cites Marlowe's *Massacre at Paris*, xii, 3–4, and *Arden of Feversham*, I, 98–100, in support of the folio reading 'My Foole vsurpes my body' at *King Lear*, IV, ii, 28. Waldo F. McNeir[7] looks for 'a satisfactory reason, on textual grounds, for preferring either the assignment of the final lines to Albany, as in the quartos, or to Edgar, as in the Folio'. As a compromise solution he would divide the final speech, giving lines 324–5 to Albany, as his answer to Kent, and lines 326–7 to Edgar, who is younger than Albany, thus 'dividing the three concluding couplets among the three surviving principal characters, each of whom reacts to the final situation in a different way'.

© RICHARD PROUDFOOT 1969

---

1 'How Many Children Had Lady Capulet?', *Shakespeare Quarterly*, XVIII (1967), 3–6.

2 'A Crux and No Crux in *Hamlet* I, iii: Safty: Sanctity (21) and Beguide: Beguile (131)', *Shakespeare Studies*, III (1967), 43–50.

3 'A Textual Puzzle in *Hamlet*', *English Studies*, XLVII (1966), 431.

4 '*Hamlet*, III, ii, 146', *Review of English Studies*, XVIII (1967), 40–5.

5 'The Fool's Prophecy', *Shakespeare Quarterly*, XVIII (1967), 76–80.

6 'A Reading in *King Lear*', *Notes and Queries*, XIV (1967), 139.

7 'The Last Lines of *King Lear*: v. iii. 320–327', *English Language Notes*, IV (1967), 183–8.

INDEX

INDEX

INDEX

INDEX

INDEX

INDEX

INDEX